IMAGES
of America

MENASHA

CITY OF MENASHA

Your investments will be entirely appreciated.

Fine locations for factories and homes.

Situated in Northeastern Wisconsin, on the Fox River, between the beautiful lakes, Winnebago and Butte Des Mortes, which afford excellent fishing and bathing

Excellent water power, electric interurban line connected with surrounding cities, making connections with C. & N. W., C. M. & St. P. and Soo Line Railroads

This ad from the 1917 Menasha High School yearbook, *The Nicolet,* touts Menasha's natural beauty, its desirable location, and its rail connections. Though the city government is simply supporting its namesake high school in its annual, this ad copy was undoubtedly used in other venues to promote the city and attract new business ventures.

On the Cover: Main Street in Menasha is pictured in June 1910 during a convention of the Benevolent and Protective Order of Elks. Previously, Main Street was paved with cedar blocks; a thin layer of dirt on top provided an extra cushion but made the road muddy when it rained. However, concrete paving was a matter of civic pride, and efforts were made to have the work finished by the time of the convention.

IMAGES
of America

MENASHA

David Galassie with the
Menasha Historical Society

ARCADIA
PUBLISHING

ISBN 978-0-7385-9178-0

Published by Arcadia Publishing
Charleston, South Carolina

Printed in the United States of America

Library of Congress Control Number: 2012936670

For all general information, please contact Arcadia Publishing:
Telephone 843-853-2070
Fax 843-853-0044
E-mail sales@arcadiapublishing.com
For customer service and orders:
Toll-Free 1-888-313-2665

Visit us on the Internet at www.arcadiapublishing.com

To Teresa, Adrianne, and Allison and in memory of my parents, Philip and Lylase Galassie, who instilled in me a love of history.

Contents

ACKNOWLEDGMENTS

Generous thanks and praise go to the staff of the Menasha Historical Society (MHS), headed by its president, Nancy Barker. I am especially indebted to her, as she took my pitch to do this book, and over the course of many months, stoked the fires of interest within the society and kept it alive. To Paul Brunette, thank you. Your review of my proposal and vote of confidence helped carry the day. Special thanks also go to MHS Resource Center director Katie LaMore, MHS Resource Center assistant director Jean Chew, and MHS board members Tom Konetzke, Richard Loehning, and Bob Smarzinski.

The staff of the Menasha Public Library was also very generous and patient with me in providing photographs, especially Joe Bongers, head of adult services, and Pattie Stanislawski. They supported my many trips to the reference desk and, on more than one occasion, fielded my inquiries via email. I cannot thank them enough. Thank you to Mike Thomas of the Neenah Public Library for providing images, too.

To my wife and daughters, you have my gratitude for your love and support and for indulging me in this pursuit. Thanks to my sister Mary Fritsch; her husband, Ken Fritsch; my brother John Galassie; and my dear friends Kila Wilson, Bob Johnstone, and Alex Arlington. Your support of my writing endeavors over the years has never wavered, and I have drawn so much inspiration from your faith in me.

I am indebted to the fantastic editors at Arcadia Publishing, particularly Jeff Ruetsche, midwest publisher, who nurtured my proposal to carve out a niche for Menasha at Arcadia, and to Winnie Rodgers. Your generous assistance throughout this process helped to realize this dream.

And to the citizenry of Menasha over the years, I thank you for providing an exciting story of bravery, innovation, commerce, and industry and an unwavering faith in a brighter tomorrow.

My sincerest hope is that this book will be not just a nostalgic look back for my generation, but also a stepping-stone for future generations to learn more of their hometown's rich and exciting history.

Unless otherwise noted, all images appear courtesy of the Menasha Historical Society.

INTRODUCTION

This book traces the historical journey of Menasha, from the arrival of French explorers to the area in the 1600s, through its charter as a village in 1853, to its incorporation as a city in 1874 and beyond as it industrialized and became an economic and political power within the state.

In 1634, the French explorer Jean Nicolet, seeking a route to the Orient, encountered and made peace with the Winnebago Indians in the Fox River Valley. Some say that the exact location of his landing is unknown, though it was believed that the Winnebago had villages at Green Bay and on Doty Island. Archeologist and Menasha mayor P.V. Lawson Jr. asserted that the landing occurred on Doty Island, and the event is now commemorated there, near Smith Park with a monument established in 1906. The Fox, or Outagami, arrived some time after the Winnebago, establishing settlements on Doty Island after the French decimated Fox settlements west of Little Lake Butte des Morts because they felt the Fox were hindering their fur trade. In time, the Fox and Winnebago moved away, and the Menominee tribe moved in. As part of a treaty in 1831, the US government established a settlement in Neenah near what is now East Wisconsin Avenue, by what was known then as Winnebago Rapids. This mission was an effort to "civilize" the tribe, to teach them farming techniques, how to establish a mill, and generally how to live among the white settlers to whom they would end up selling their land. This experiment failed, and by 1835, after a smallpox outbreak killed a third of the tribe, the whole effort was abandoned. Still, the government convinced the tribe to sell their land, and in 1836, the Menominee sold their rights to six and a half million acres for $772,000 in an action called the Treaty of the Cedars.

Both Neenah and Menasha were subsequently named by Sarah Collins Doty, wife of Judge James Duane Doty, an early territorial governor of Wisconsin. Doty Island was named by the Menominees in his honor during treaty negotiations, and they were even prepared to deed the entire island to Doty as payment for his legal services. The federal government, however, denied this payment as part of the treaty, and eventually, Doty took the government to court and lost. Still, the name *Doty Island* remained in common usage. The Winnebago name for water is *nee-nah*. *Menasha* is a Native American word meaning "the settlement on the island." Sources vary as to whether it is of Winnebago or Menominee origin.

The first permanent settler in Neenah was Harrison Reed in 1843. In 1848, his younger brother Curtis Reed arrived as the first settler in Menasha. Curtis Reed saw visions of a great industrial city on the shore of the Fox River and allied himself with Charles Doty, Governor Doty's brother, who was assigned to watch over the governor's land interests in Menasha while he was away on political matters. Curtis Reed, on behalf of Governor Doty, purchased land as a site for a city by borrowing funds from a businessman named Harvey Jones, a friend of a friend of the Reverend O.P. Clinton. But Jones, too, had a vision. He wanted to build a dam that would enable development of a city constructed on the Neenah side of the river. Soon, a competition developed over who would be successful in taming the river by building a canal to help harness the waterpower needed for industry. Governor Doty preferred Curtis Reed's property, and Menasha was consequently chosen for the canal. But Jones was not defeated; he constructed a canal of his own on the Neenah side. As a result, both cities gained the advantages of steamboat traffic on the river, and trade and development prospered. Soon, Neenah and Menasha had many flour mills in operation, driven by the waterpower available and never at a loss for raw material as Wisconsin had become a major wheat producer in the United States.

Moreover, with the advantages of its direct rail lines to Milwaukee, as well as the increasing demand for flour during the Civil War, Neenah and Menasha's flour output quickly grew to be second only to Milwaukee's in the state.

In time, however, the flour industry left the upper Fox Valley and relocated to Minnesota, and nothing underscored the flour mills' demise more than having one of the area's flour moguls selling his milling technology to a fledgling company by the name of Pillsbury. Also undercutting the flour industry was the increasing paper business, which proved rather profitable. By 1890, flour milling was quickly being surpassed by paper interests, and in 1908, the last mill closed.

Menasha, as such, is a confined city. With Neenah right across Nicolet Boulevard, Appleton encroaching from the north, and Little Lake Butte des Morts to its west, Menasha has little room for growth, save for its efforts to move east towards Calumet County along Wisconsin Highway 114.

Reinventing itself in the 1980s with the marina project, Menasha scrapped much of its downtown to reinvigorate its commerce and embrace what brought the city its original glory in the 1850s—the Fox River. Now with the closing of a paper mill on Doty Island, Menasha has gained 12 acres on the shoreline opposite downtown to develop and reenergize its living space. Its 2006 redevelopment plan provided a conceptual design for a multiphase mixed-use development including a two-acre riverfront park.

With a history of consistently reinventing itself, Menasha has, at critical junctures in its history, made dramatic decisions that changed its very core. From a rapids in the wilderness, a city was born that tamed the river, putting its waterpower to work for itself, first with flour mills, then with wood products and paper mills. With water routes initially and later railroad connections to the commerce centers of Milwaukee and Chicago, Menasha became a second-to-none industrial center for northeastern Wisconsin. This book documents those changes and puts a face on its civic leaders and industry giants.

The average citizen of Menasha today most likely cannot tell you who Elisha D. Smith was, yet he or she knows his namesake, Smith Park, and the public library he endowed. Change is in the wind and is happening quickly. As I write this, so many changes have occurred in Menasha's landscape, it seems the entire city has transformed. Yes, the modernist reminds us that progress is good, but a definitive record of what Menasha once was is in order, and this book will serve as a bellwether in our efforts to define and depict the history of Menasha. As the documentarian Ken Burns said, "History isn't really about the past—settling old scores. It's about defining the present and who we are." I believe it is time again to redefine Menasha for all to see.

One

EARLY MENASHA

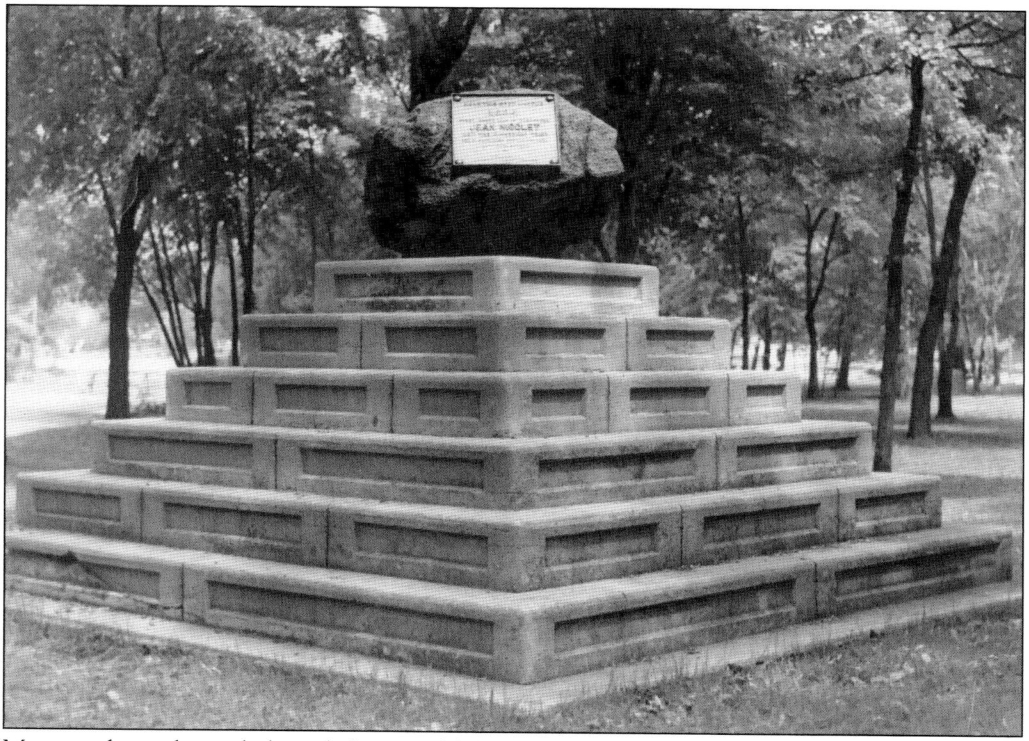

Many early explorers believed they would find an easy route to Asia rather than be satisfied to explore and settle North America. In 1634 Jean Nicolet, an emissary of Gov. Samuel de Champlain of New France (Quebec, Canada), landed at Red Banks on the shore of Green Bay. Nicolet expected to meet Asians on his voyage and donned an elaborate Oriental robe before landing. Brandishing two pistols, he fired into the air to impress upon the Winnebago Indians who met him that he was in authority. Later, after traveling down the Fox River, Nicolet came ashore near what is today's Smith Park, where this monument commemorates his landing. It was erected by the Women's Clubs of Menasha and unveiled in 1906.

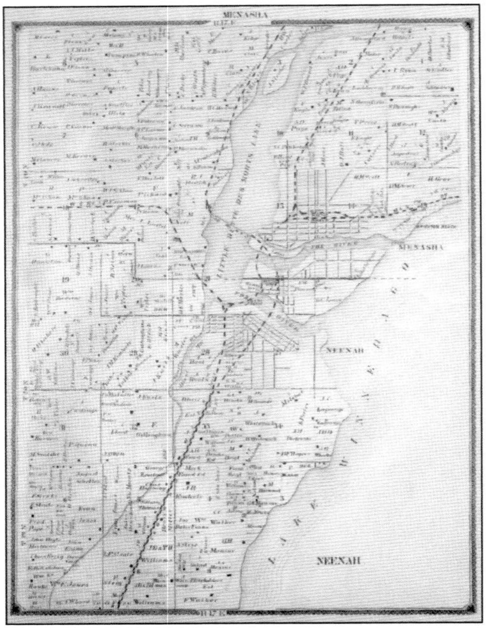

Little Lake Butte des Morts (northwest of Menasha) on these maps took on its French name, translated as "Hill of the Dead," due to the large burial mound located adjacent to the lake. In 1730, French forces, tiring of Indian interference in their fur-trapping activities, ambushed the Fox Indians near Dendo Island, adjacent to today's Washington Street. (The channel separating Dendo Island from Doty Island became Garfield Avenue after it was filled in.) The Fox and Winnebago had been warring for six weeks when the French arrived and allied themselves with the Winnebagoes. The Fox buried their dead in a communal grave on the eastern edge of Little Lake Butte des Morts, a large burial mound that lasted until the Chicago & North Western Railway constructed a major railroad bridge on the site. (Both, author's collection.)

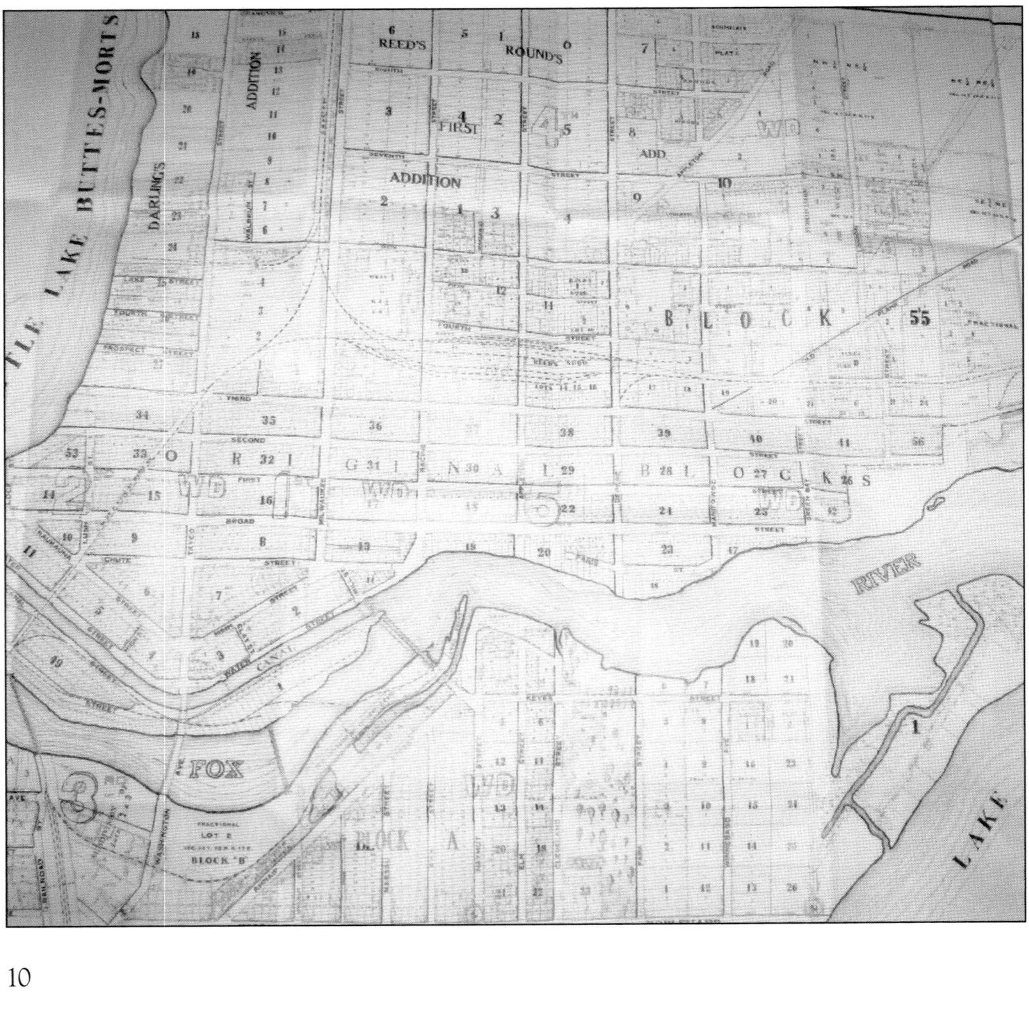

O'-Check-Ka, or Chief Four Legs, was the last Ho-Chunk (Winnebago) chief to reside on Doty Island. This illustration was painted at the Treaty of Green Bay in 1827 by the noted portrait engraver of Native Americans James Otto Lewis (1799–1858) when Wisconsin was still a part of Michigan Territory. Chief Four Legs died in 1830 at the age of 40, and two years later, his village was abandoned.

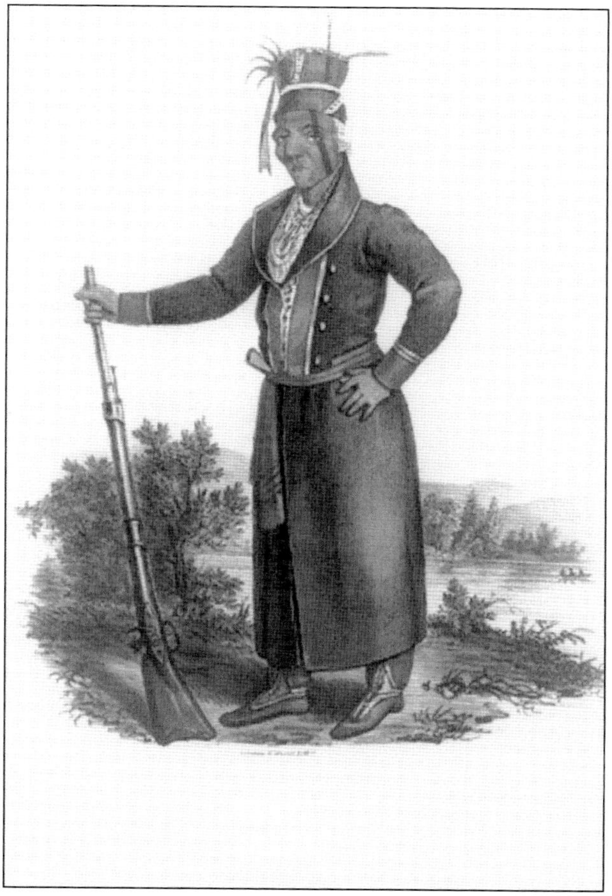

In 1847, Judge Doty facilitated the passage of an act within the state legislature to grant him and his business partners the authority to dam the Fox River at each channel around Doty Island. Discord arose among them, so Curtis Reed and Judge Doty dammed the north channel (Menasha) while Harrison Reed and Harvey Jones carried the cause for the south channel (Neenah). Because of these differences, two towns were destined to be developed instead of the one originally envisioned.

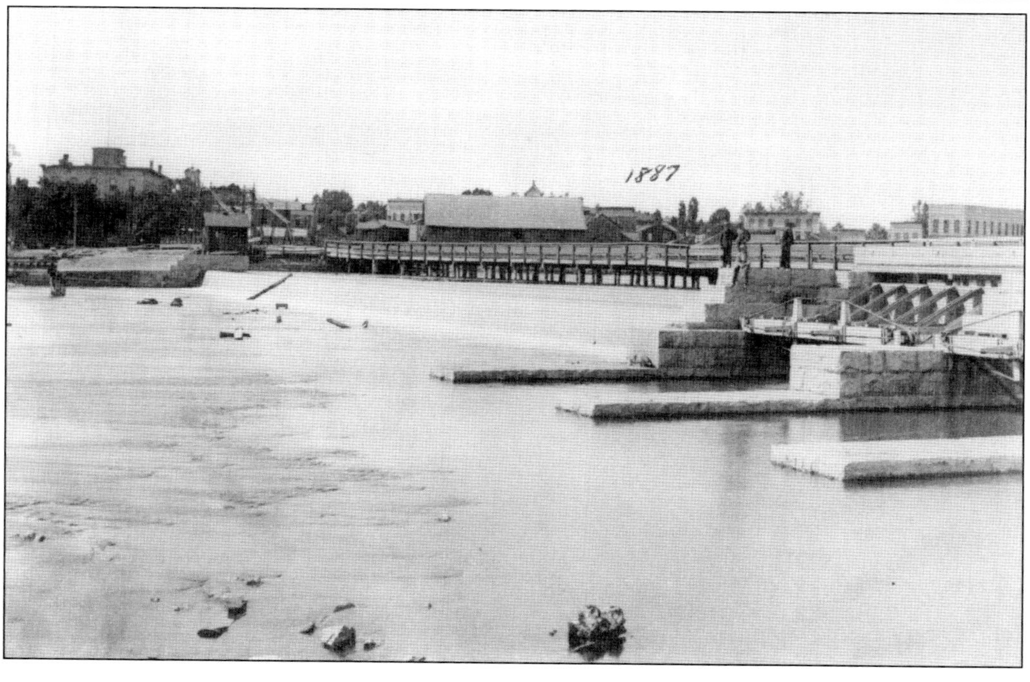

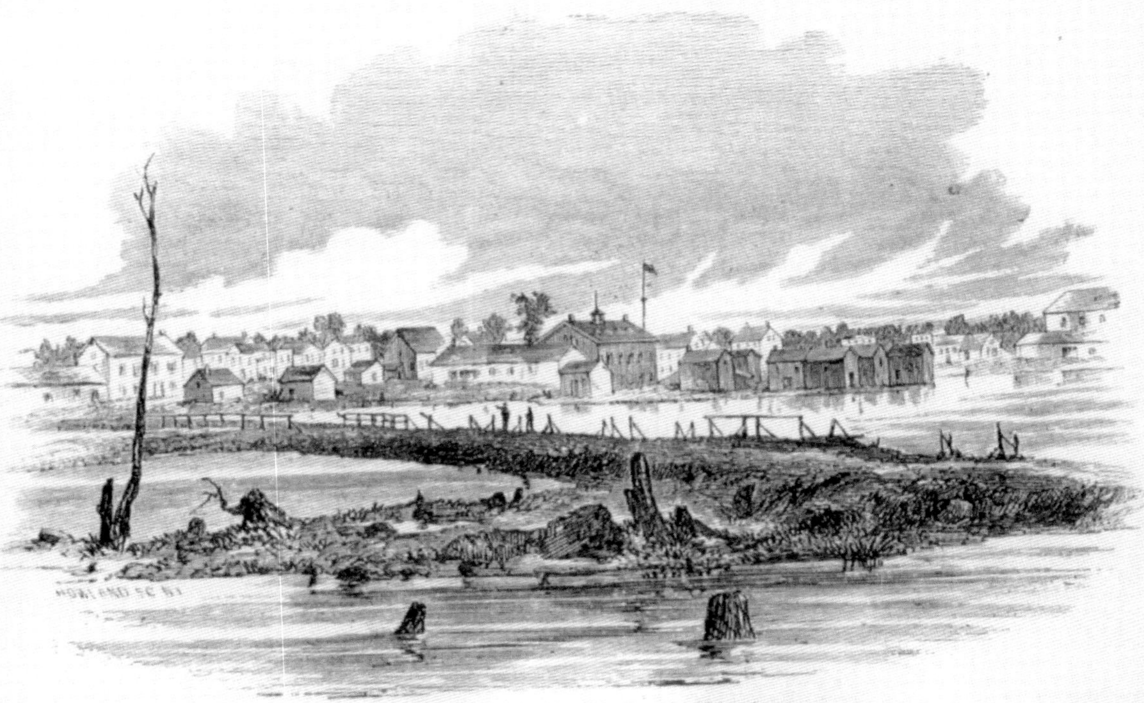

From daguerreotype by J. F. Harrison

Menasha in 1855

In 1853, Menasha was the first of the two towns to officially incorporate. Incorporation gave Menasha a governing board of two wards with three trustees each and a host of other village offices to include a clerk, treasurer, assessor, constable, justice of the peace, and many others. Curtis Reed was elected as the first village president, an office in which he eventually served five terms. Reed laid out the town square of Menasha at the convergence of Main, Chute, and Milwaukee Streets, despite the thinking at one time that downtown might become the area surrounding Broad and Appleton Streets due to the proximity of the steamboat landing. This engraving based on a J.F. Harrison daguerreotype shows Menasha in 1855, as seen from Doty Island. Paper as an industry had not yet come to Menasha. What few factories there were at the time were flour mills and wood-related industries. Notice the wooden structures close to the water's edge and the rough-hewn nature of the river.

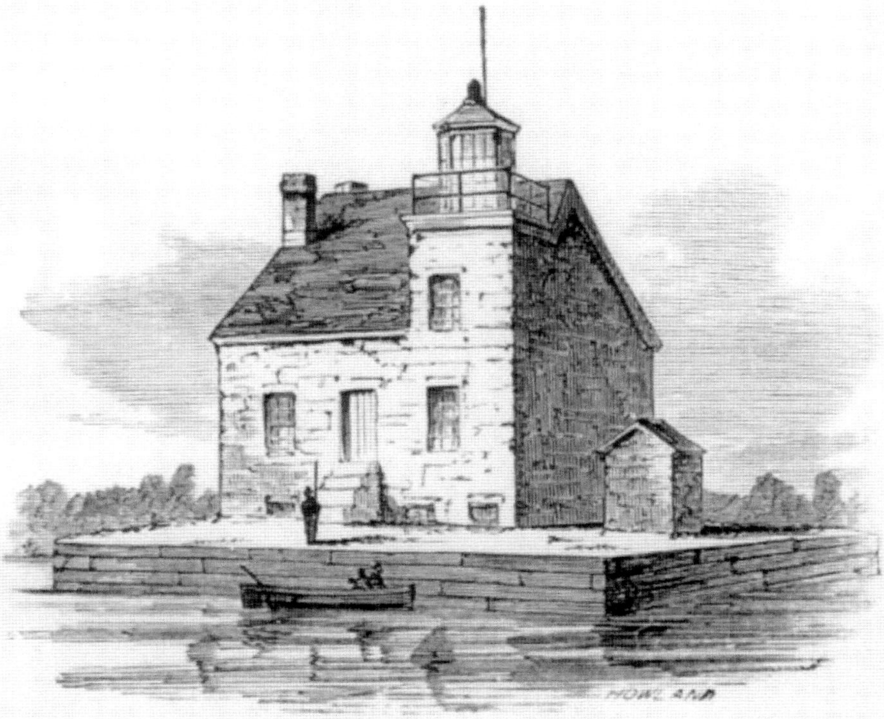

Menasha Lighthouse, Lake Winnebago, in 1855

In the middle of the 19th century, there was a lighthouse at the Menasha entrance to the Fox River. The island, which was known as Lighthouse Reef, was designated as the site of the federal lighthouse on April 28, 1852. Territorial governor James Doty, then a congressman, pushed for the appropriation of $5,000. On July 26, 1855, the lighthouse was completed at a cost of $6,000 and was put into service with Jerry Crowly as its first keeper. After an incident where Crowly nearly froze to death while returning from shore, the lighthouse was abandoned. In later years, skaters tore up the wood for firewood, and finally, in 1880, someone set fire to the entire building. After a few hard winters during the 1880s, the ice had practically demolished the blackened walls, and by 1886, nothing remained of the building. Today, no trace of the lighthouse exists, and the island it sat upon is gone.

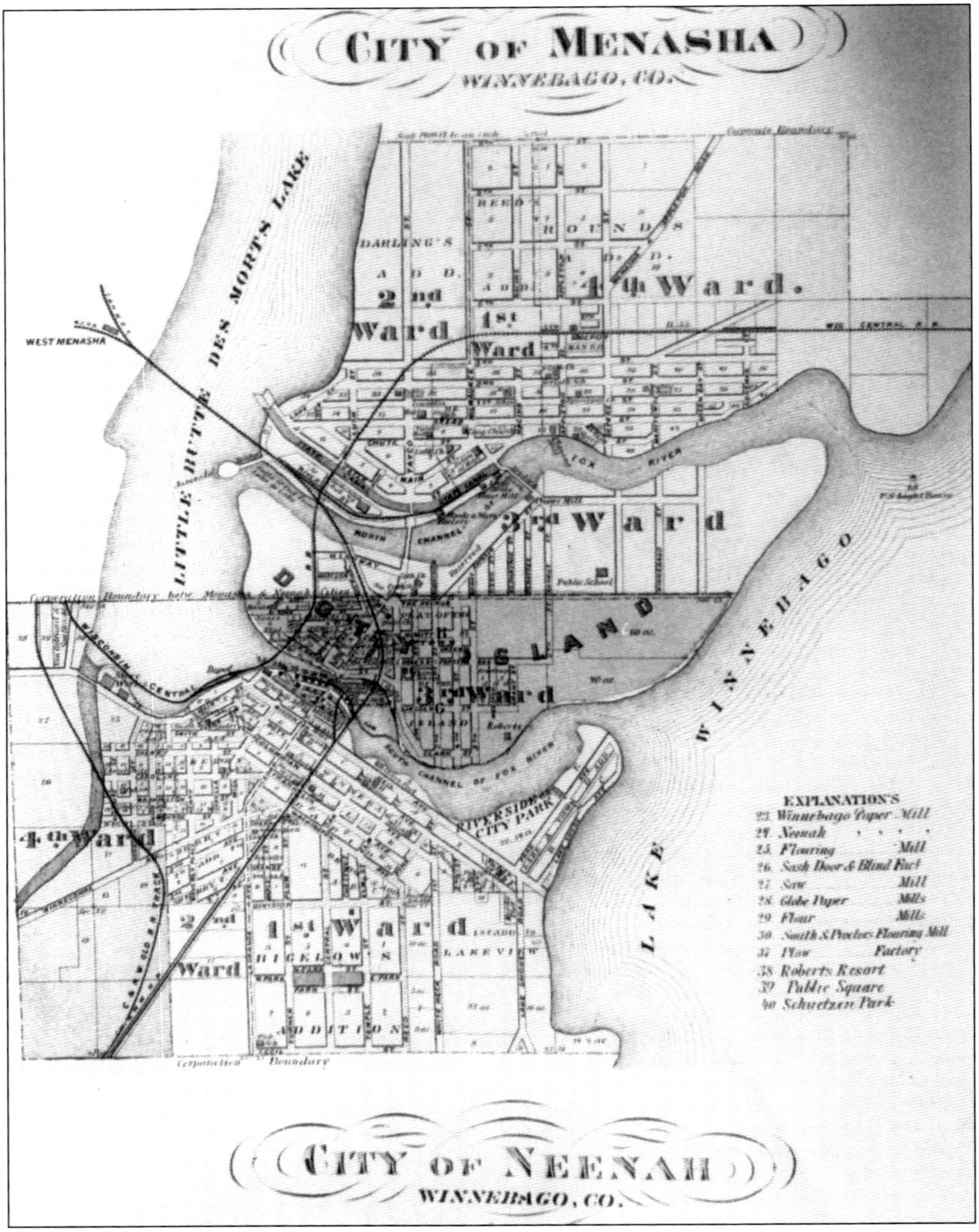

This 1877 map highlights Doty Island. Early histories are vague as to how Doty Island was divided in half, but separation was largely guided by the sectional lines originally used in laying out the two towns. Eventually, Nicolet Boulevard, or the "Avenue," reached from Lake Winnebago to Commercial Street (Neenah)/Washington Street (Menasha) and became the dividing line with a 100-foot jog to the north at this intersection before continuing west. The significance of Doty Island cannot be overstated in the history of Menasha and its twin city, Neenah. The development of the two cities largely paralleled each other, yet plans to consolidate the two were brought up from time to time, beginning as early as 1869. Even after the two villages had incorporated into cities in 1873 and 1874, consolidation was again considered in 1881, 1887, 1896, and into the 20th century. But, after so much time, the debate was not enough to overcome the years of rivalry and animosity to create the longed-for "Island City." (Author's collection.)

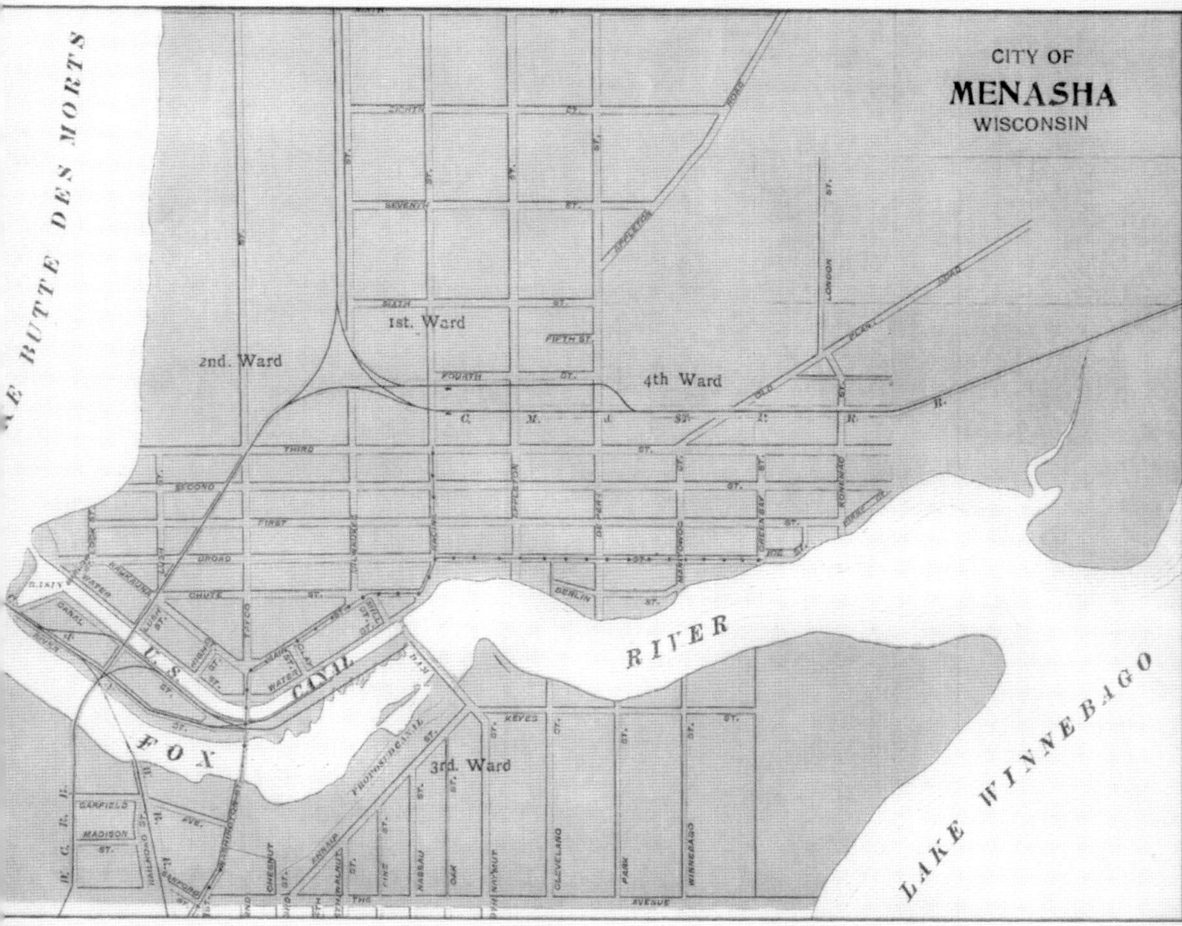

This pre–World War I map of Menasha (1909) shows the changing names of many streets and the increasing sophistication of transportation assets within the community. At this point, Berlin Street still exists near the Fox River. During the anti-German sentiment of World War I, Berlin Street became Paris Street and remains so to this day. Other name changes occurred since the 1877 map was created: Penaysee Street became Oak Street, Keshaynie Street became Nassau Street, Osko Street became Pine Street, Neaht Street became Walnut Street, Ahnair Street became Ahnaip Street, and Waubacon Street became Chestnut Street, though that street has since disappeared altogether with mill construction near the river. This map shows the route of the interurban, as denoted by dotted lines that show its origins at Broad and Green Bay Streets, turning down Racine Street and onto Main Street before journeying on to Neenah across the Tayco and Washington Street Bridges. (Author's collection.)

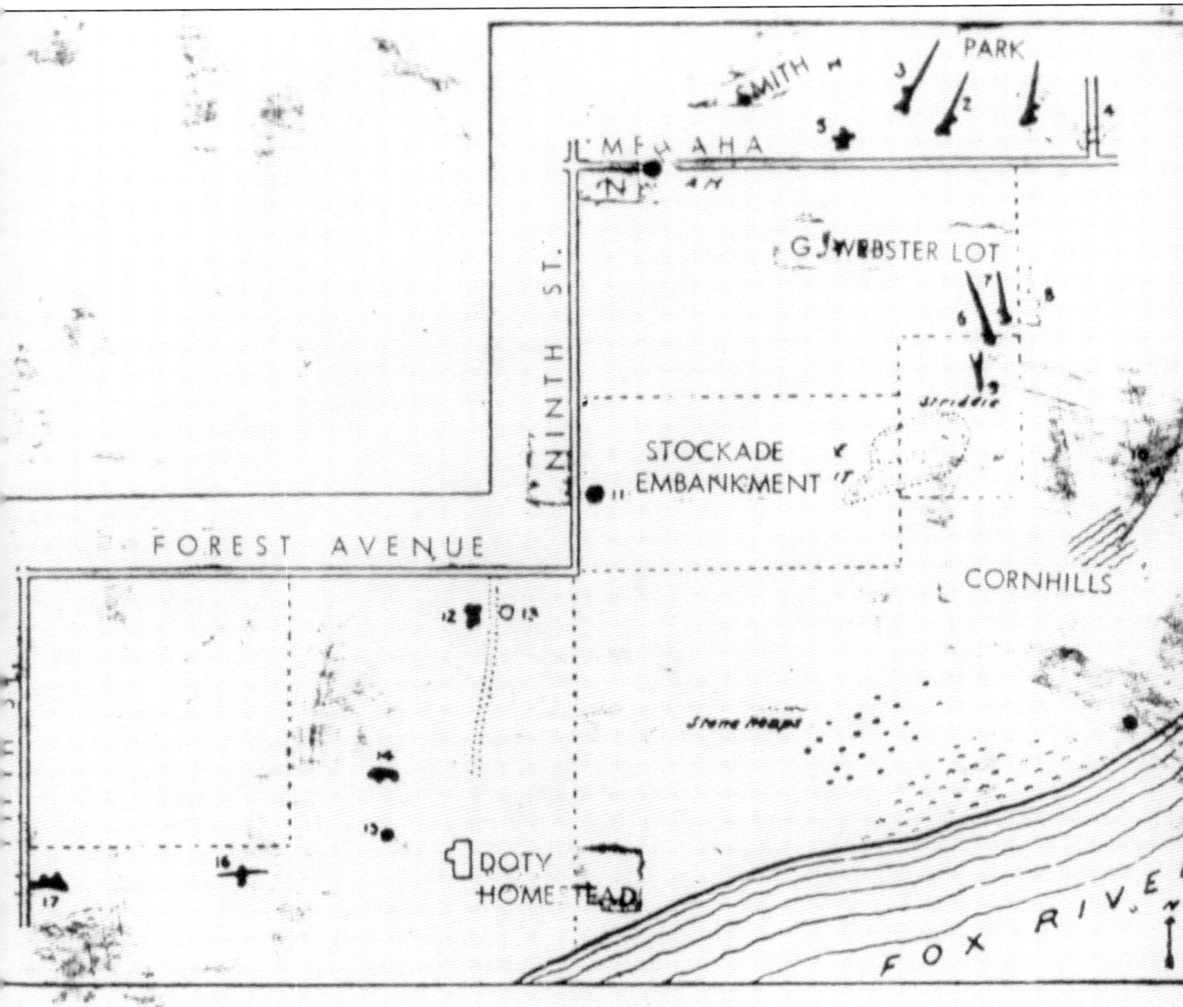

Fig. 5.

This map shows the Indian burial mounds on Doty Island. More than 20 mounds were visible on the island at the end of the 19th century, stretching from Smith Park westward towards Neenah's Fifth Street. The only mounds that survive today are in the park and are listed on the top of the map as nos. 1 through 3. Those three mounds are in the shape of long-tailed animals sometimes referred to as panthers, but they are more likely representations of water spirits prominent in Native American beliefs. The mounds were built to serve a variety of purposes, but most were intended to be the final resting place of the builders' people. Archaeologists have labeled the builders of the mounds as the "Effigy Mound People" and believe they erected mounds across Wisconsin and parts of Minnesota, Illinois, and Iowa. The dates of construction are believed to be between AD 700 and AD 1100.

Two

Getting Around

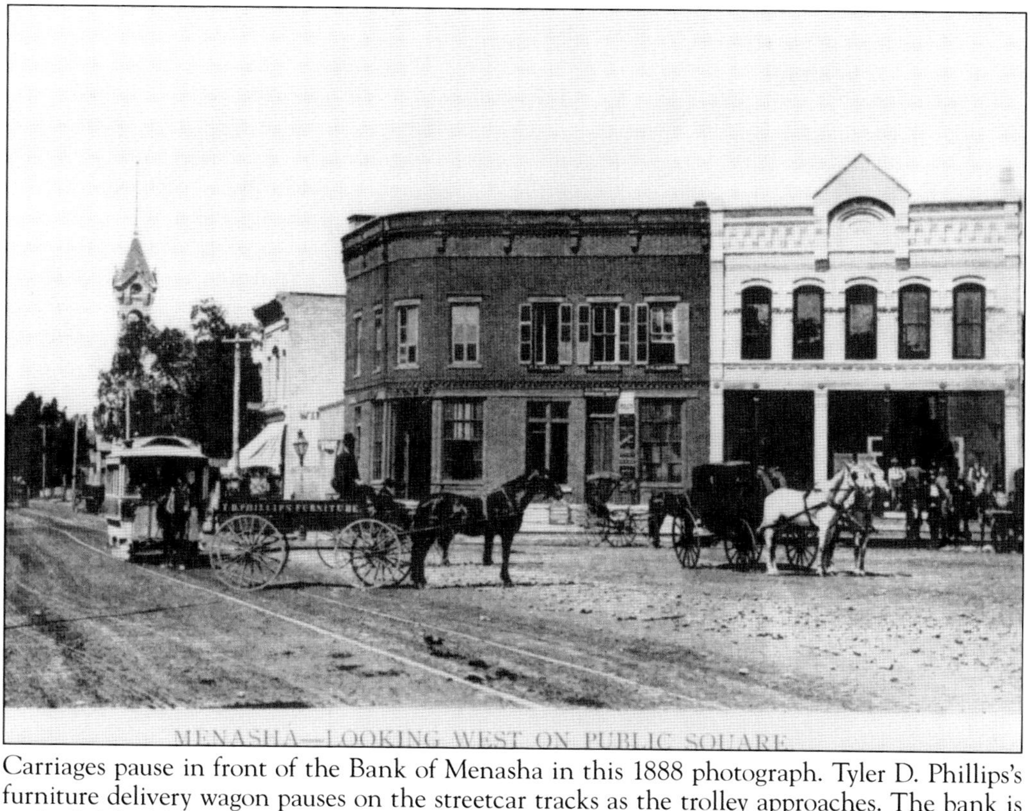

Carriages pause in front of the Bank of Menasha in this 1888 photograph. Tyler D. Phillips's furniture delivery wagon pauses on the streetcar tracks as the trolley approaches. The bank is in the left building. P.V. Lawson Jr.'s law office is located on the second floor. A barber shop and sample rooms fill the other building. City hall, with its signature bell tower, looms beyond the trees. (Courtesy of Menasha Public Library.)

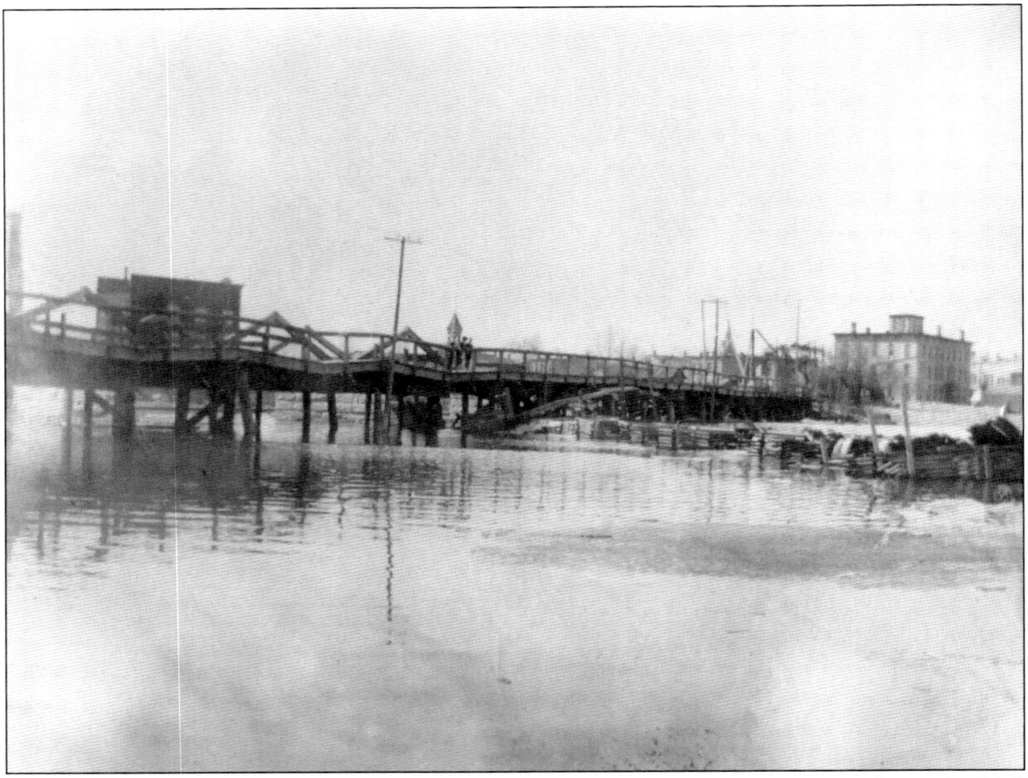

Above, this view of the Fox River, looking towards the Island Paper Company, shows the Mill Street Bridge. The National Hotel lies at the north end of this bridge, and the bridge tender's shack is in the foreground. Contrast this view of the bridge with that of the sturdier Mill Street Bridge below, looking east in about 1900. One can see St. Mary's Catholic Church rising in the distance, and Menasha High School is obscured by the Elisha D. Smith Library. The Mill Street Bridge was not just a means of joining the community with Doty Island; it also served as an impressive gateway into the heart of downtown.

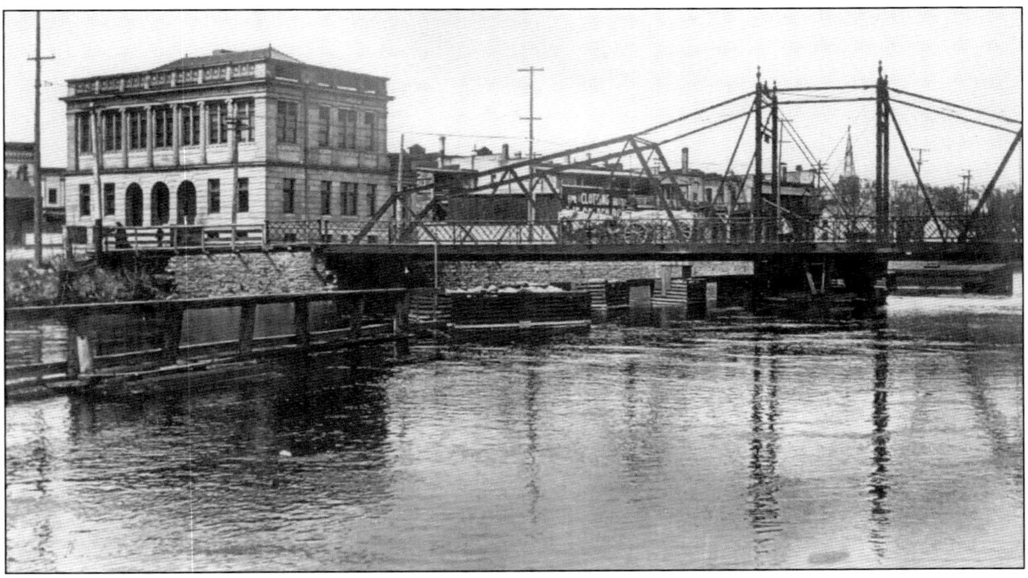

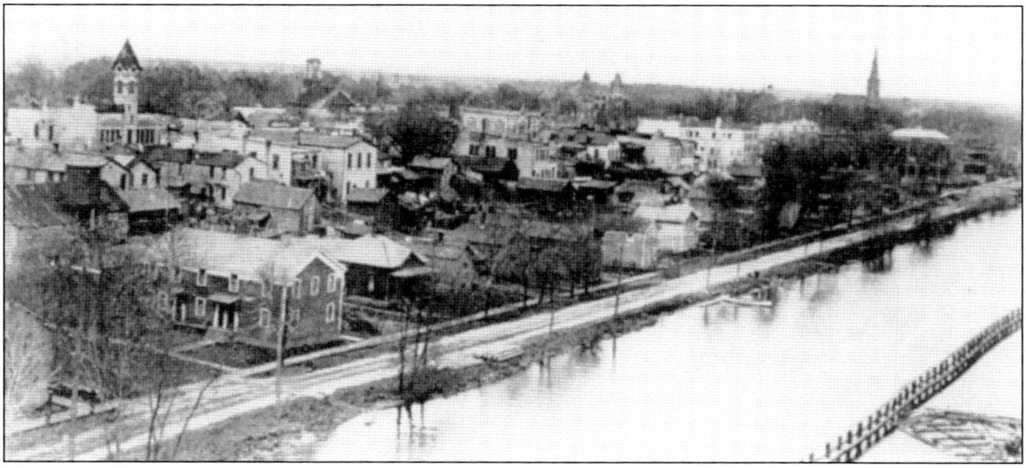

This panoramic view of Menasha's waterfront emphasizes the Fox River's importance to the community. In the distance, one can see the iconic landmarks of city hall, Menasha High School, and St. Mary's Catholic Church. The log boom in the river kept shipping lanes open while preventing the escape of valuable assets into open waters. (Courtesy of Menasha Public Library.)

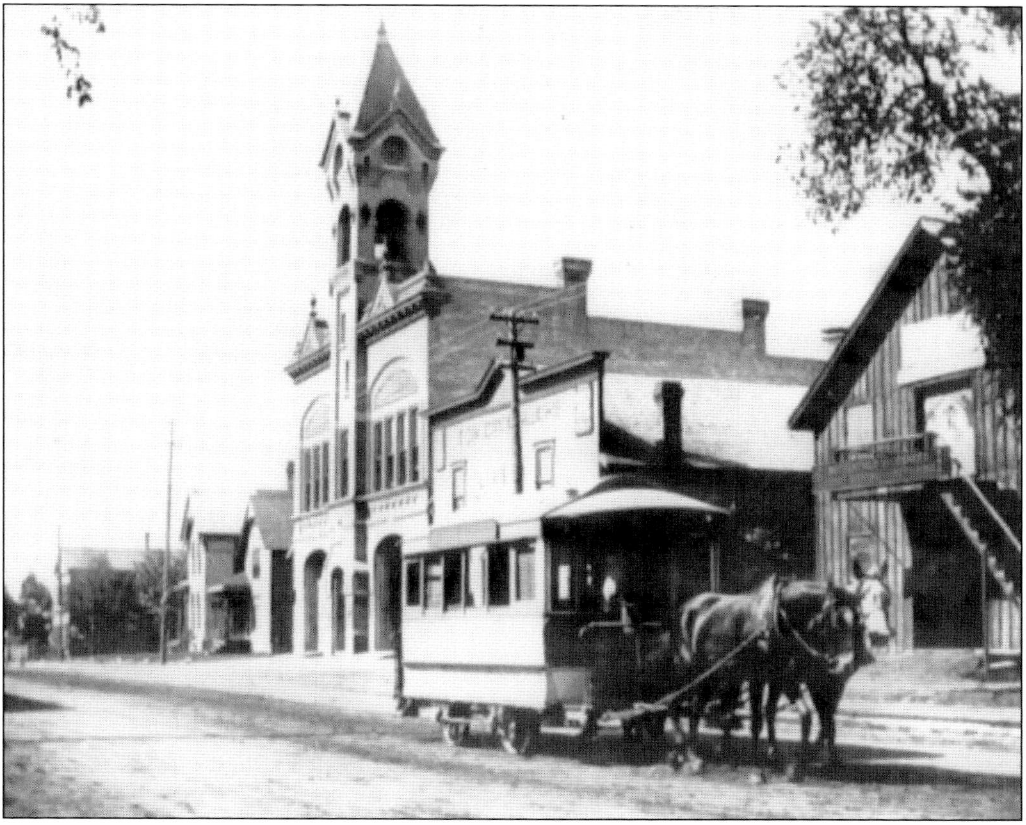

Moving slowly down Main Street, the horse-drawn streetcar, sometimes known as a dinky, passes the recently completed city hall. The horse-drawn streetcar combined the low cost, flexibility, and safety of animal power with the efficiency, smoothness, and all-weather capability of a rail right-of-way. Nevertheless, the economies associated with electric power eventually led to the replacement of the more-costly horsecars on June 18, 1898.

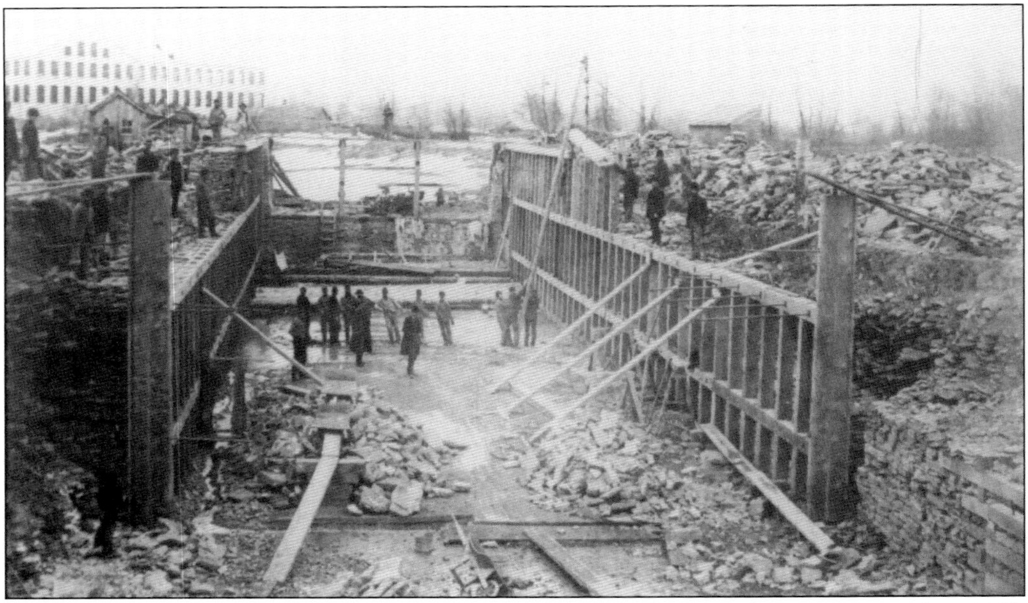

This 1889 photograph shows the rebuilding of the Menasha lock, first constructed in 1853. Rebuilding was necessary to better handle shipments of timber, coal, and pig iron, as well as pleasure craft. By 1856, a lock, dam, and canal system was completed from Portage to Green Bay. In 1884, the US Army Corps of Engineers took responsibility for the locks system for the next 100 years. The building in the background is the George A. Whiting Paper Company. (Courtesy of Menasha Public Library.)

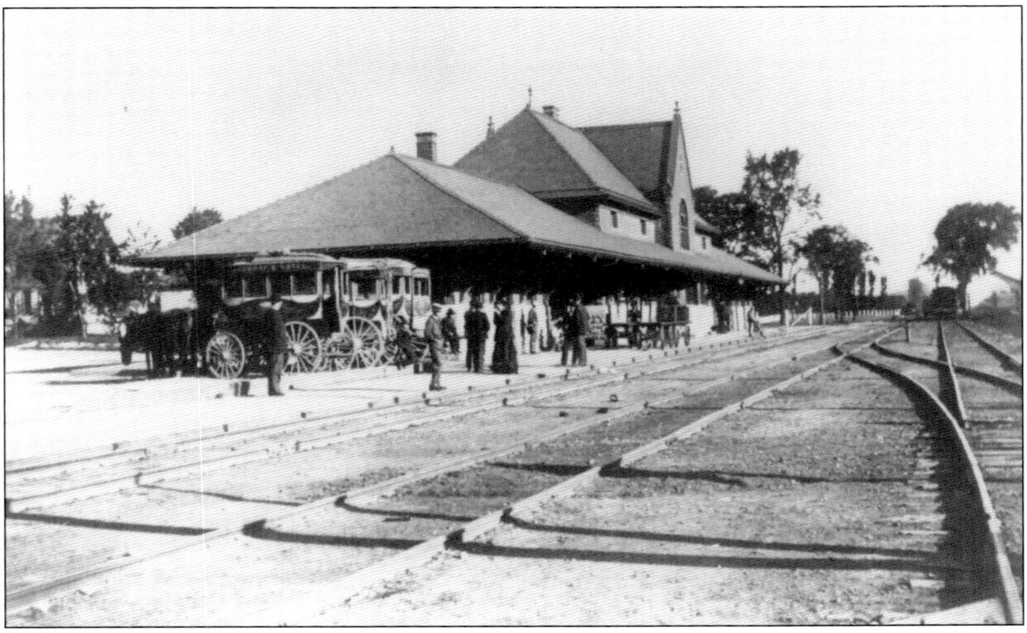

Built in 1892 in the Victorian Romanesque style, the Chicago & North Western Railway station was strategically located on Doty Island, practically straddling the line between Menasha and Neenah. Notice the transfer carriages of the Landgraf Hotel, ready to take passengers to that lodging in Menasha, just over the Tayco Street Bridge. The citizenry took pride in having a train depot larger than that of nearby Appleton or Oshkosh. (Courtesy of Menasha Public Library.)

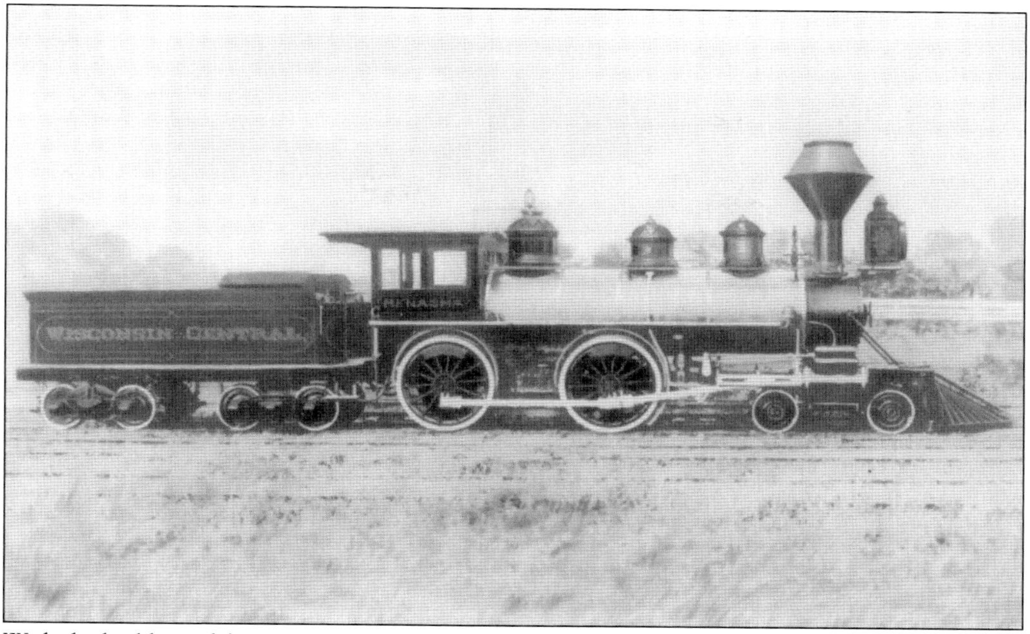

With the building of the Wisconsin Central Railroad, a branch of the Milwaukee and Northern was built from Menasha to Hilbert in 1871 to give the Wisconsin Central a connection to Milwaukee. Originally named the Menasha, this 35-ton engine was one of an order for five engines placed and delivered in 1871. These were said to be beautiful machines—adorned in green, gold, and red paint with shiny brass bands around their boilers.

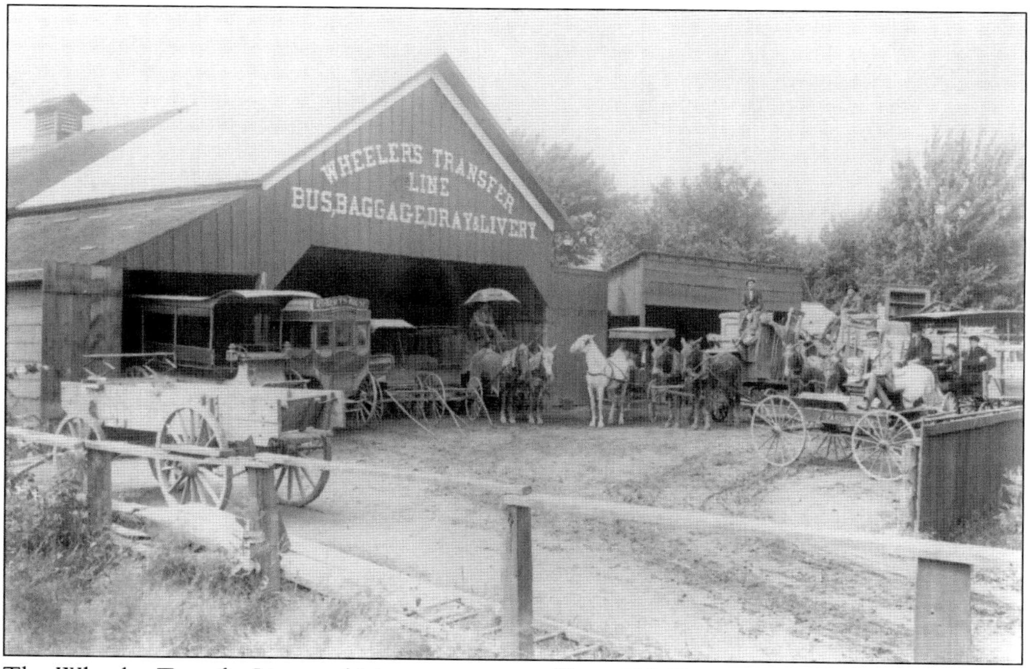

The Wheeler Transfer Line and Livery was originally at 328 Tayco Street, between Main and Chute Streets. Founded in 1894, the company eventually moved to Chute Street, just west of what became Menasha Furniture. Notice the coach used by Roberts Resort for passenger transfer from the train stations to the resort at the end of Doty Island. (Courtesy of Menasha Public Library.)

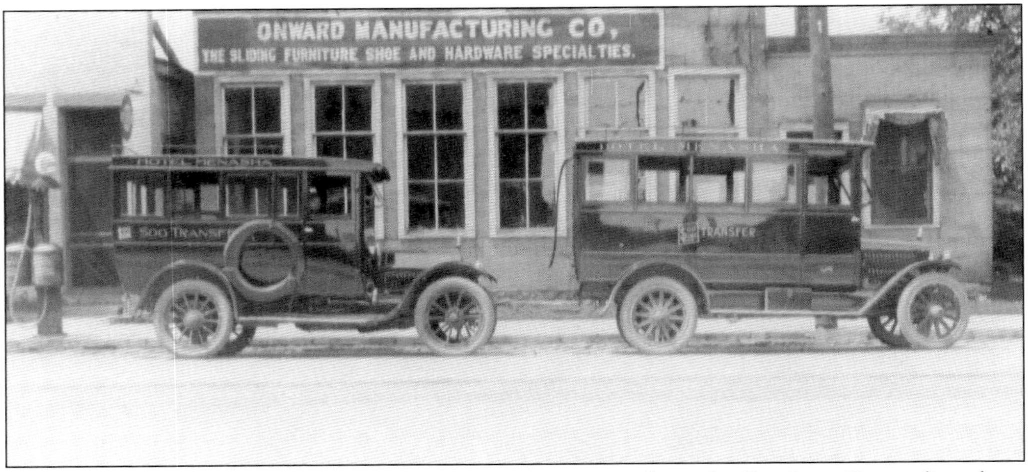

These conveyances were used to transport weary passengers from the Soo Line Depot directly to the Hotel Menasha. Notice the gas pump behind the first vehicle. The early pumps were visible gas pumps with a clear glass cylinder of usually 5 or 10 gallons on top of the pump, so one could see what he or she was getting, or if the gas was dirty, a big problem at that time.

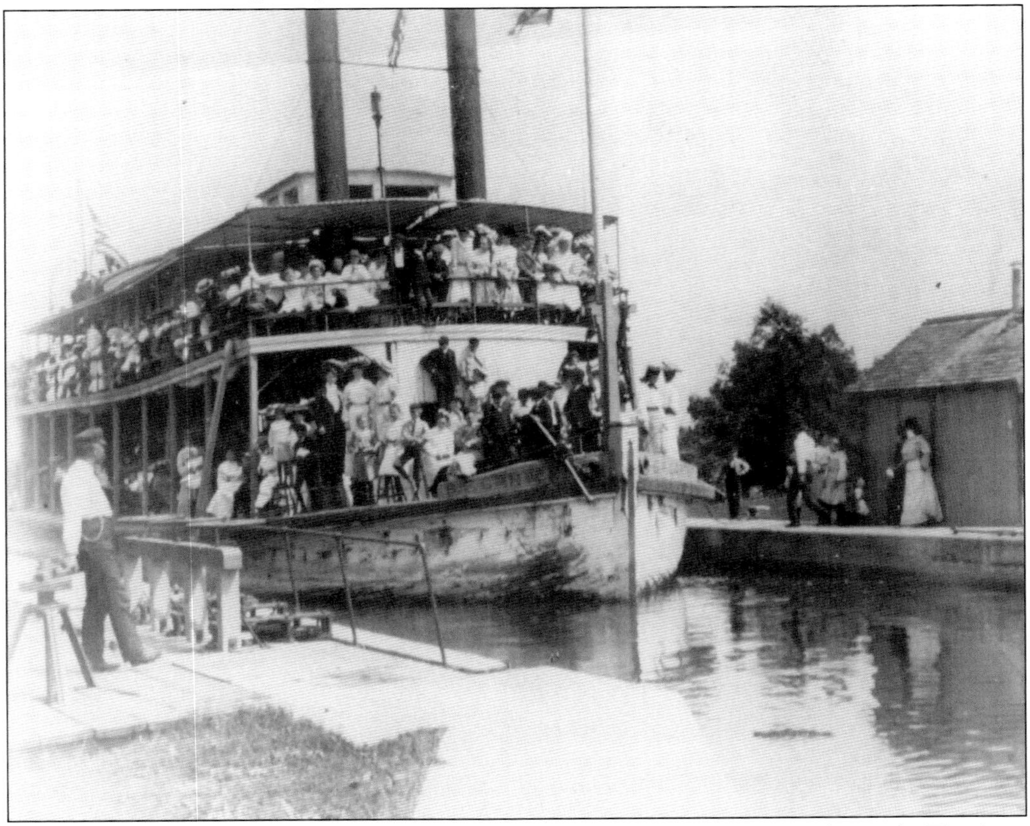

In this photograph, the excursion boat *B.F. Carter* heads through the Menasha Lock. This boat would take passengers to High Cliff Park (the only state-owned recreation area located on Lake Winnebago) with a one-way fare that cost 10¢. The lock master is leaning against the crank, which opened and closed the lock gates. *The B.F. Carter* was launched in the spring of 1876 and operated until 1910. (Courtesy of Menasha Public Library.)

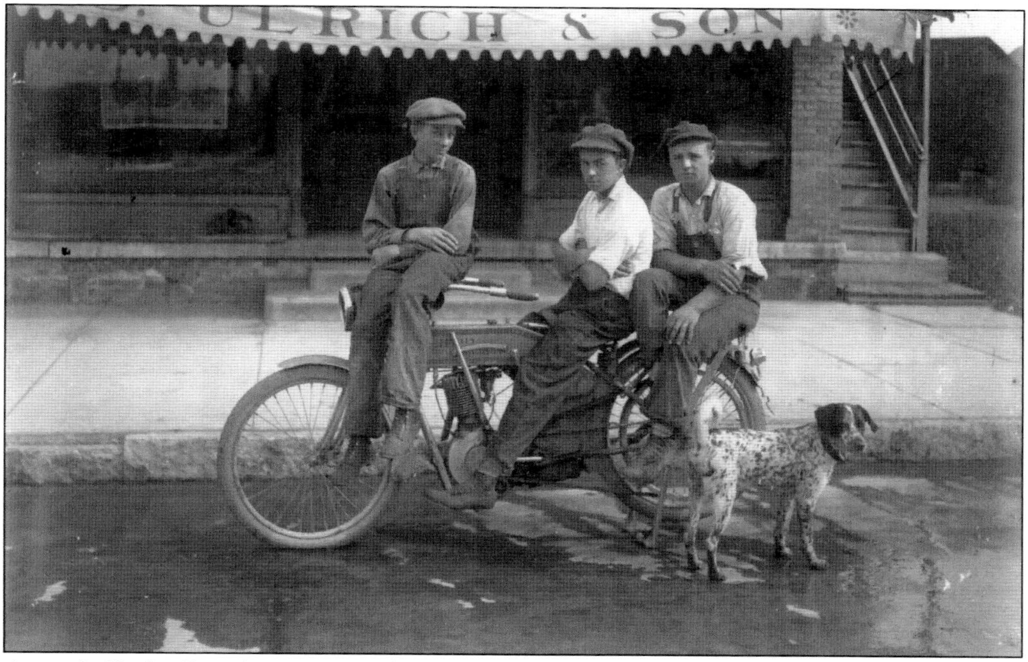

An early Harley-Davidson motorcycle graces the entrance to Ulrich Meat Market at Main and Tayco Streets. Many motorcycles in this era were simply regular pedal-bicycle frames with engines. Pictured from left to right are Joe Ulrich, Sheldon ?, and Frank Ciske. Spot the dog completes the quartet.

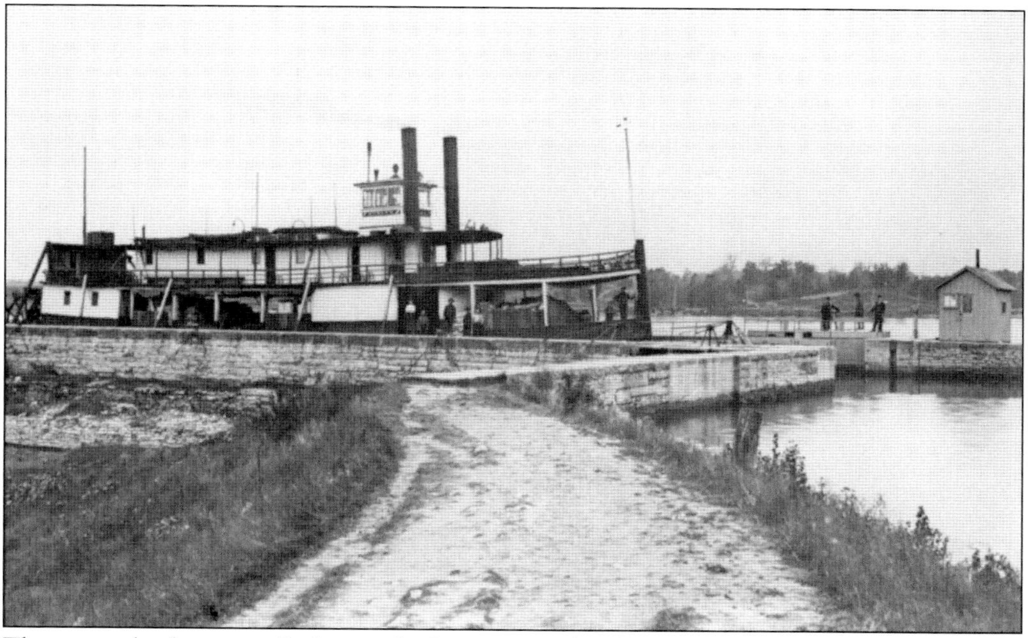

The stern-wheel steamer *Evelyn* was built in 1883 to handle the coal trade between Green Bay and Oshkosh. At 143 feet long and under the command of Capt. John Crawford, she was later sold to the Oshkosh Steamboat Company and dismantled in 1907. Her hull was destined to be used as a hunting lodge on the marsh at the head of Lake Butte des Morts. (Courtesy of Menasha Public Library.)

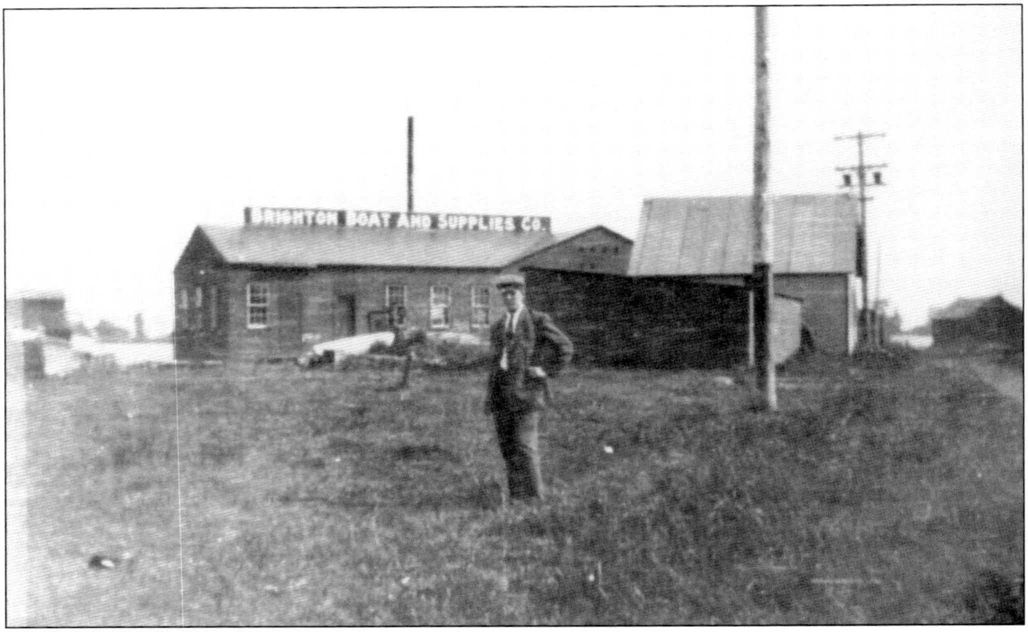

The Brighton Boat and Supply Company, seen here in 1907, was located on Konemac Street at the corner of Second Street near present-day Jefferson Park. Incorporated in 1905 with $5,000 in capital, the principal stockholders were Andrew Lind, L.H. Moore, and John A. Olmstead, who managed the premises. By 1910, six craftsmen were employed at the facility. (Courtesy of Menasha Public Library.)

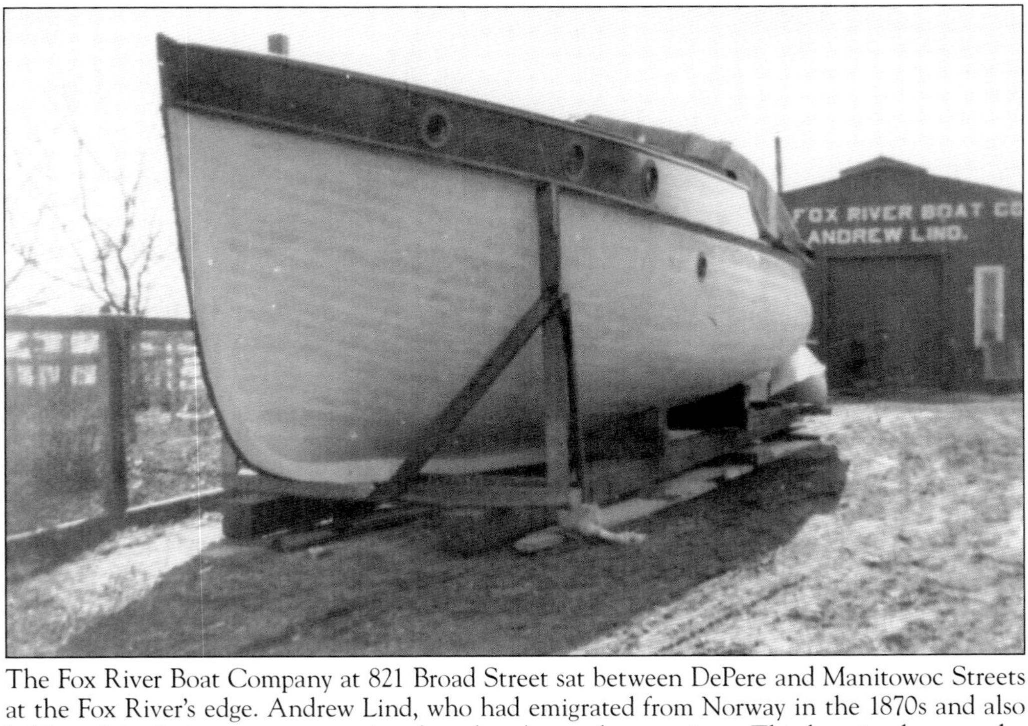

The Fox River Boat Company at 821 Broad Street sat between DePere and Manitowoc Streets at the Fox River's edge. Andrew Lind, who had emigrated from Norway in the 1870s and also held stock in their nearest competitor (see above), was the proprietor. This location became the Menasha Water Filtration Plant in the 1930s. (Courtesy of Menasha Public Library.)

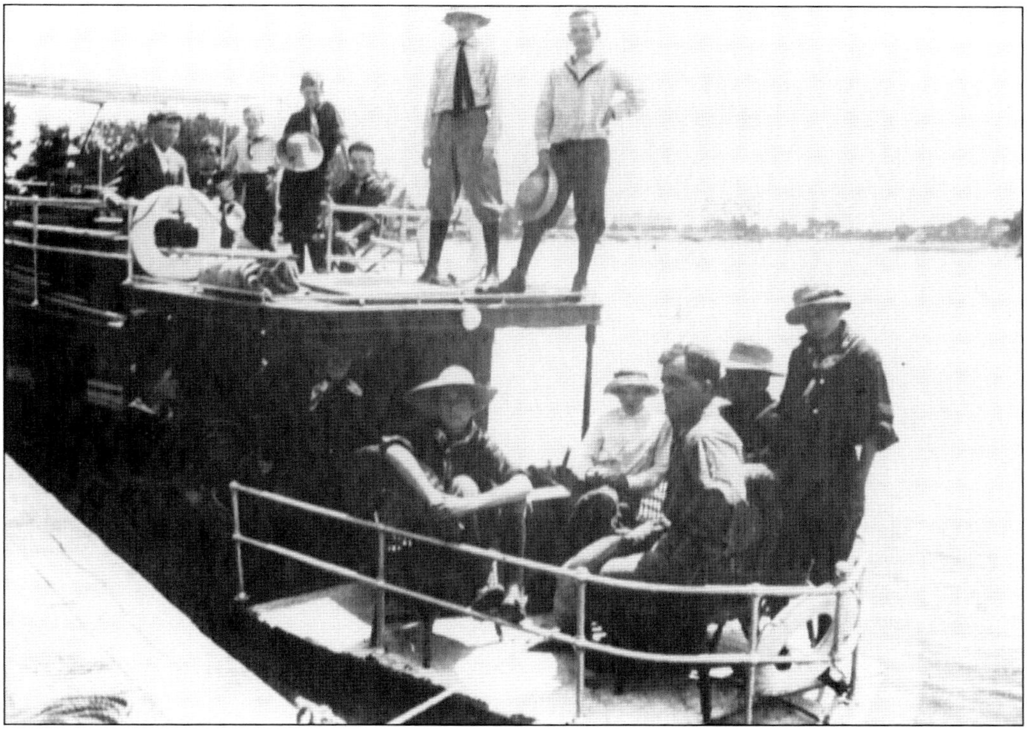

The *Adonis*, a boat owned by the George Loescher family, long-standing Menasha hardware merchants, carried a group of Boy Scouts on an outing in this July 11, 1911 photograph. Notice the boys' standard fashion of the time: knickerbockers, or knickers, which were short pants that buckled at or just below the knee.

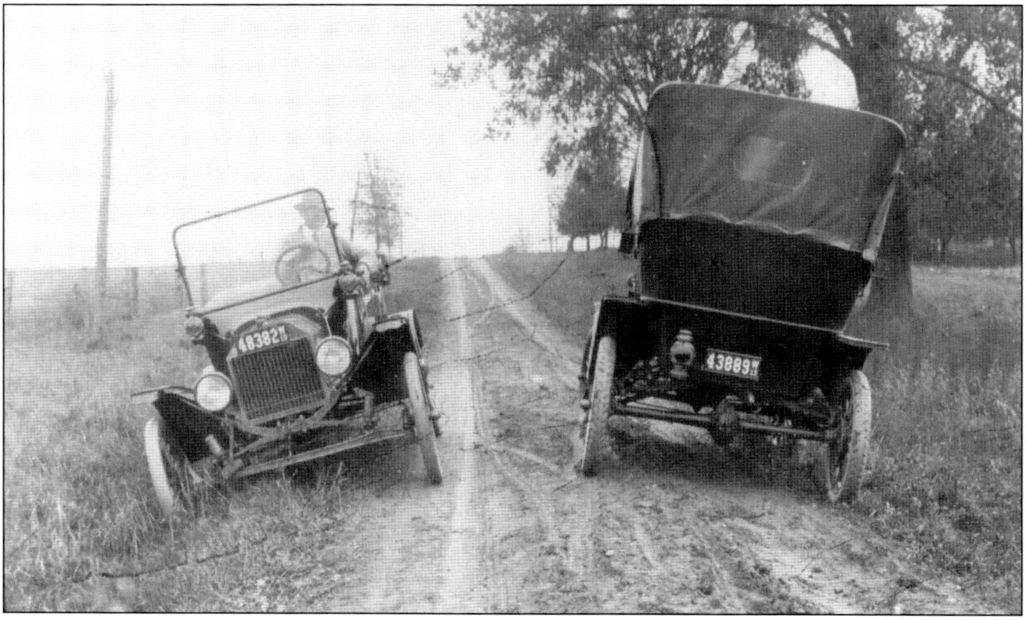

This view of Appleton Road between Menasha and Appleton is representative of road conditions outside of most towns in 1915. The autos are both Ford touring cars—a 1915 model on the left, and a 1912 model on the right.

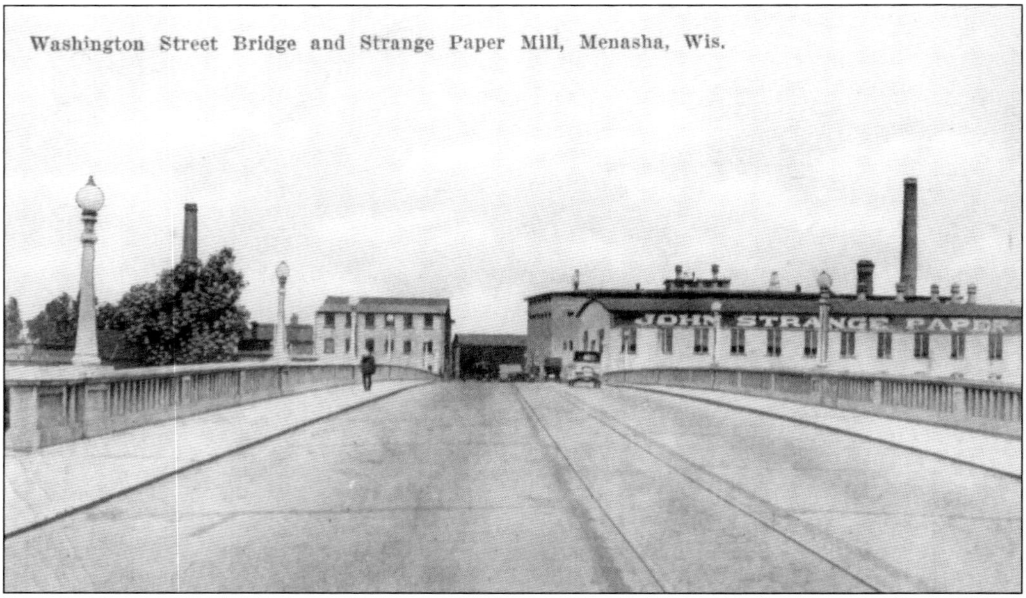

Built in 1919, the Washington Street Bridge connects Doty Island to the island in the Fox River, containing River Street and Menasha Wooden Ware. From there, the Tayco Street Bridge continued to the mainland. In this view facing north, John Strange Paper Company is on the right, and the Menasha Woolen Mill on the left.

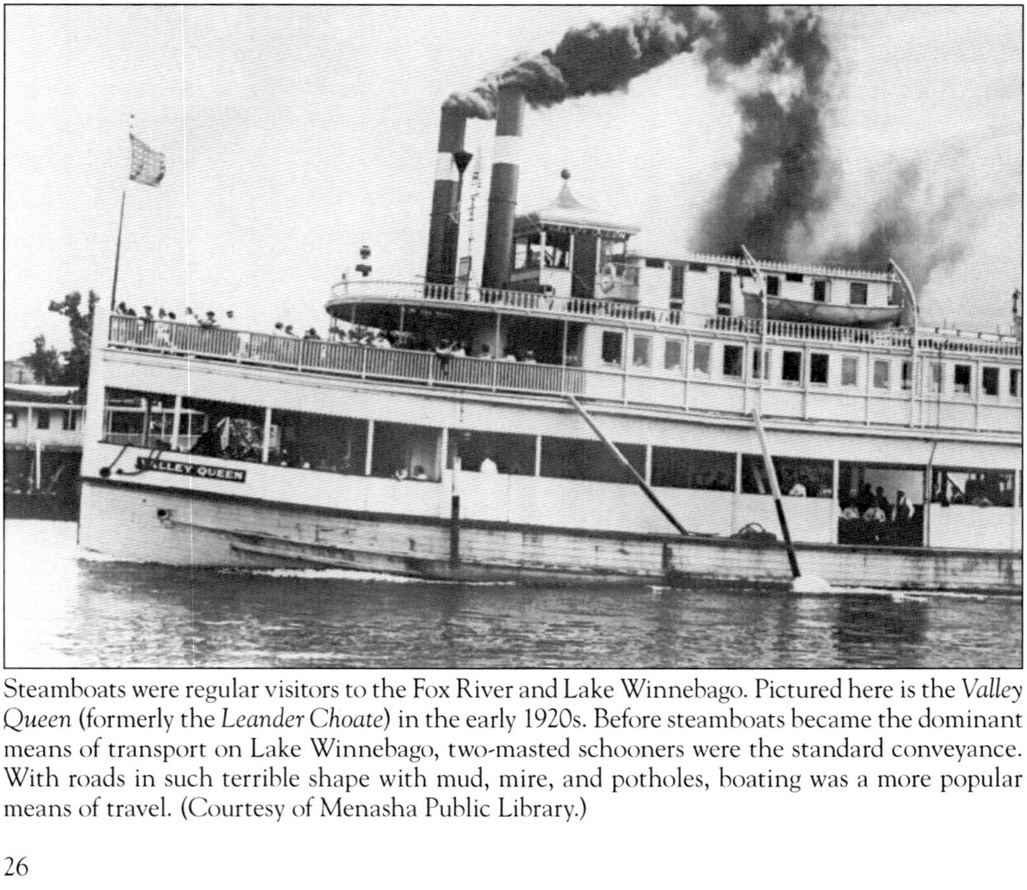

Steamboats were regular visitors to the Fox River and Lake Winnebago. Pictured here is the *Valley Queen* (formerly the *Leander Choate*) in the early 1920s. Before steamboats became the dominant means of transport on Lake Winnebago, two-masted schooners were the standard conveyance. With roads in such terrible shape with mud, mire, and potholes, boating was a more popular means of travel. (Courtesy of Menasha Public Library.)

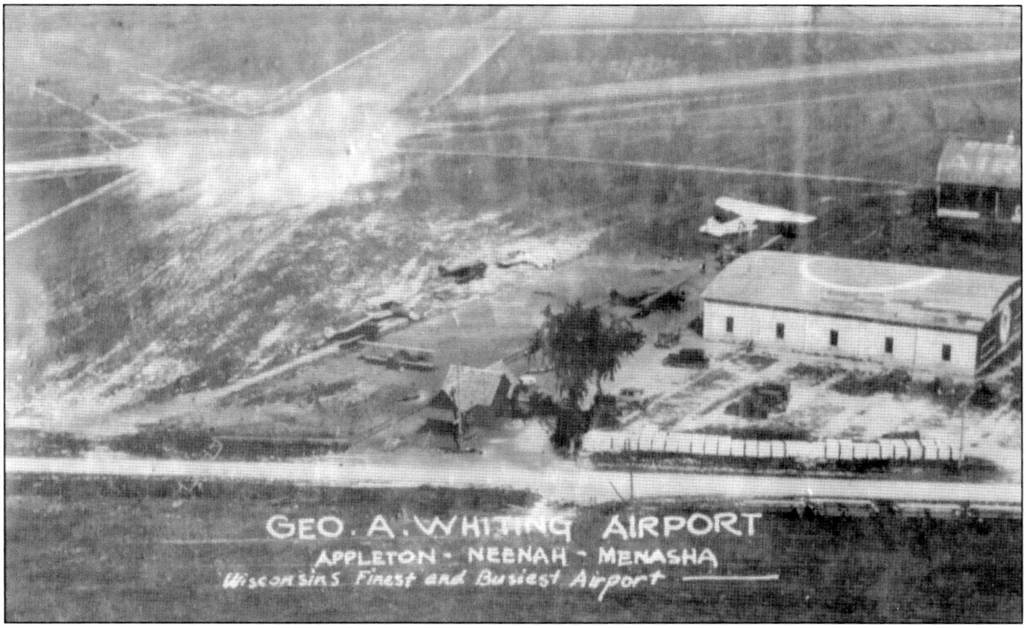

These 1920s views of the George A. Whiting Airport, located north of Menasha at Airport Road and State Road 47, are symbolic of aviation in its early years. George A. Whiting of the George A. Whiting Paper Company was a major investor in this airport and became its namesake. Situated on leased land from the Wittman farm north of Menasha, the airport had two 1,600-foot runways. The airport opened for use in March 1928 but lasted only until 1930, when it was closed due to its losing money on airmail operations. In later years, the telltale shape of the hangar was still evident, as it became a Goodwill store and, later, a hardware store.

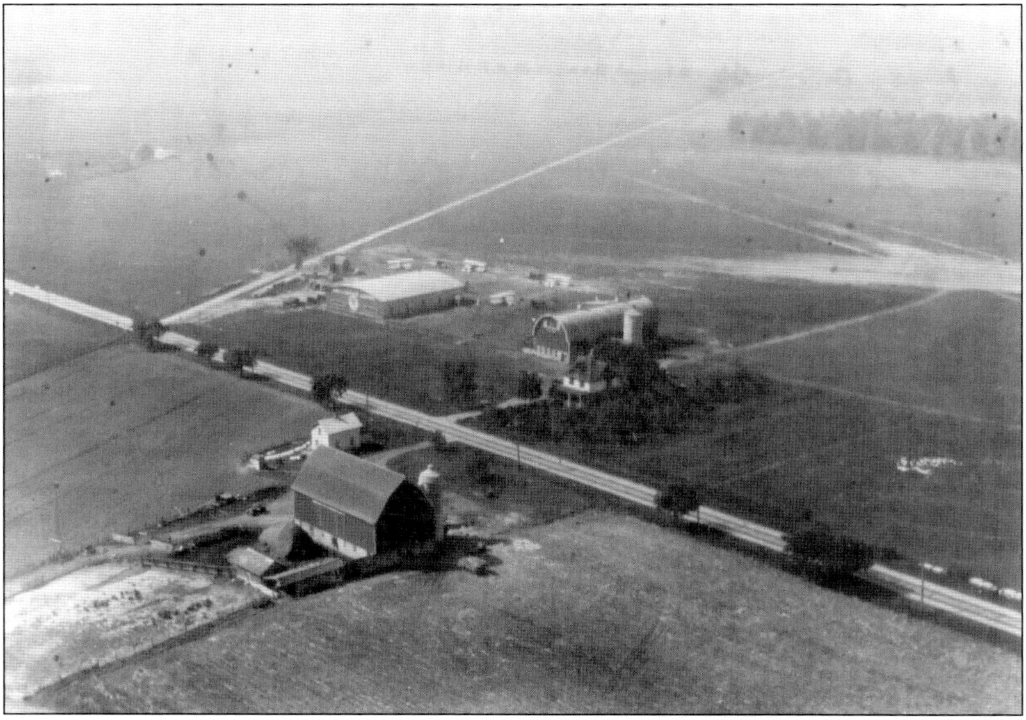

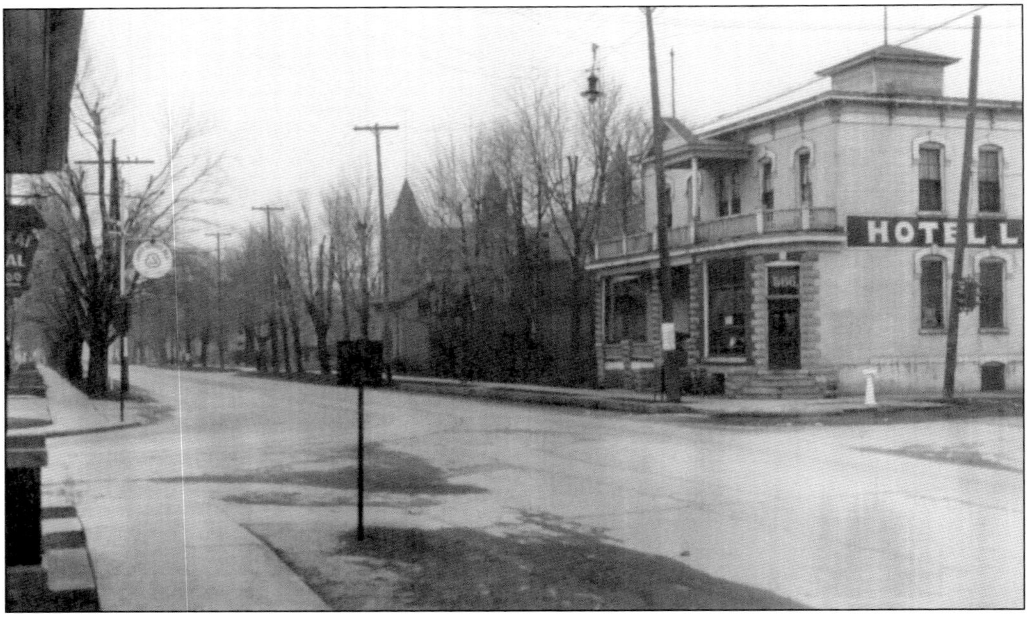

In this view of the Third and Racine Street intersection in the 1920s, the sign on the pole outside the Hotel Lenz designates Racine Street as US 41. The spires of Menasha High School are visible through the trees beyond the hotel. Also of note is the porcelain bubbler at the street corner.

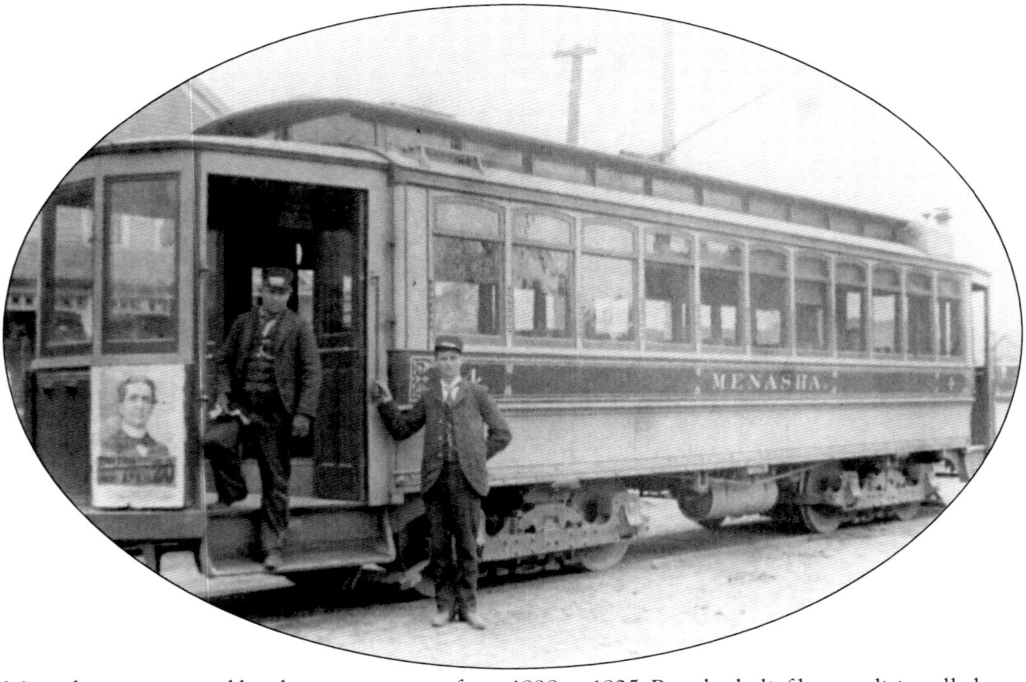

Menasha was serviced by electric streetcars from 1898 to 1925. Popular belief has traditionally been that streetcar service ended because of the rise of the automobile. But for Neenah and Menasha, at least, the official reason cited in a news article of the time was simply that the streetcar company (Wisconsin Traction, Light, Heat, and Power Company) did not want the responsibility of paying for new bridges. The same news item argued that there was sufficient motor bus service to take up the slack. Streetcar service lasted in Appleton and Oshkosh until 1930.

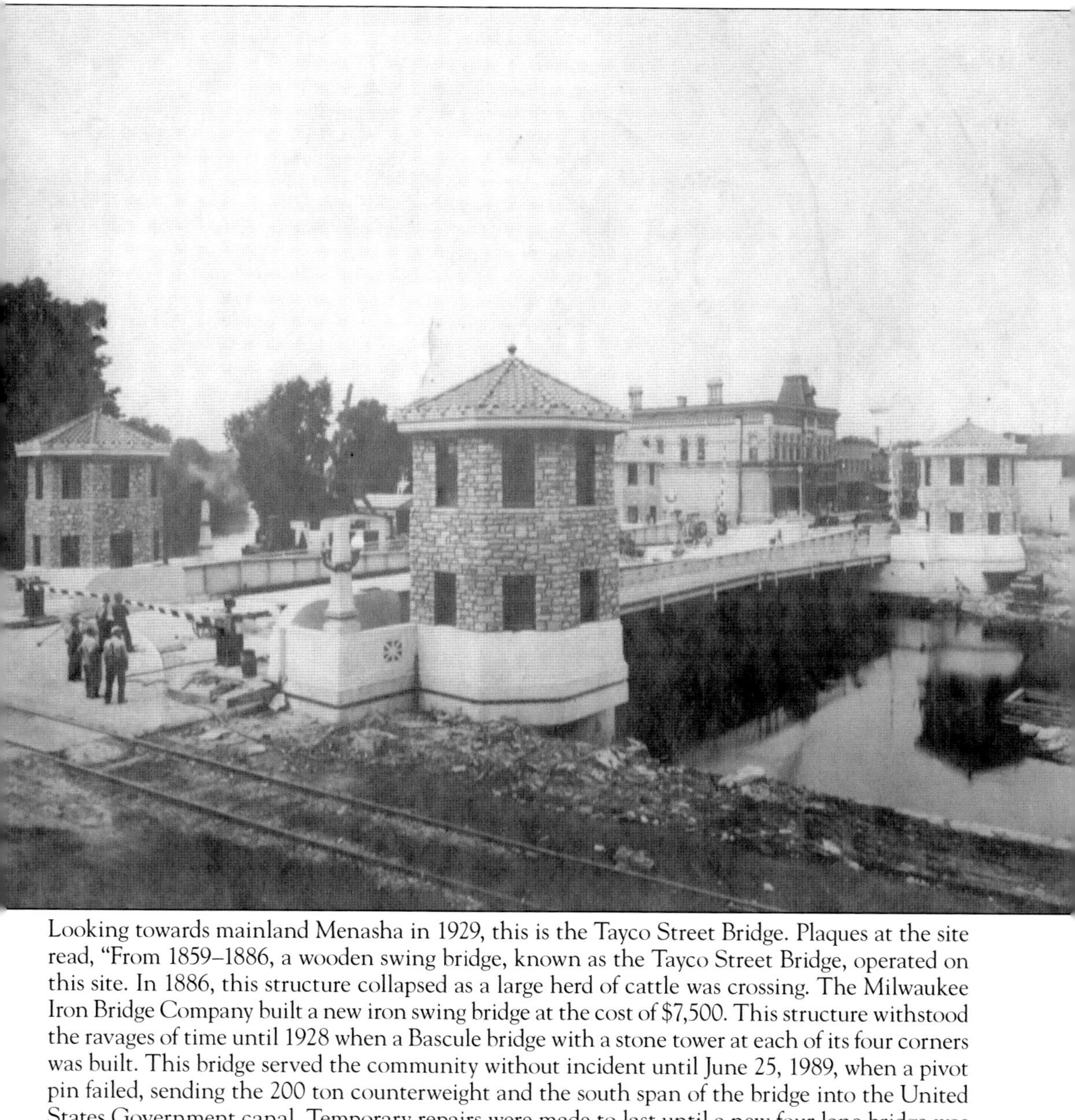

Looking towards mainland Menasha in 1929, this is the Tayco Street Bridge. Plaques at the site read, "From 1859–1886, a wooden swing bridge, known as the Tayco Street Bridge, operated on this site. In 1886, this structure collapsed as a large herd of cattle was crossing. The Milwaukee Iron Bridge Company built a new iron swing bridge at the cost of $7,500. This structure withstood the ravages of time until 1928 when a Bascule bridge with a stone tower at each of its four corners was built. This bridge served the community without incident until June 25, 1989, when a pivot pin failed, sending the 200 ton counterweight and the south span of the bridge into the United States Government canal. Temporary repairs were made to last until a new four lane bridge was built in 1993 at a cost of 3.2 million dollars." (Courtesy of Menasha Public Library.)

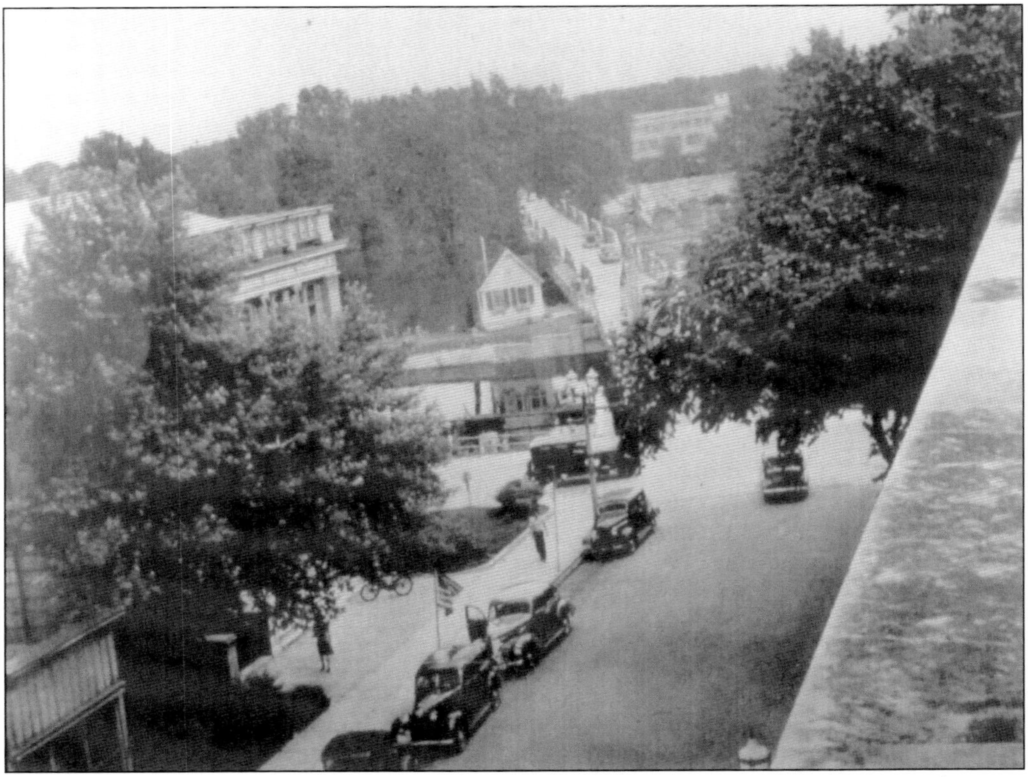

This photograph, taken in the 1940s from the roof of the Hotel Menasha, shows the Mill Street Bridge in its glory days. The Neoclassical architecture of the Elisha D. Smith Public Library made a grand first impression for newcomers arriving from the Doty Island side of town to downtown. (Courtesy of Menasha Public Library.)

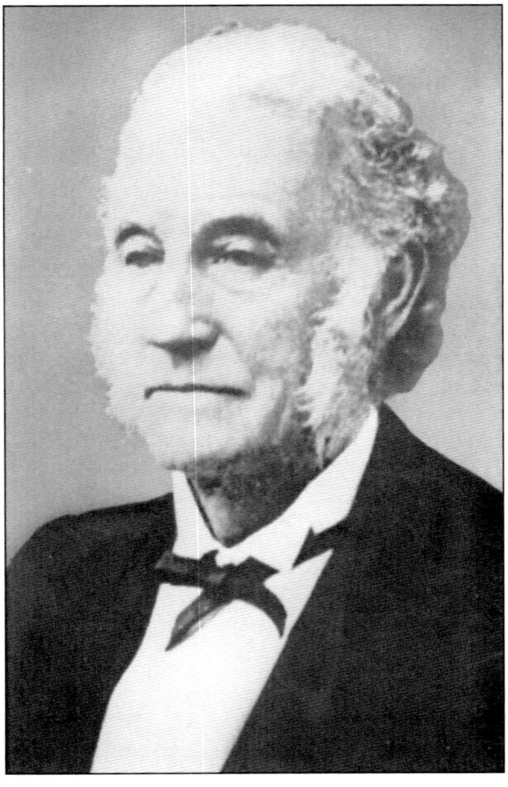

Railroad organizer Judge George Reed, brother of Harrison and Curtis Reed, helped organize the Wisconsin Central Railroad in February 1871 at the National Hotel. He became the first vice president and general counsel for the line. The city of Reedsville, Wisconsin, is named after him. Judge Reed lost his life in a hotel fire in Milwaukee in 1883.

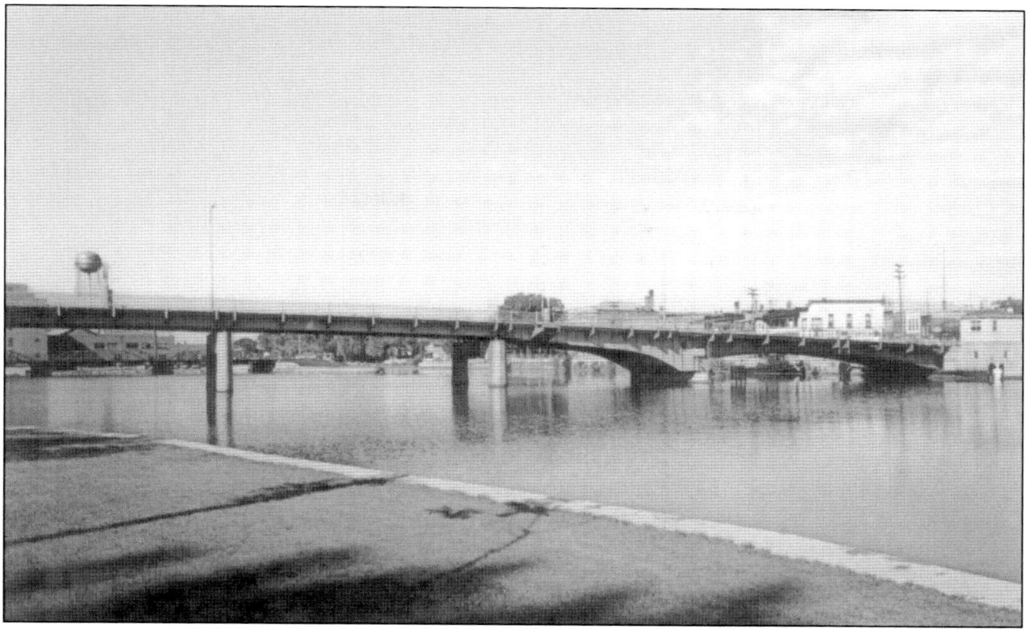

The completion of the new Racine Street Bridge, seen above during its August 1951 opening, allowed the dismantling of the Mill Street Bridge, below, which had serviced Menasha in various incarnations at that location for well over 60 years. This new bridge was dedicated to the memory of founding father Curtis Reed and was built at a cost of $585,000. The bridge extended Racine Street across the Fox River from the old steamboat landing downtown. On the Doty Island side, the short street in front of the George Banta Company, where this bridge ended, was dedicated as Curtis Reed Plaza. (Above, author's collection.)

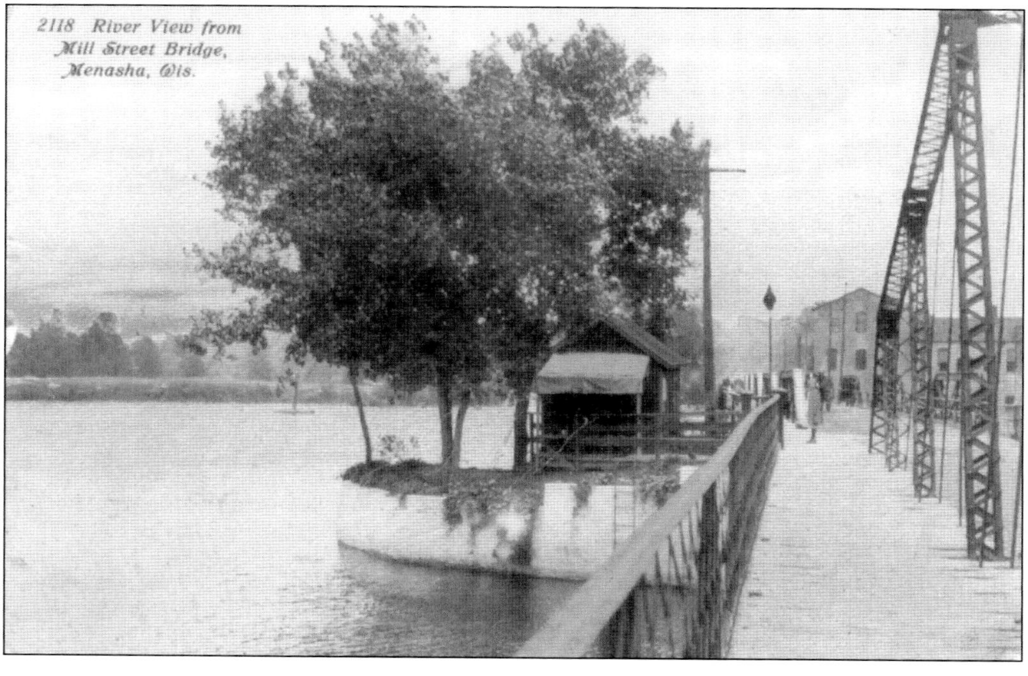

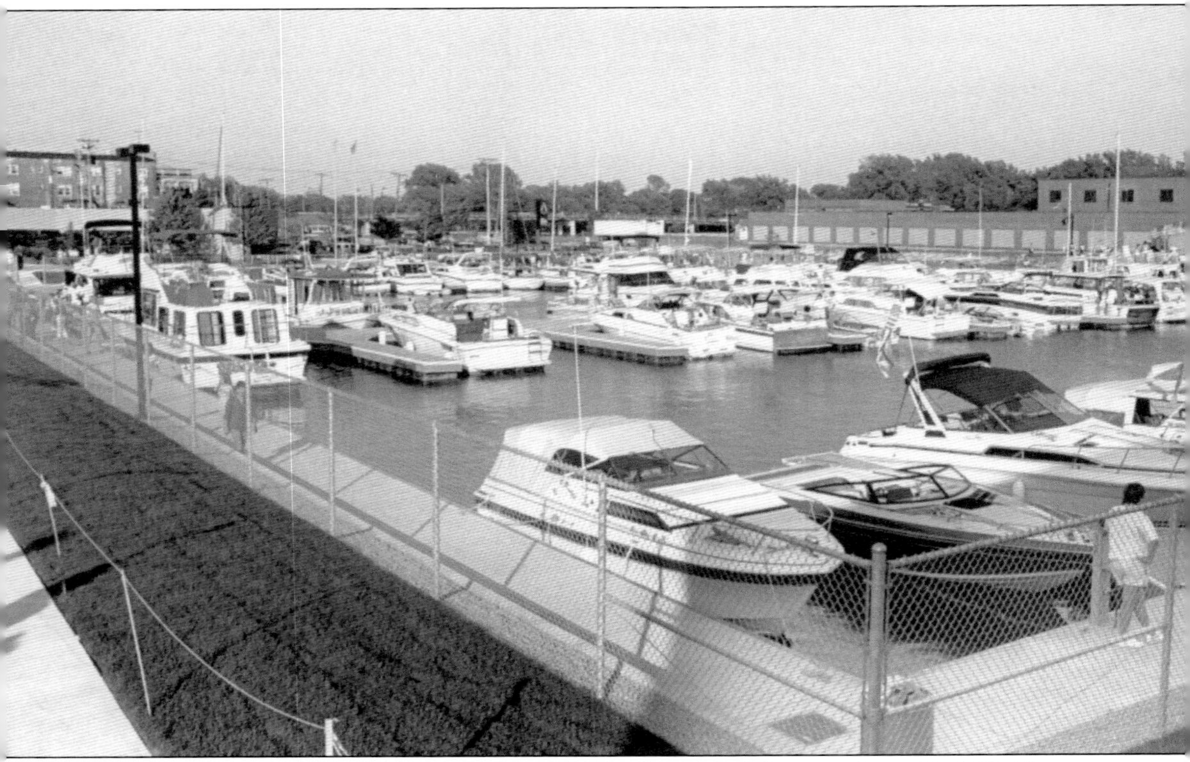

The Menasha Marina is filled to capacity on the day of its dedication, May 16, 1987. The marina has 87 seasonal boat slips, and users have walking access to restaurants and shops downtown. Construction for the marina took out a considerable section of downtown real estate including a major portion of the south side of Main Street across from the old Bank of Menasha corner.

Three

Paper Mills and Wood Products

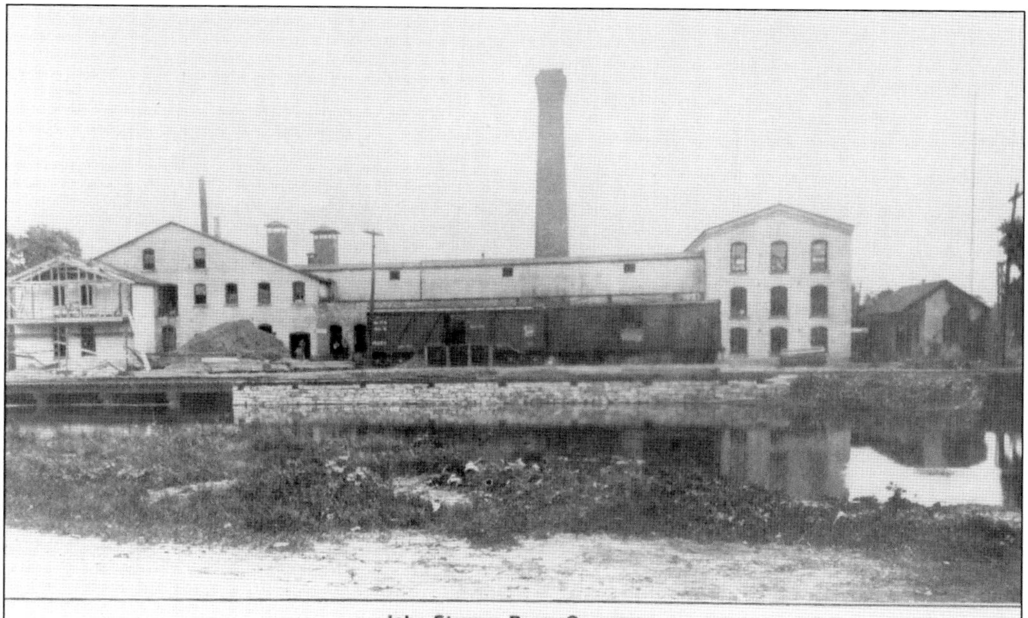

The John Strange Paper Company grew out of the old John Strange Pail and Tub Factory, which was founded in 1881. Incorporated as John Strange Paper in 1891 and located off the Tayco Street Bridge, it made Kraft paper, the kind used for brown paper grocery and lunch bags. In 1969, the Menasha Corporation bought out and gained full ownership of the John Strange Paper Company, which was then renamed the Menasha Paperboard Mill.

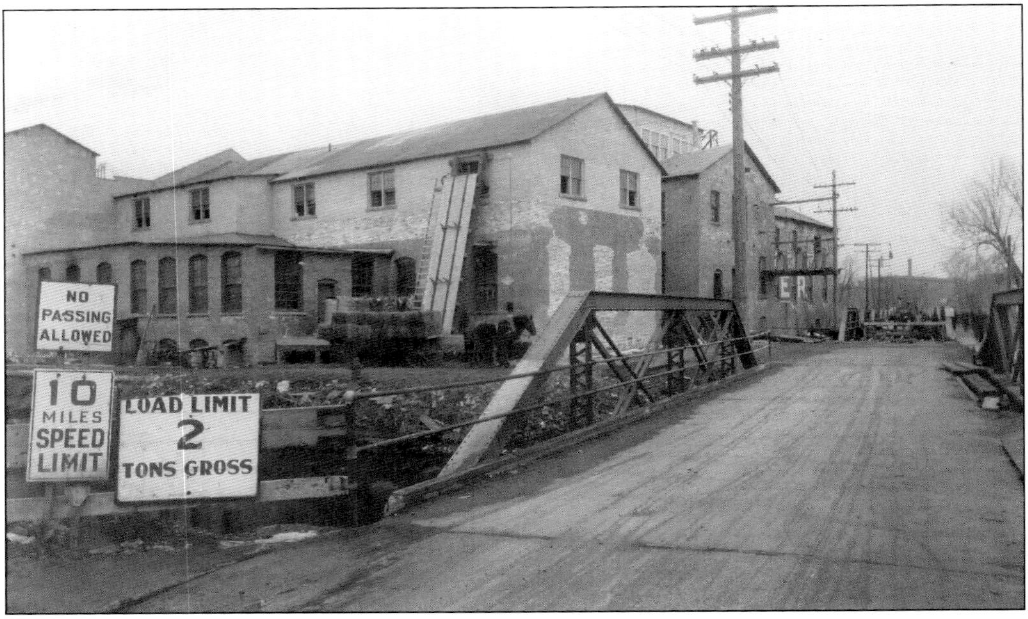

The Island Paper Company, located on the small island situated between the Fox River and the Lawson Canal, was organized by John Strange's brother Alexander and several investors. Reachable by the Mill Street Bridge, the company made paper from straw, which they called "strawboard." Reportedly, this created an obnoxious smell in the area. (Courtesy of Menasha Public Library.)

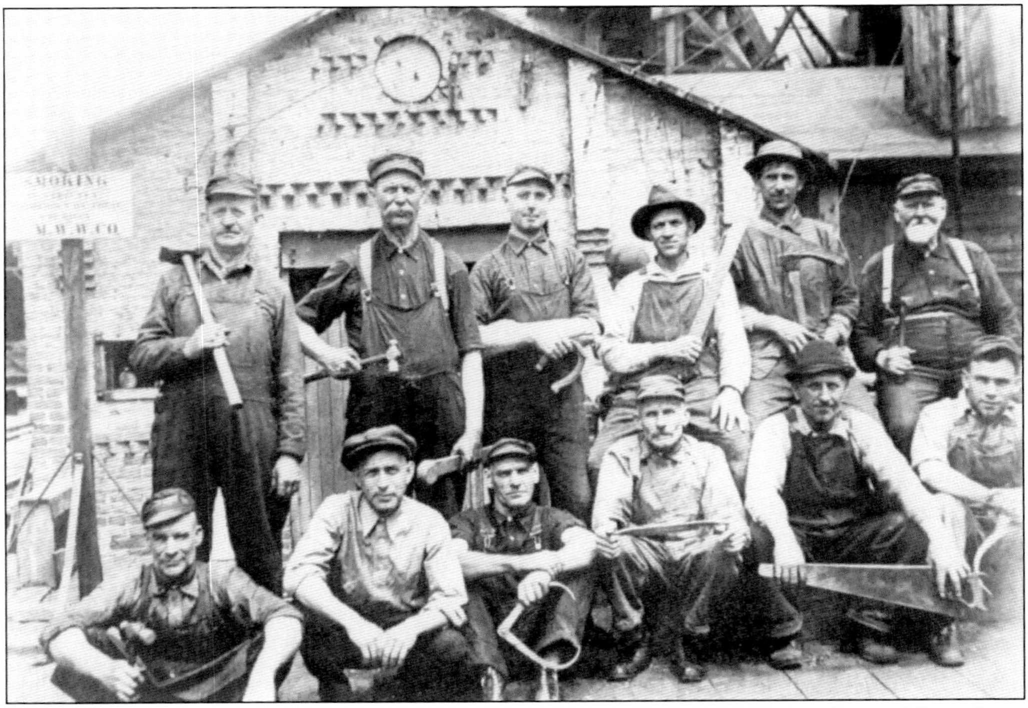

The blacksmiths who cared for the horses of Menasha Wooden Ware pose in front of their shop, displaying the tools of their trade. Albert Christofferson is in back, third from the left; Adolph Gartzke is fifth from the left. The other tradesmen are unidentified. Notice the "no smoking" sign posted prominently in deference to the flammable nature of the company's product.

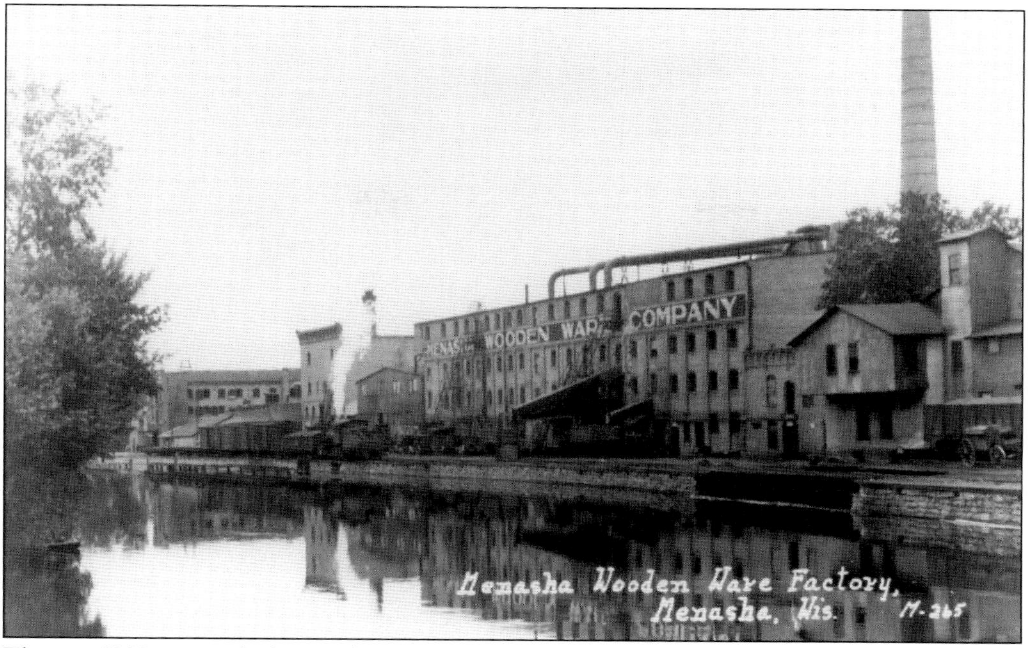

This is a 1929 postcard of Menasha Wooden Ware. An early manufacturer of storage containers such as barrels, kegs, and butter tubs, the Wooden Ware evolved into today's Menasha Corporation, an industry leader in packaging, logistics, and marketing services. The Wooden Ware operated in this location until the fire of 1964 caused operations to leave Menasha proper. (Courtesy of Menasha Public Library.)

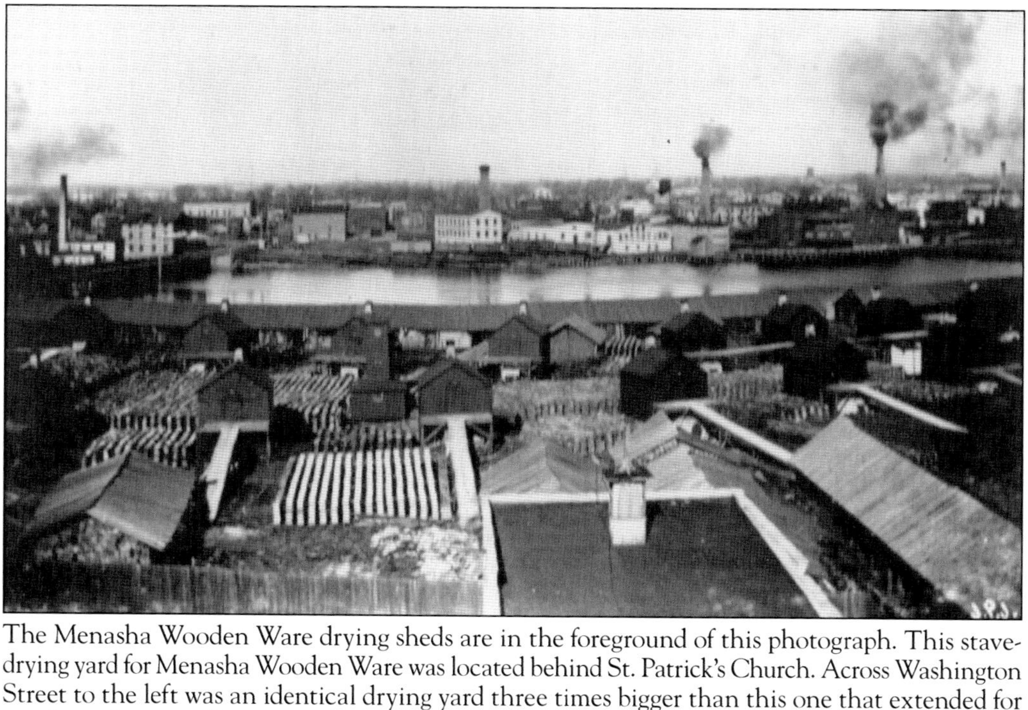

The Menasha Wooden Ware drying sheds are in the foreground of this photograph. This stave-drying yard for Menasha Wooden Ware was located behind St. Patrick's Church. Across Washington Street to the left was an identical drying yard three times bigger than this one that extended for a mile to the west. Staves are the narrow strips of wood placed edge to edge to form the sides of a barrel. The white building in the background is the John Strange Paper Company.

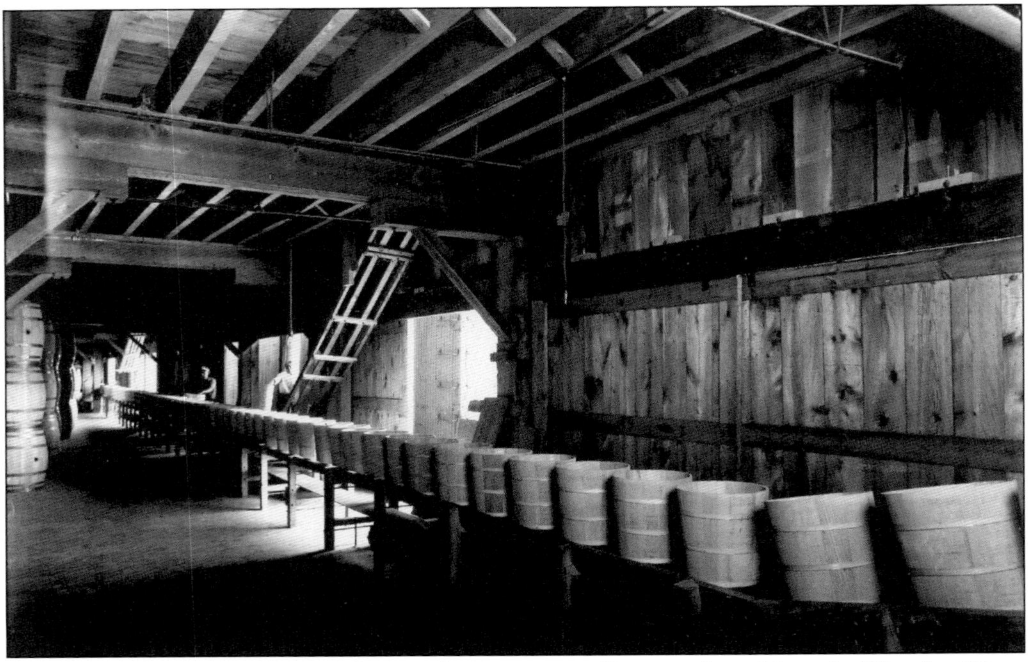

Assembly line automation is evident in this conveyor of butter tubs at Menasha Wooden Ware. Notice the Soo Line boxcar adjacent in the background. To save time and money, the finished product went right from the assembly line to the shipping container. (Courtesy of Menasha Public Library.)

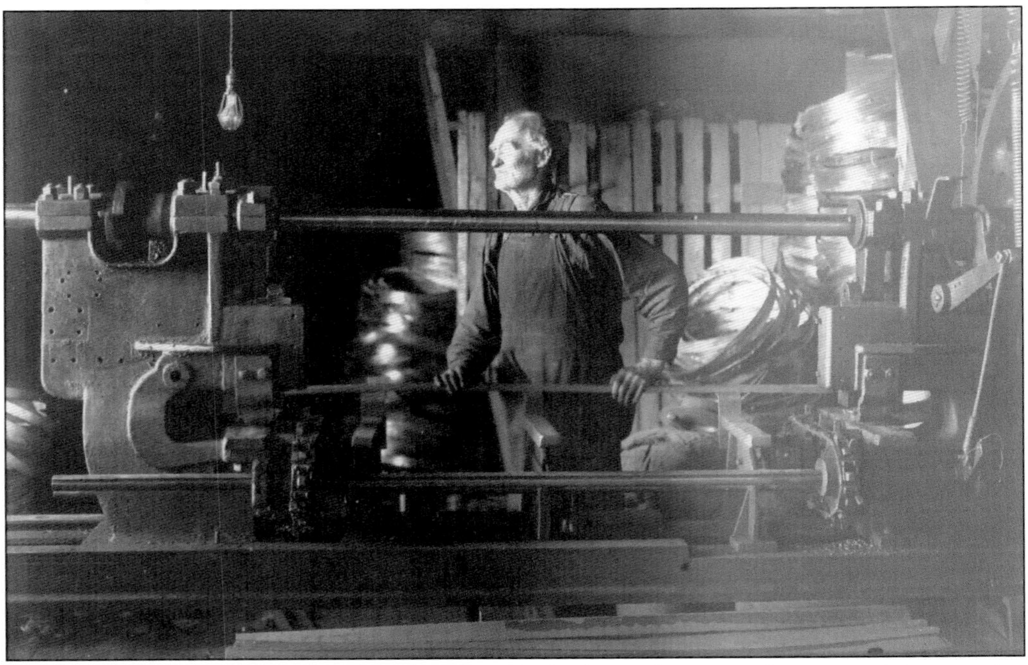

James Hart, a hooper for Menasha Wooden Ware, feeds a brass plate into a shaping machine, creating the hoops stacked behind him. He is 75 years old in this photograph; his career with the Wooden Ware Company spanned 61 years. Today, plastics and corrugated cardboard have replaced most wooden containers, largely making his job obsolete. (Courtesy of Menasha Public Library.)

Traditionally, a cooper is a barrel maker or, by definition, any artisan who makes wooden-staved containers of a conical form of greater length than width, bound together with hoops and possessing flat ends or heads. Examples of a cooper's work include, but are not limited to, casks, barrels, buckets, tubs, and butter churns, as well as items with obscure names like hogsheads, firkins, tierces, rundlets, puncheons, pipes, tuns, butts, pins, and breakers. These 1931 photographs illustrate just how hands-on work at Menasha Wooden Ware could be for Mary Sahosky, right, and John Remich, below, who uses a metal framework to set up construction of a pail. (Courtesy of Menasha Public Library.)

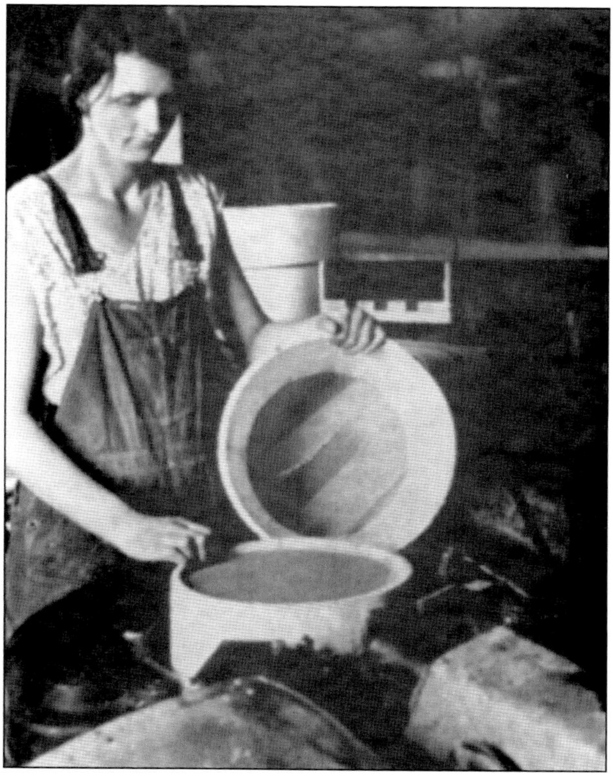

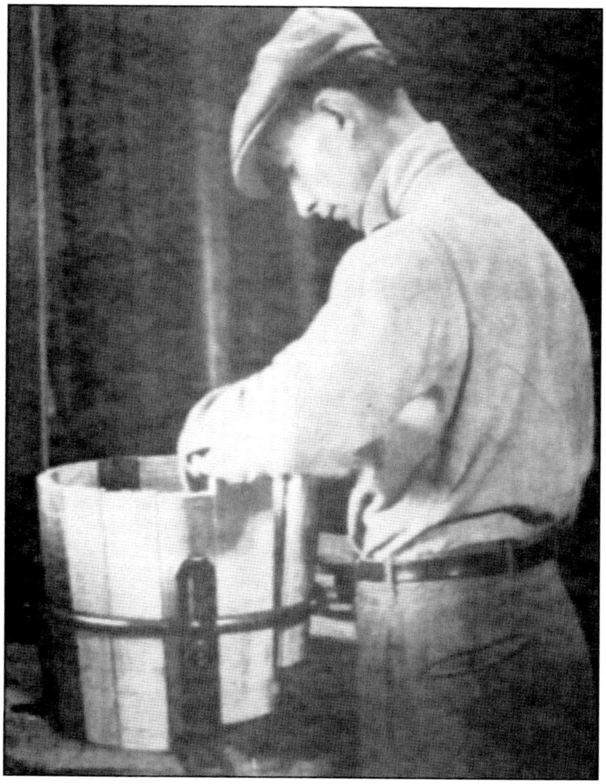

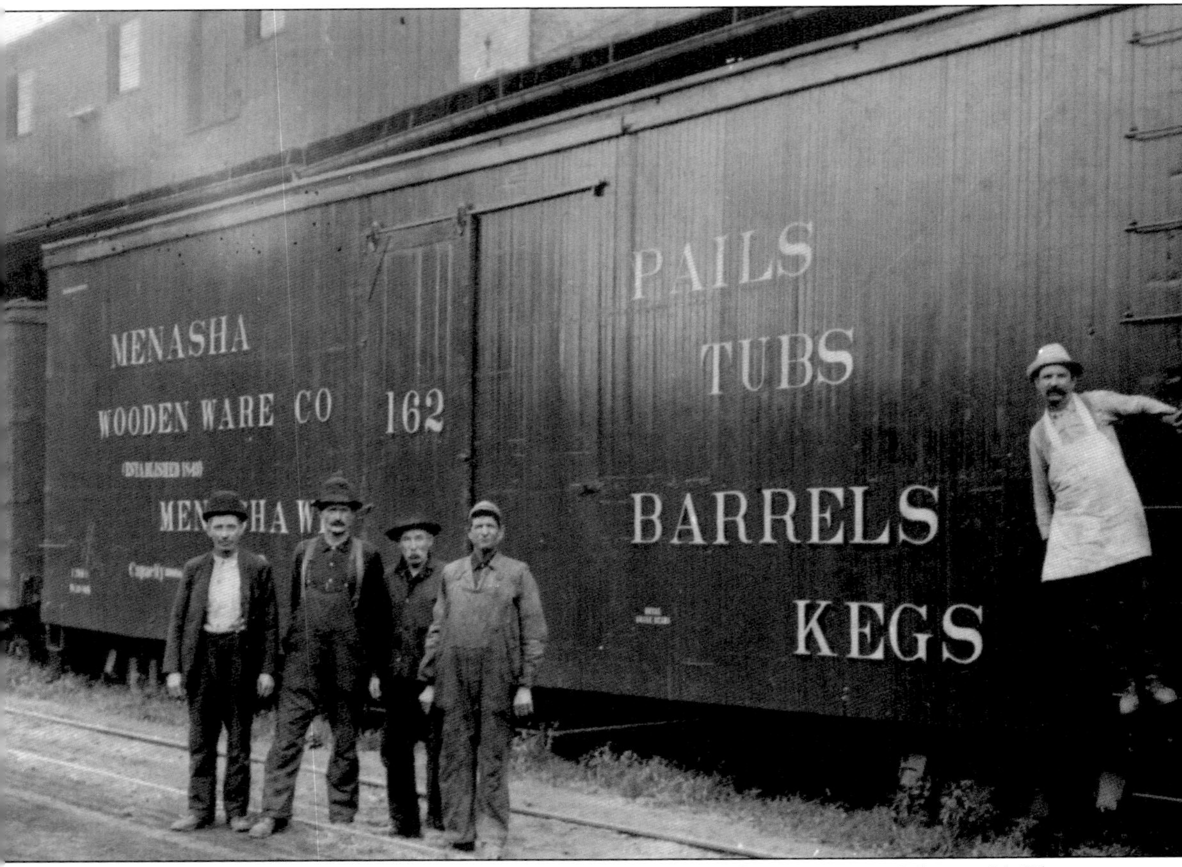

This iconic photograph from 1905 inspired model train enthusiasts around the world. That same year, Charles Smith, son of Menasha Wooden Ware founder Elisha D. Smith, began purchasing old oversized circus boxcars to ship his products. Painted a deep kelly green, these boxcars were 10 feet high, whereas traditional boxcars were 8 feet high. (See the differences in height in the photograph.) Soon, it was possible to have a scale model Menasha Wooden Ware boxcar in one's model railroad layout, which gave even more weight to Wooden Ware's reputation worldwide.

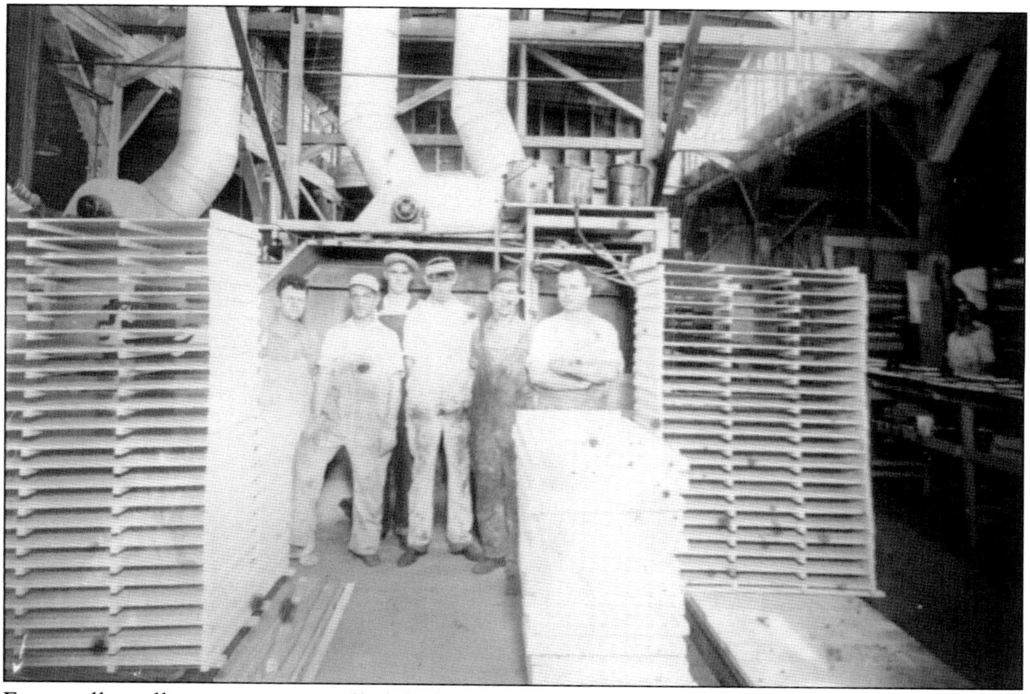

Eventually, pallets, sometimes called skids, would provide a much quicker turnaround in loading and unloading the boxcars. A pallet is a simple flat structure that supports goods in a stable fashion while being lifted by a forklift or other jacking device. Above is the pallet department at Menasha Wooden Ware. In 1931, a workload study was conducted in which it took three days to unload a boxcar containing 13,000 cases of unpalletized canned goods. When the same amount of goods was loaded into the railway trucks on pallets, or skids, the task took only four hours. Contrast that with the image below of the Menasha Wooden Ware boxcar with butter tubs loaded the old-fashioned way. (Above, author's collection.)

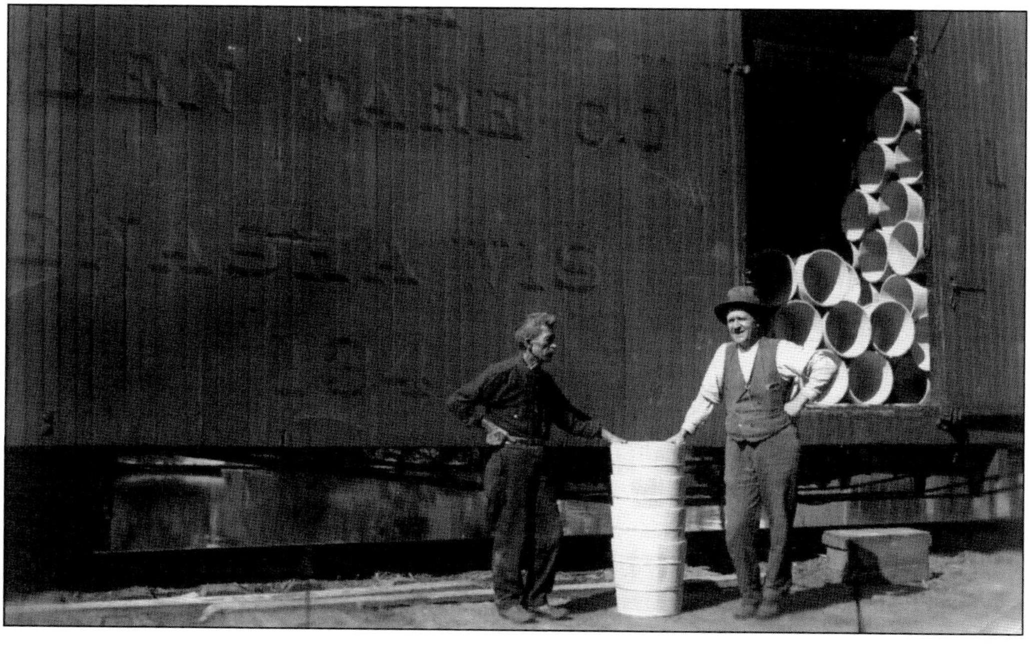

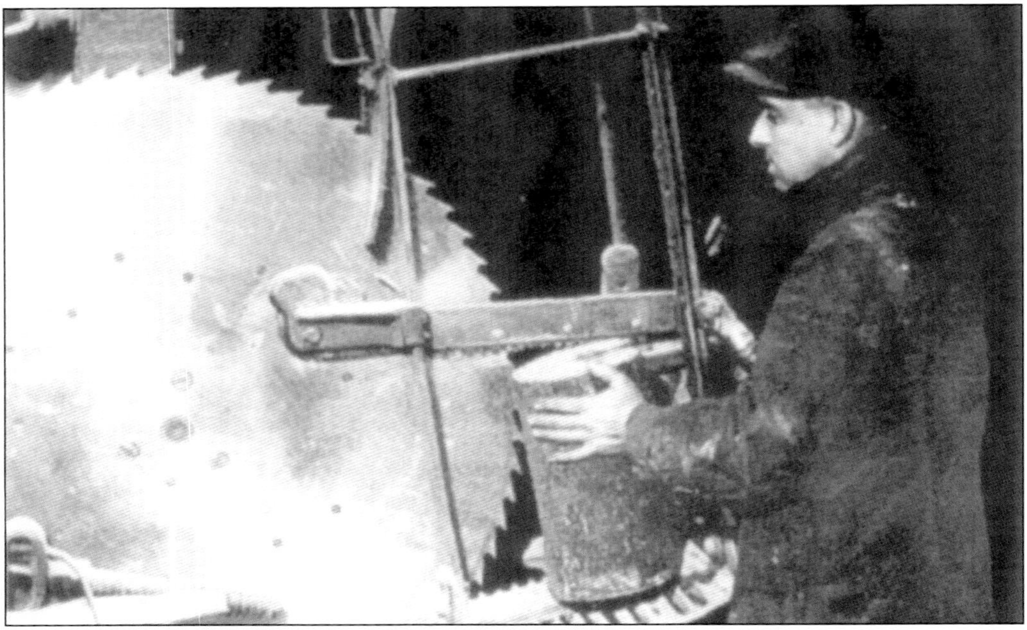

Charles Buck was a sawyer and saw filer for the Menasha Wooden Ware Company. As it would be many years before Occupational Safety and Health Administration (OSHA) regulations would become a staple in the workplace, one has to wonder what safeguards there were, if any, to provide a measure of safety for employees in this environment. (Courtesy of Menasha Public Library.)

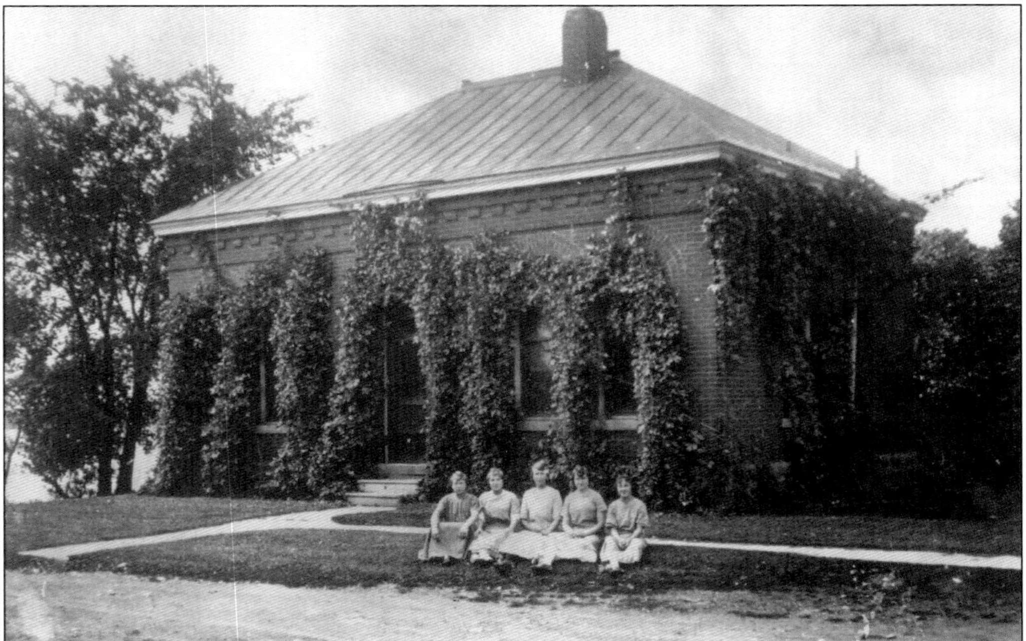

George A. Whiting Paper Company office workers pose in front of their ivy-covered offices in about 1912. The company, located on River Street in Menasha and founded by George A. Whiting and Theodore and William Gilbert, was known as Gilbert and Whiting until 1886, when George A. Whiting bought the Gilbert interest. The next year, Gilbert, along with his four sons, founded his own paper company. (Courtesy of Neenah Public Library.)

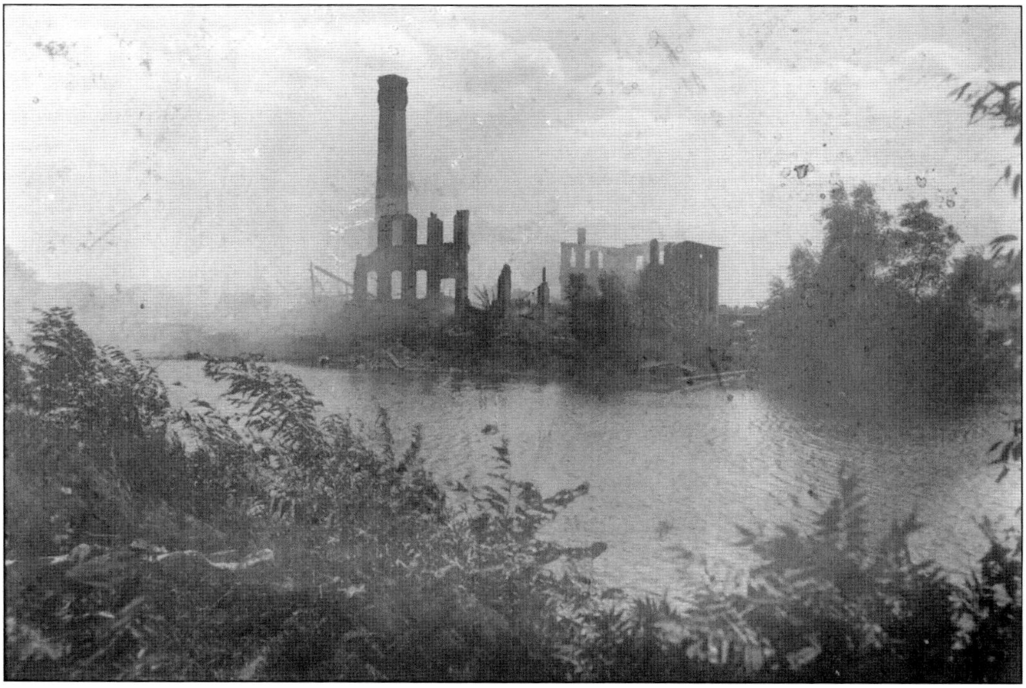

The George A. Whiting Paper Company explosion in 1888 is the worst disaster in Menasha's history. On August 23, 1888, the boiler house caught fire. But in fighting the flames, firemen unknowingly turned a stream of cold water onto a hot bleaching drum, causing an explosion that threw debris hundreds of feet toward a crowd that had gathered to watch the fire. Ten tons of boiler debris shot out of the building into an open lot 200 feet away, striking the bystanders. Eighteen were killed, and seven were badly injured. Most of the dead had suffered fatal head injuries.

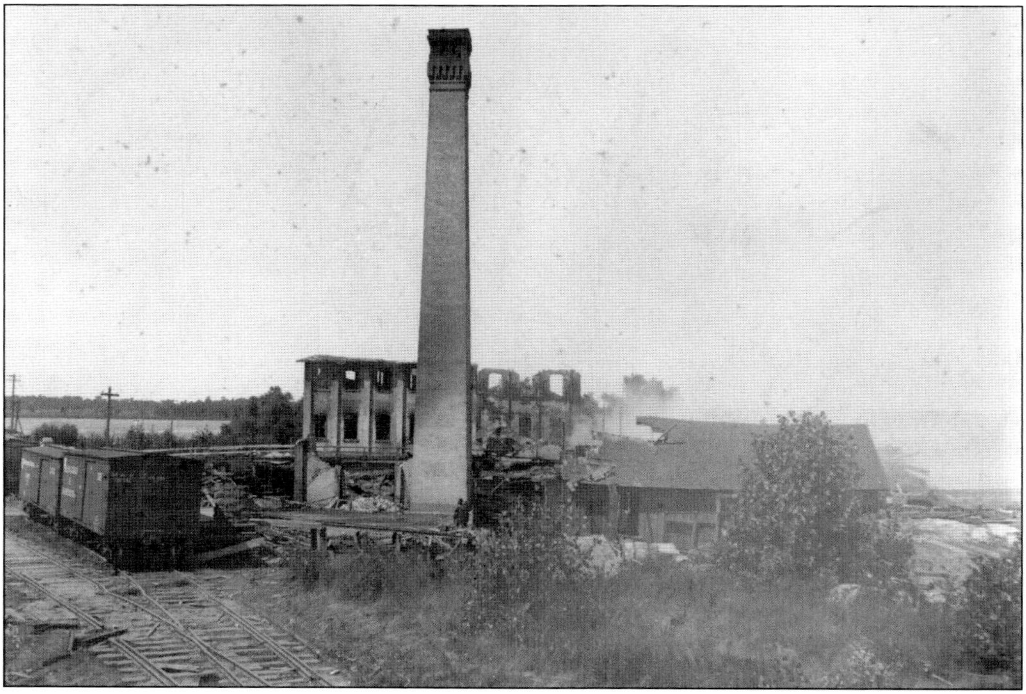

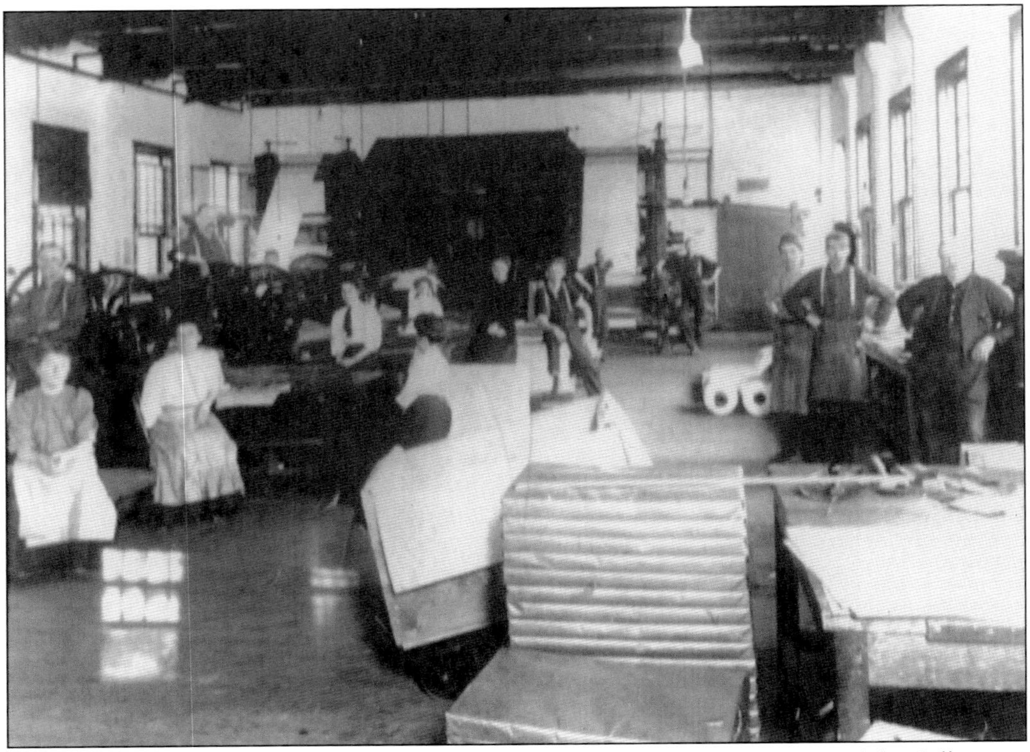

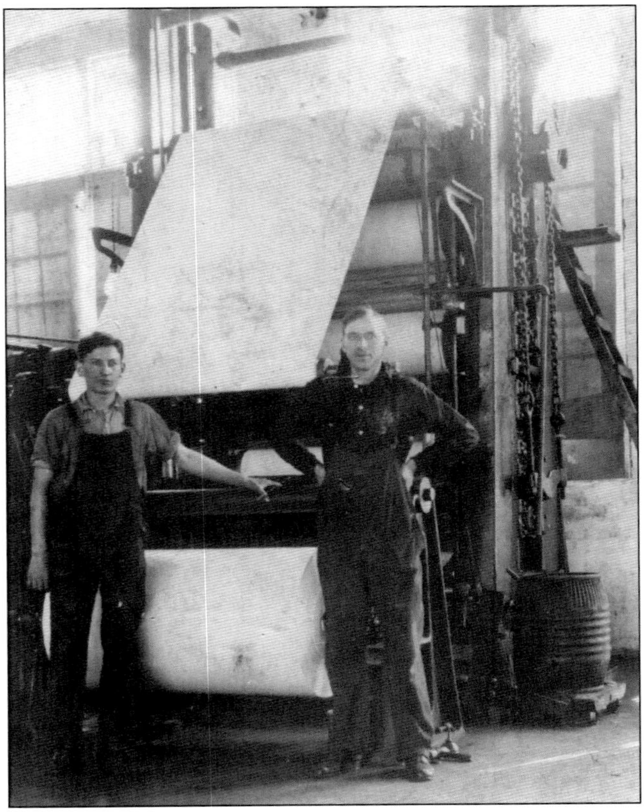

This 1909 view of the Gilbert Paper Company finishing room portrays the integration of women into the workplace in the early 20th century; however, working side by side with the men did not mean equal pay or other rights. The woman second from the left is Josephine Kolasinski. Notice the stacks in the foreground wrapped in heavy brown Kraft paper.

Howard LaSage, on the left, poses with a fellow worker in front of a supercalender press at the Gilbert Paper Mill. In paper manufacturing, the rollers are known as calenders, and the process of smoothing the surface of the paper by pressing it between cylinders, or rollers, is known as calendaring. An additional set of rollers, called supercalenders, produce an even smoother, thinner paper, typically used for magazines, catalogs, and directories.

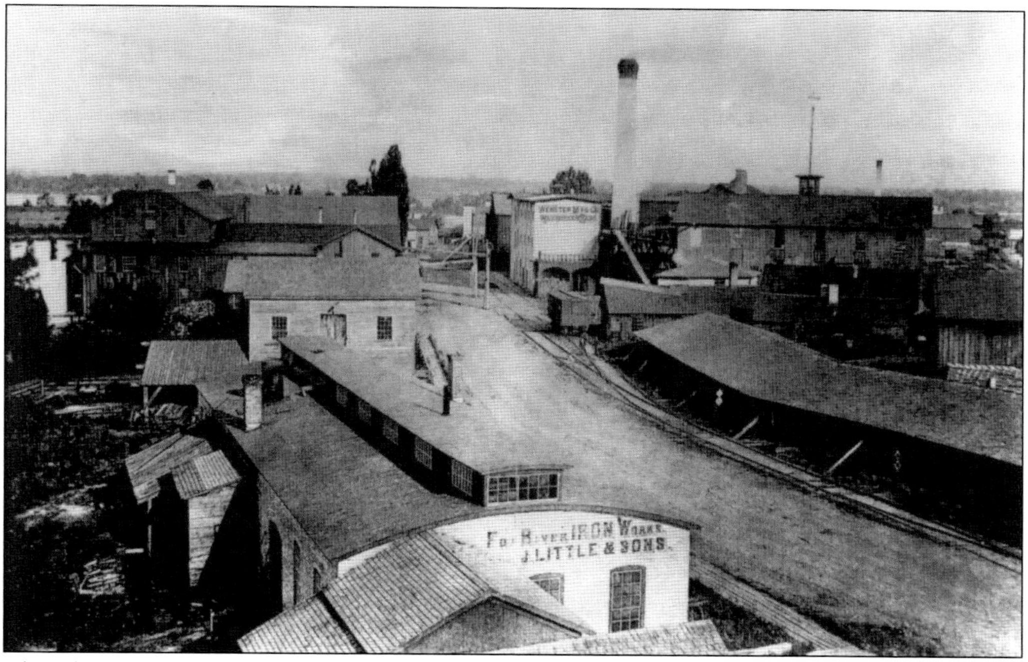

This photograph illustrates Menasha's diversification of industries. Just down the road from the iron works is a manufacturer of wagon stocks and chairs. Sometimes, the industries complemented each other; for example, there were foundries in Menasha that were in business to specifically manufacture machine parts for paper mills.

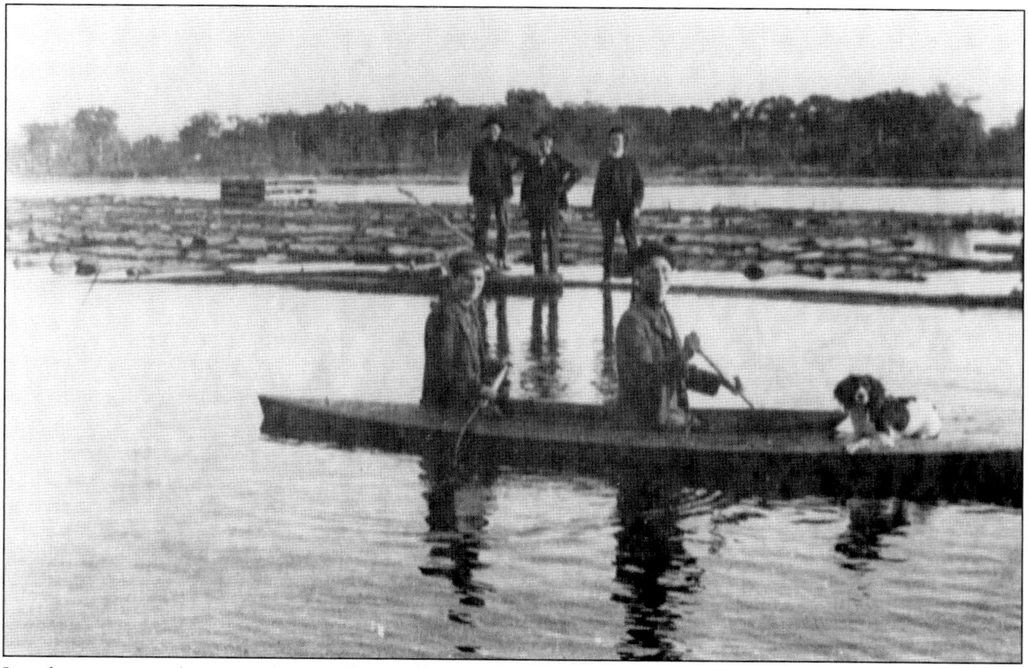

Log booms were barriers designed to collect and contain floating logs as they were guided to their respective mills. One can surmise that these logs were destined for Menasha Wooden Ware. The man in the front of the boat is William Kraus, and his dog's name is Flirt. This boom was by the 500 block of Broad Street.

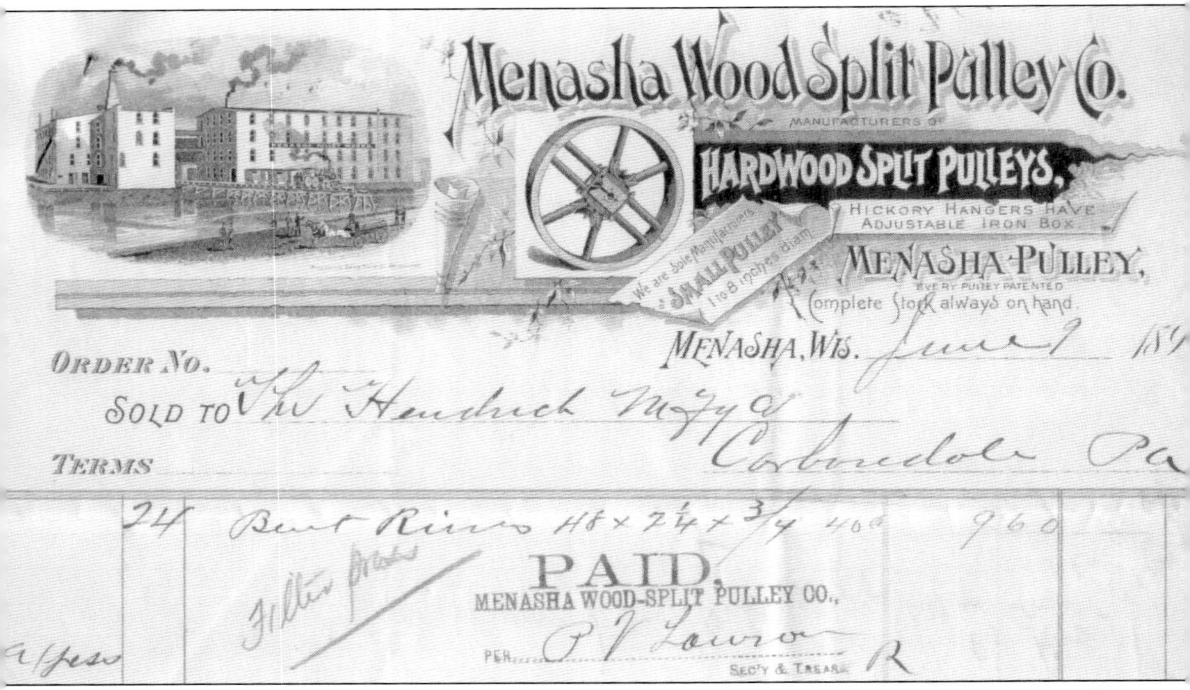

The Menasha Wood Split Pulley Company was founded by P.V. Lawson Jr., attorney, author, politician, orator, and mayor. His factory made wood split pulleys, which were exported all over the world. The factory reportedly made 150 pulleys daily, as well as other wood specialized goods such as hand trucks and cogs. At the time of this receipt, Lawson had already been mayor from 1886 to 1889 and would serve additional terms in 1893 and 1896. (Author's collection.)

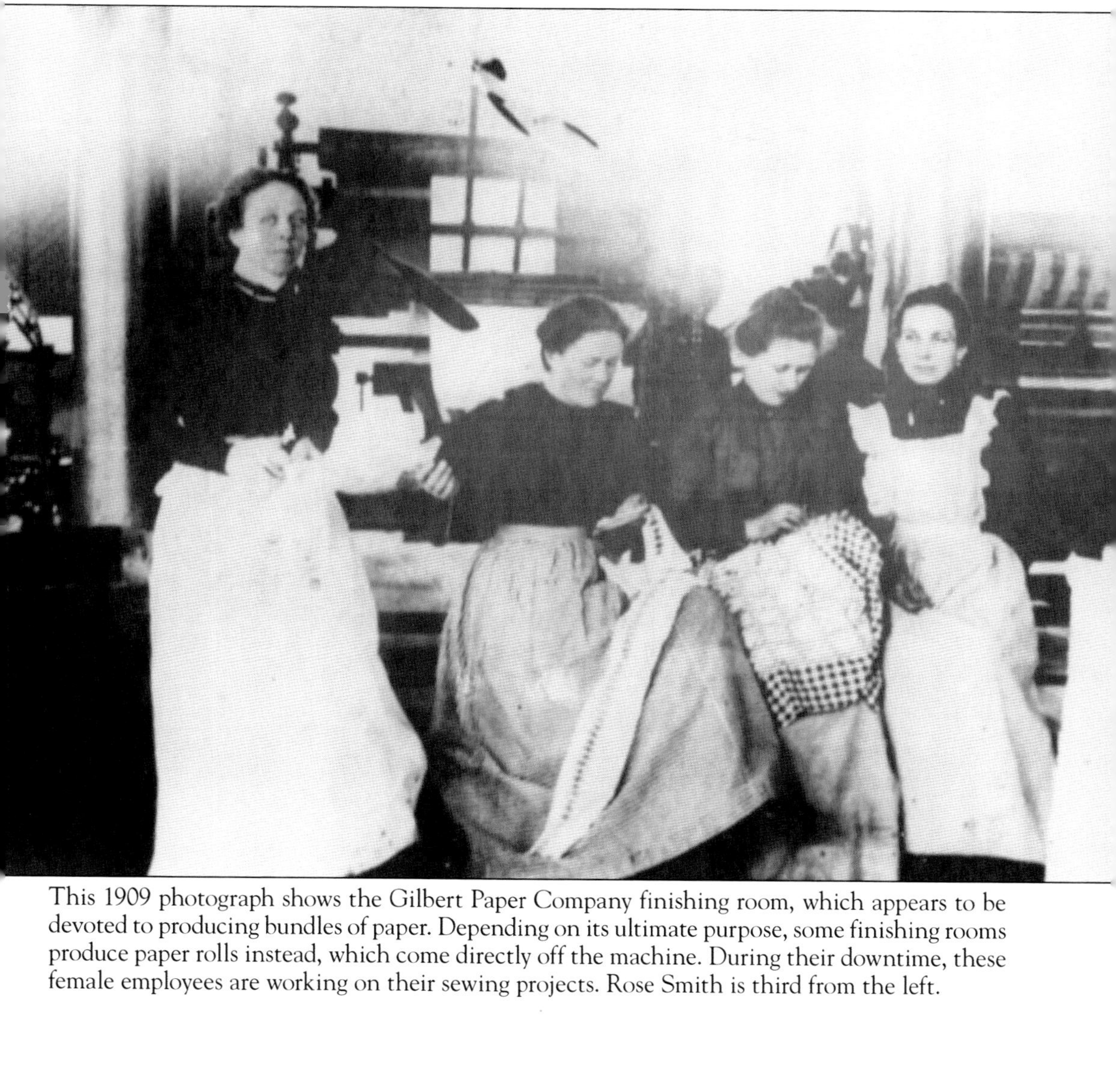

This 1909 photograph shows the Gilbert Paper Company finishing room, which appears to be devoted to producing bundles of paper. Depending on its ultimate purpose, some finishing rooms produce paper rolls instead, which come directly off the machine. During their downtime, these female employees are working on their sewing projects. Rose Smith is third from the left.

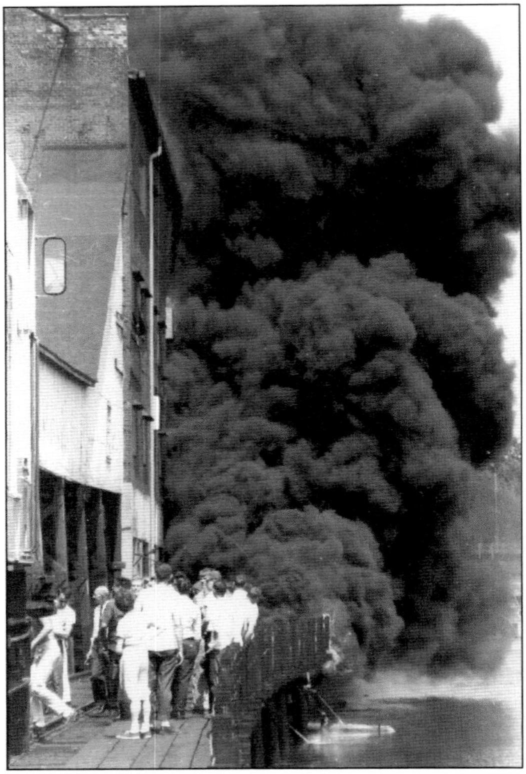

The Menasha Wooden Ware fire of July 17, 1964, ended an era. A railroad employee, using an acetylene torch to repair a track on a wooden trestle next to the box plant, set fire to the trestle. Although the fire was quickly controlled, burning embers were still carried by a swift breeze and engulfed the building, destroying it and three boxcars. Two weeks after the fire, the company's board of directors announced that a new 185,000-square-foot corrugated box plant would be constructed in an industrial park three miles south of Neenah. New corporate offices adjacent to the new plant were planned as well, and the office staff left Menasha the next year.

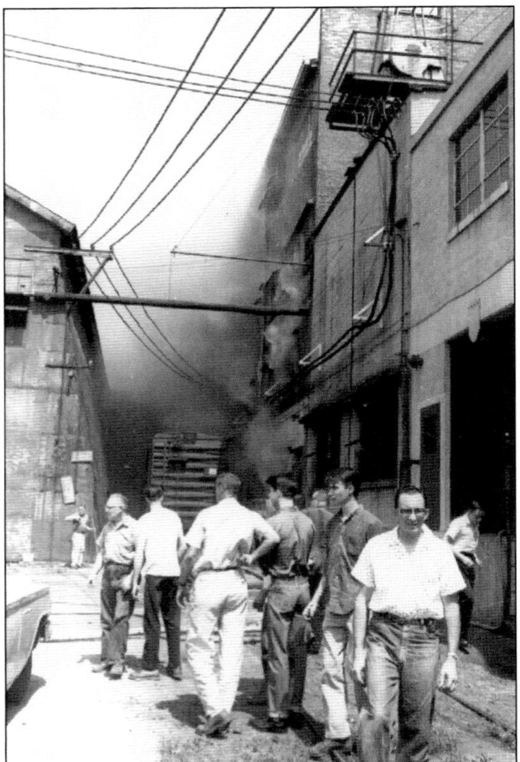

Four

COMMUNITY

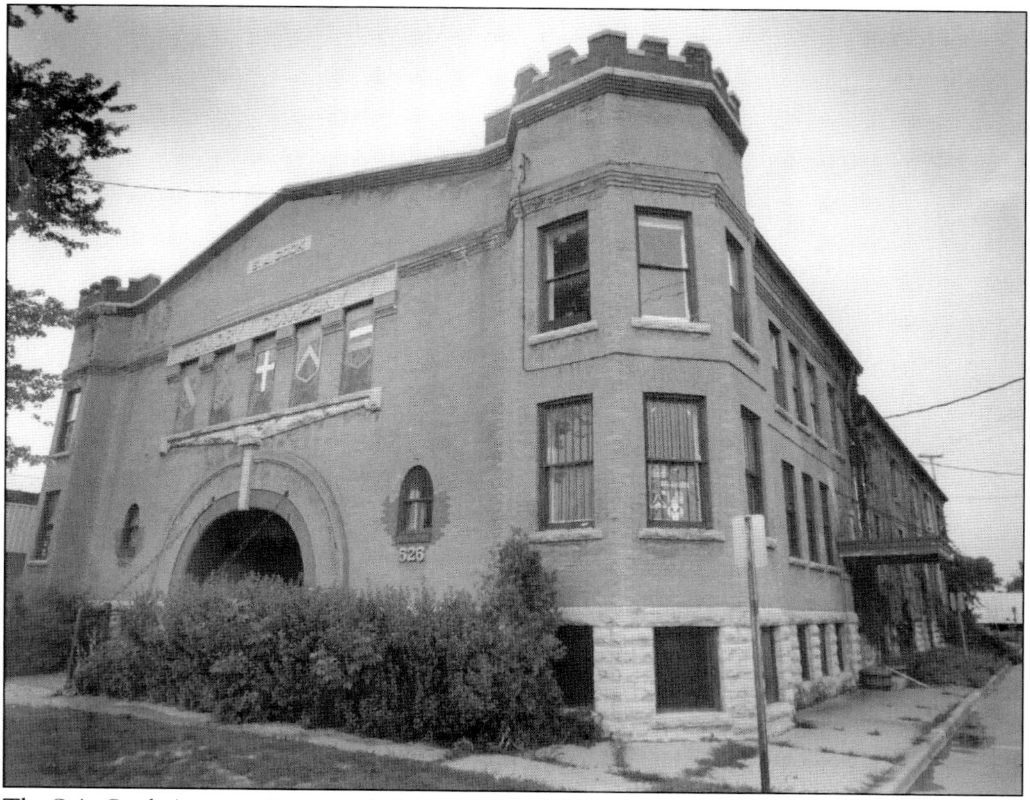

The S.A. Cook Armory, Company I, shown here in 1987, was dedicated in 1906 to house Company I of the Wisconsin National Guard. Championed by Republican congressman S.A. Cook, the armory was strategically located midway between the principal milling districts of Neenah and Menasha at a time when labor unrest resulted in several violent strikes.

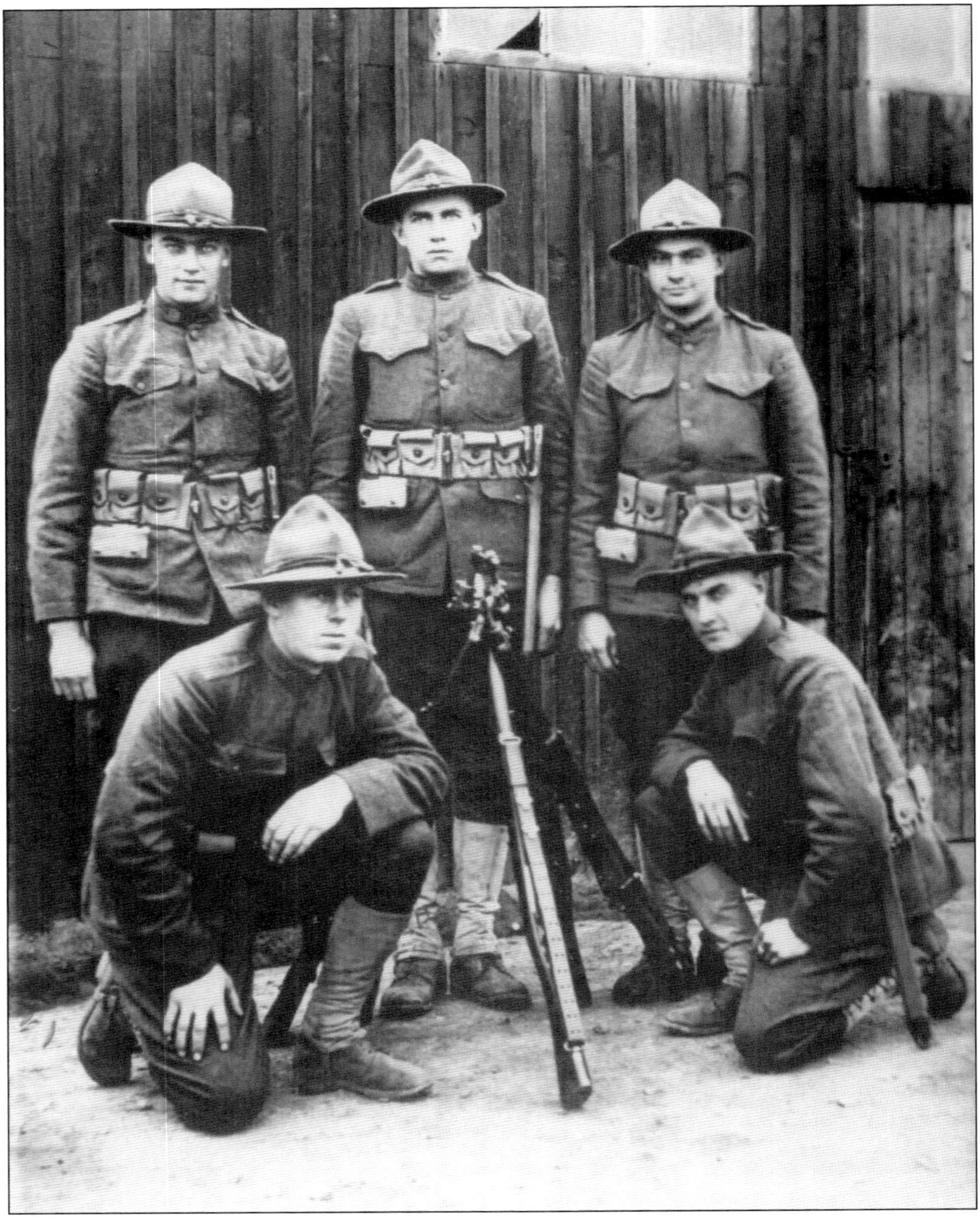

Company E members are pictured around the time of World War I, or the Great War, as it was also known at the time. Until Company E, a new unit of the Wisconsin National Guard, was mustered into service on August 5, 1917, Menasha had no military units since the Civil War. The unit served in France and in the Army of Occupation, returning home in June 1919. Company E had three officers and 149 enlisted men. Fifteen men from Menasha were killed in action or died in service during World War I. In this photograph from left to right are (first row, kneeling) Clarence Smith and Oliver Baenke; (second row, standing) Alfred Baenke, John Scanlon, and Ed Tratz. The Baenke brothers and Ed Tratz returned from the war to work for Marathon Corporation. John Scanlon became an alderman and was later elected mayor of Menasha from 1946 to 1955.

The Young Mens' Social Club state basketball champions of 1905–1906 pose for this photograph. They are, from left to right (front row) Bert Bell and Ben Metternicht; (second row) three unidentified boys; (third row) Joe Fitzgibbon, ? Gaerdner, ? Grode, and Joe Bruehl. Basketball as a sport had only been in existence since 1892, and peach baskets (with intact bottoms) were still being used until 1906, when they were finally replaced by metal hoops with backboards.

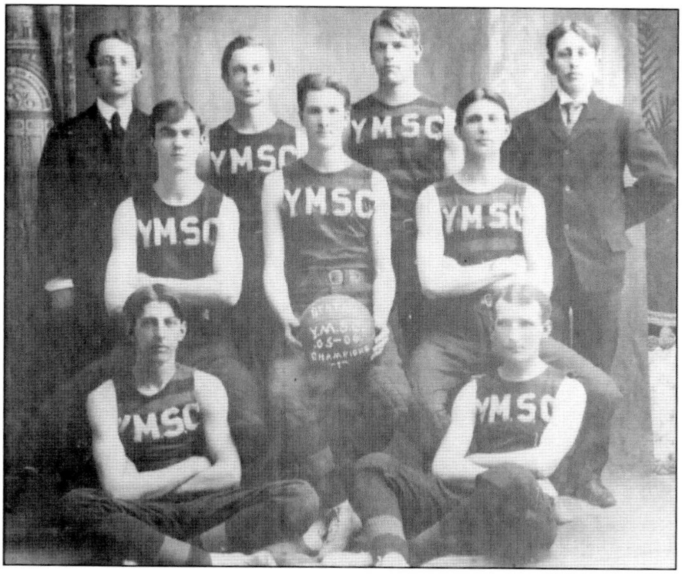

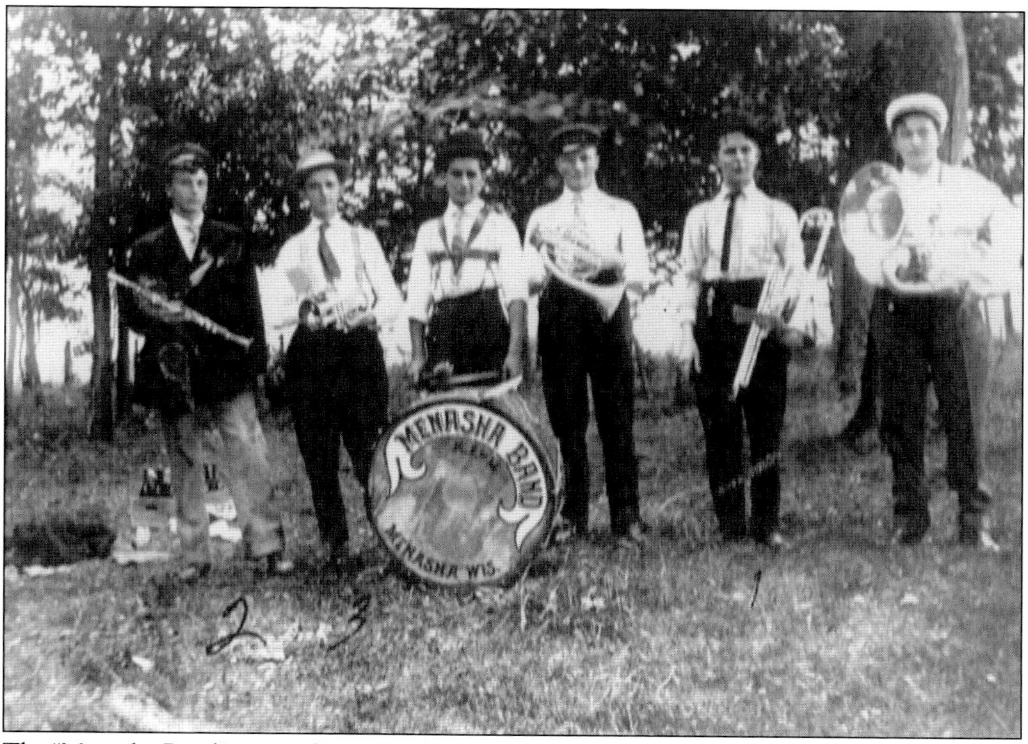

The "Menasha Band" graces this November 1907 postcard. Community bands in the 19th century and early 20th century were a source of civic pride and a piece of Americana that has largely gone by the wayside. Though its six members' names aren't available, the writer of this postcard relayed to his friend, "Hurrah for the little German Band."

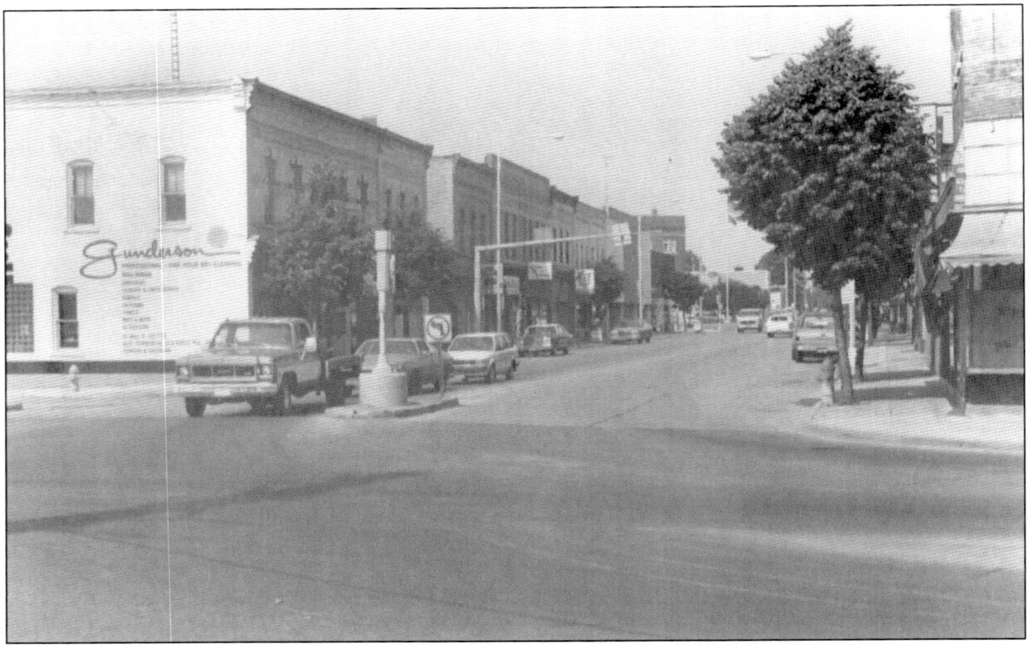

These before and after views of Main Street looking west were photographed from the intersection of Main and Racine Streets. The initial image dates from the 1970s or 1980s. All of the businesses on the south side of Main Street were razed in the 1990s and replaced with a new office building and parking lot, leaving only the Hotel Menasha as a link to the past. In the first photograph, one can see the Hotel Menasha as the last building before the Bank of Menasha, seemingly at the end of Main Street in the photograph's center. In the second image, the three-floor building with 10,000 square feet per floor was home to the new George Banta Company headquarters until 2007.

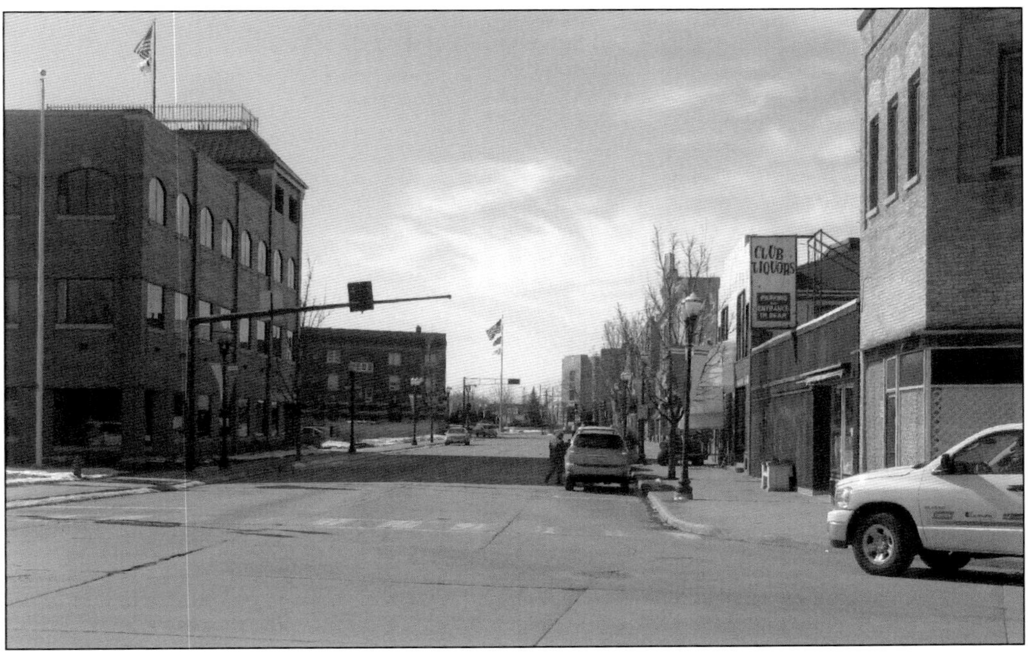

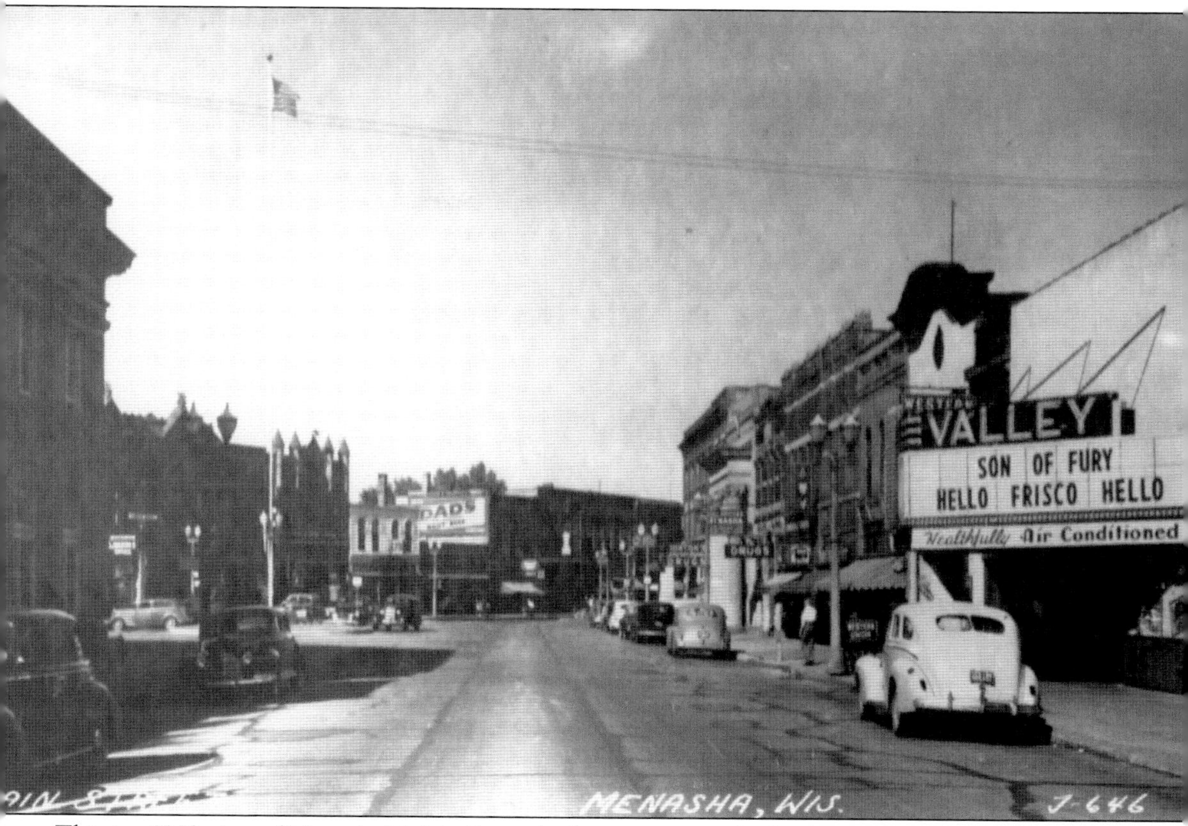

This is a 1943 view of Menasha's Main Street looking east towards the downtown square. Notice Schultz Brothers' Five and Dime below the Dad's Root Beer billboard. Years later, the Valley Theater was razed, and a new First National Bank was built on its site. The bank's old location, identified by the classic columns past the theater, was Menasha City Hall until 1987. The steeple of St. Mary's Catholic Church rises above in the distance. The Bank of Menasha on the left would be replaced with a newer structure in 1963, and the Left Guard restaurant, owned by Green Bay Packer great Fuzzy Thurston, would be situated just west of it.

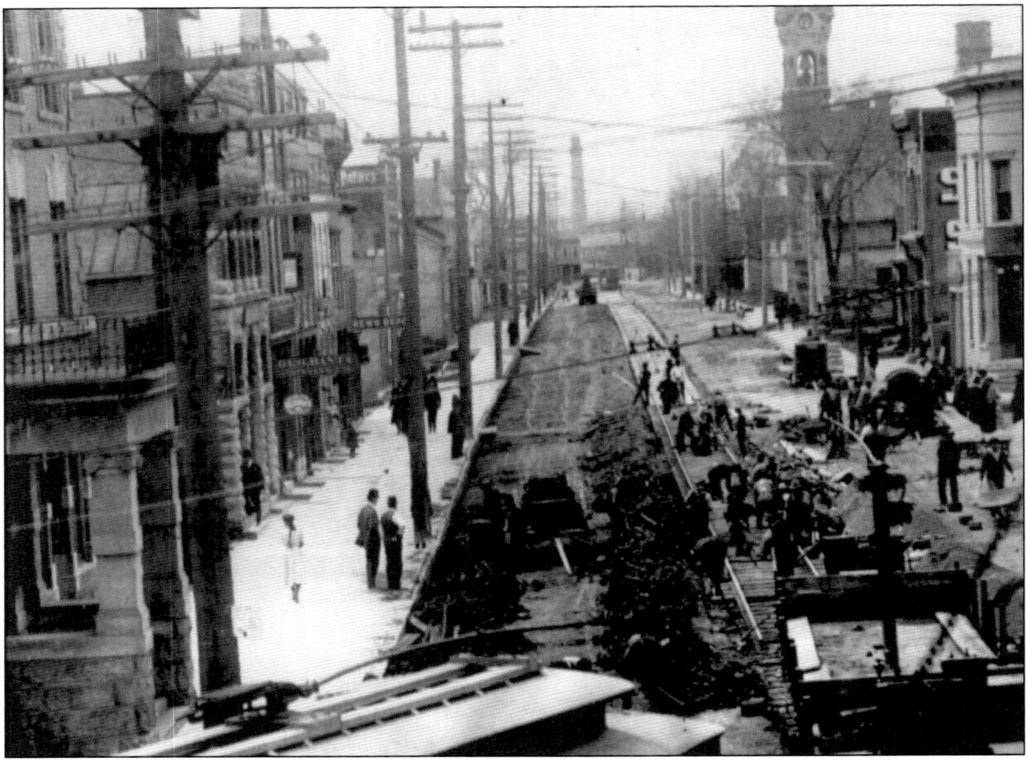

This view of Main Street looks west from the Hotel Menasha in about 1910. This was the first cement street in Menasha, and all the cement was hand mixed. The bell tower is the city hall and fire station building. An electric streetcar is visible in the lower left.

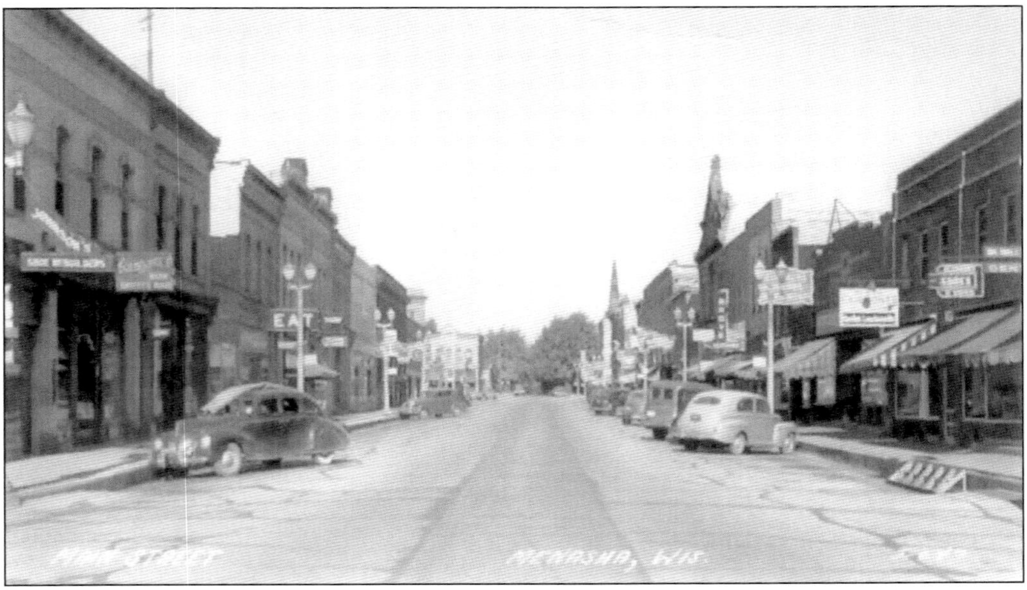

This image of Main Street faces west from Racine Street in the 1940s. Notice the Gold Label beer sign on the left, just past Johnson's Shoe Repair. Gold Label and Gem, another beer, were brewed by Walter Bros. Brewing Company, located next door to St. Patrick's Catholic Church on Doty Island.

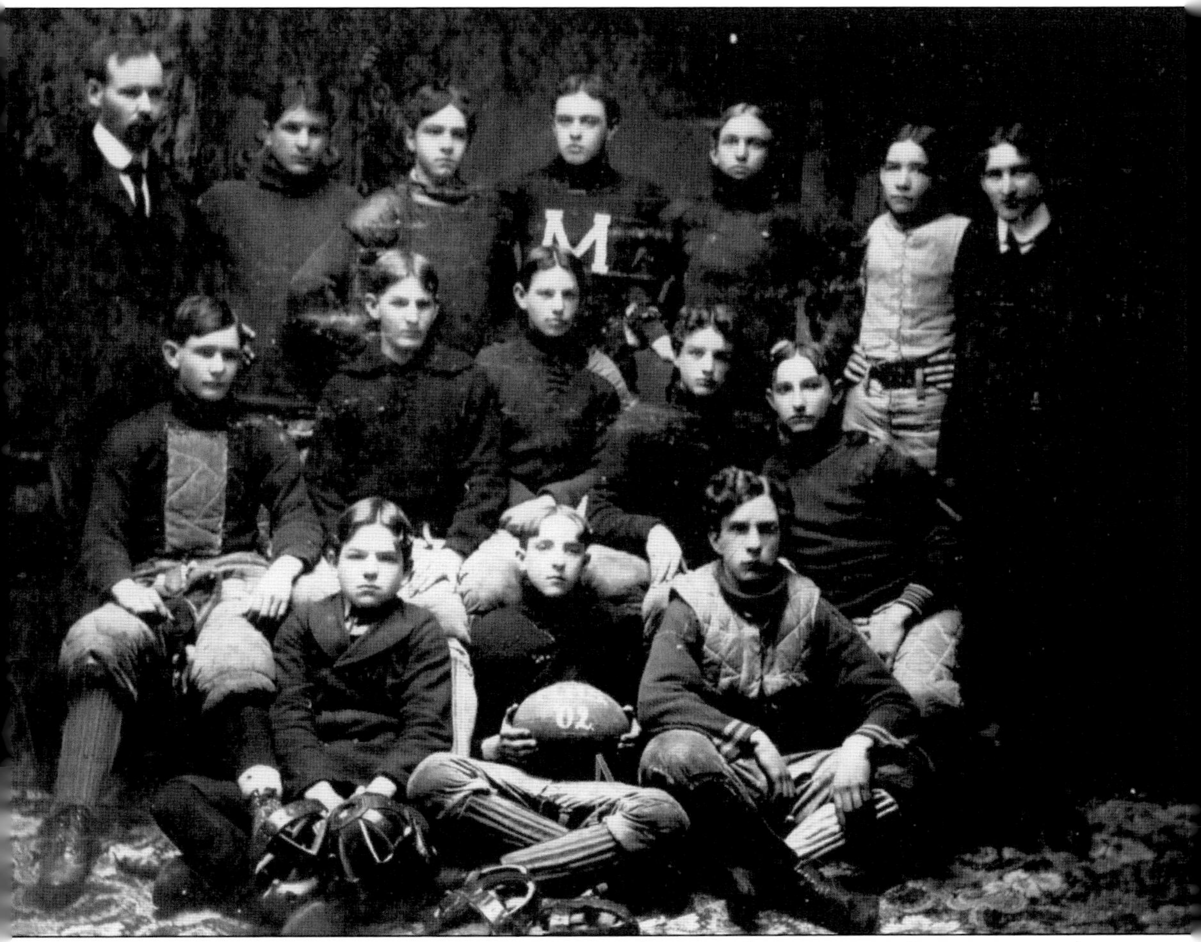

Football was first introduced to Menasha High School in 1895, but it was mostly an intramural affair and died a quick, unheralded death. In 1898, another team was organized, and a player named Nick Wagner broke his collarbone. As a result, interest again waned until 1902, when yet another team was organized. Nothing remains of their existence save for this photograph and their names. With the exception of the principal, they are identified by last name only as, from left to right, (first row) Minton, Eldredge, and Richardson; (second row) Anklam, Ellingboe, Fitzgibbon, Lawson, and Loescher; (third row) principal John Callahan, Hill, Trilling, Lenz, Johnson, Hart, and Dineen. Somehow, football captured everyone's enthusiasm in 1903, when the Menasha squad played eight games. However, they lost most of them, except for a 48–0 victory over Berlin and a scoreless tie with Oshkosh.

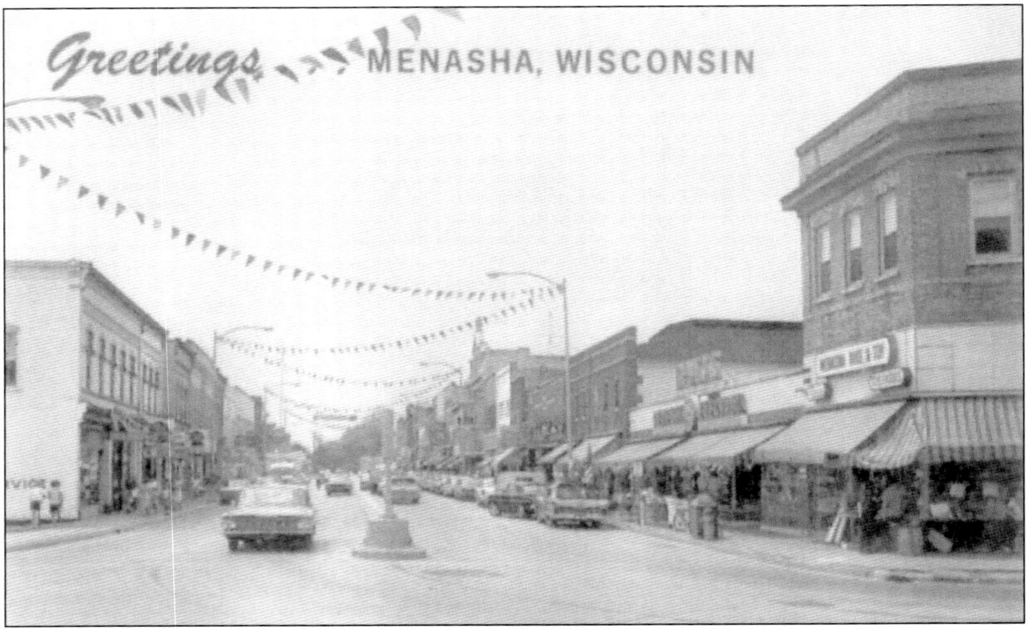

This is another view of Main Street, looking west from Racine Street in the 1970s. Cars wait for the traffic signal as they pass through downtown via Wisconsin Highway 114. This postcard highlights the downtown sidewalk sale during a Prospector Days celebration in the late 1960s. Prospector Days was a summer event created in collaboration with Neenah merchants to stimulate business in the two downtowns by sponsoring an annual parade, sidewalk sale, concerts, carnival rides, and other fun activities.

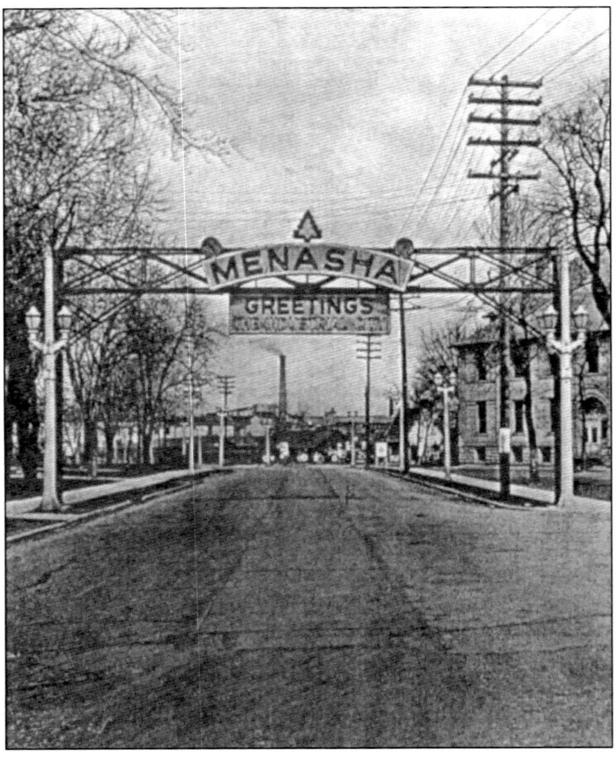

In 1929, US Highway 41 was to be rerouted through Menasha over the new Tayco Street Bridge. In a moment of civic pride, the electric sign pictured here was created by city fathers to welcome visitors to the fair city as they crossed Nicolet Boulevard. The back side of the sign was to display the words, "Good Luck," as well wishes to departing visitors. This photograph seems to be the last tangible evidence that the sign ever existed. Little else is known about it or its whereabouts.

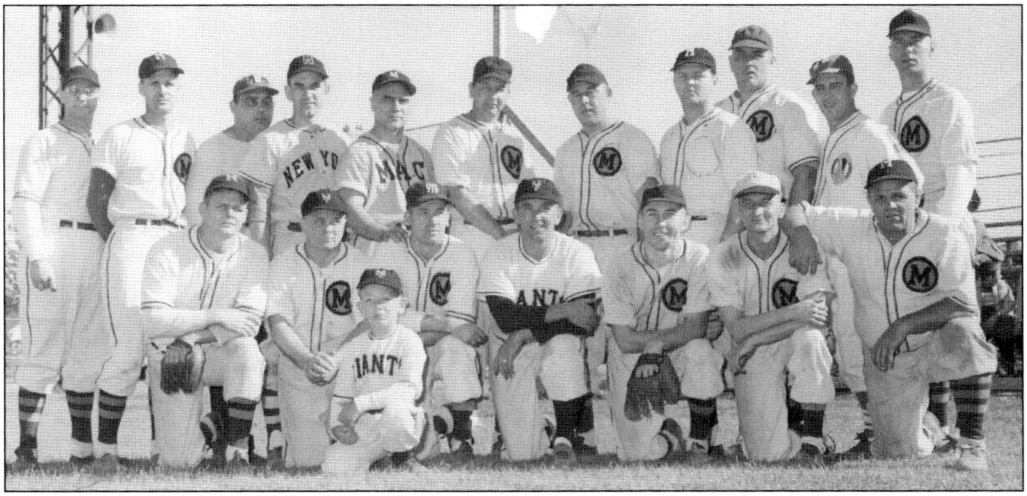

Menasha's favorite son, Dave "Koslo" Koslowski, poses with a pick-up team from the area in 1952. Koslowski's career spanned the years from 1941 to 1955. As a left-handed pitcher, he toiled for 12 seasons for the New York Giants, Baltimore Orioles, and Milwaukee Braves; he was in service for four years during World War II.

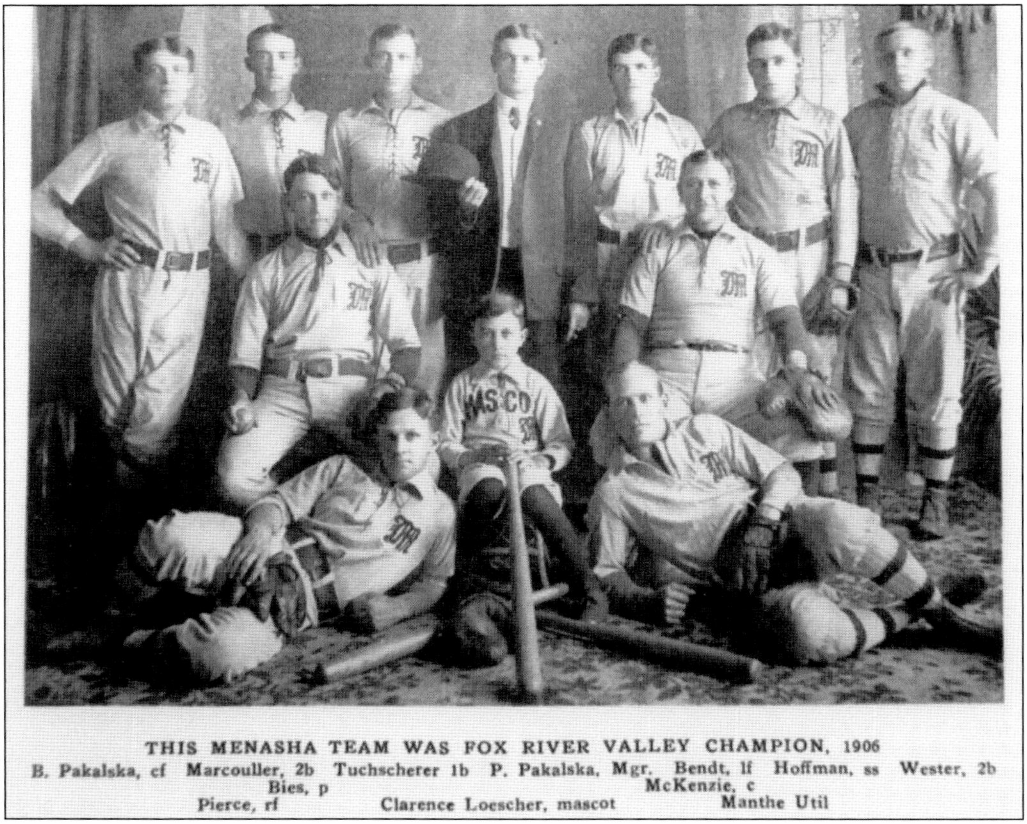

THIS MENASHA TEAM WAS FOX RIVER VALLEY CHAMPION, 1906
B. Pakalska, cf   Marcouller, 2b   Tuchscherer 1b   P. Pakalska, Mgr.   Bendt, lf   Hoffman, ss   Wester, 2b
Bies, p   McKenzie, c
Pierce, rf   Clarence Loescher, mascot   Manthe Util

Stories about how tough sports were in the old days were, apparently, not far off the mark. This photograph's caption seems to agree with that premise. Champions of 1906, every player on this Menasha baseball team had to have been vital, as Mr. Manthe is the only utility player listed, aside from the full nine-man squad.

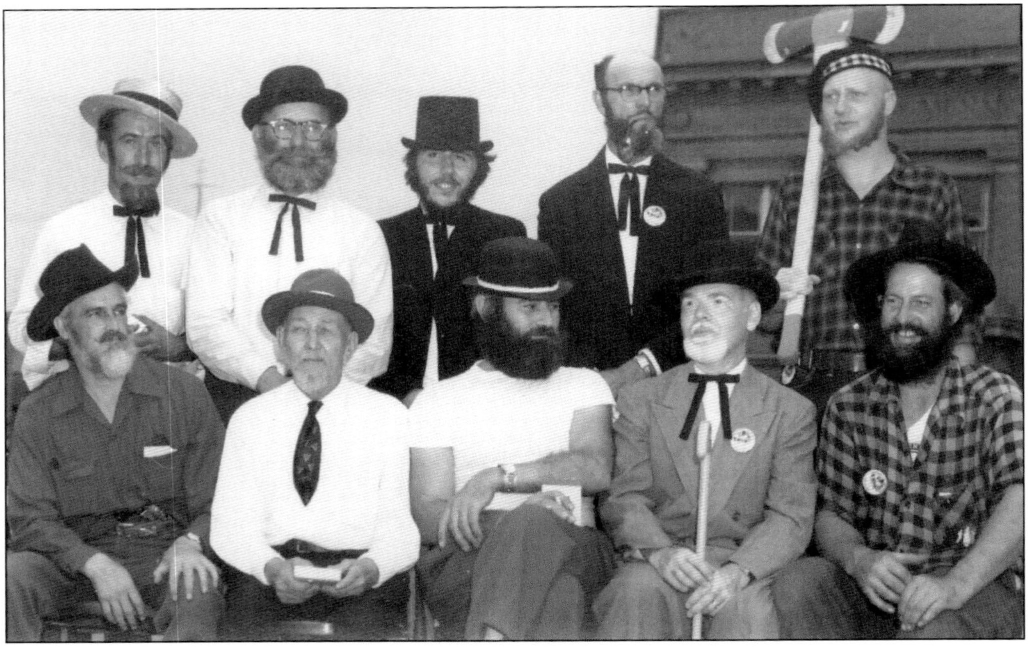

Menasha celebrated its centennial from July 2 to 5 in 1953, as it was 100 years since its inception as a village on July 5, 1853. Festivities included a beard-growing contest for the men and a bonnet contest for the ladies. Obviously, adopting the right mode of period dress also helped to make the illusion more complete. These Brothers of the Brush were not allowed to rid themselves of their whiskers until they had purchased a permit of sorts: a festive yellow pin-back button giving them permission to shave. Accordingly, the ladies, as Sisters of the Swish, were prohibited from applying make-up until they had obtained their own similar button.

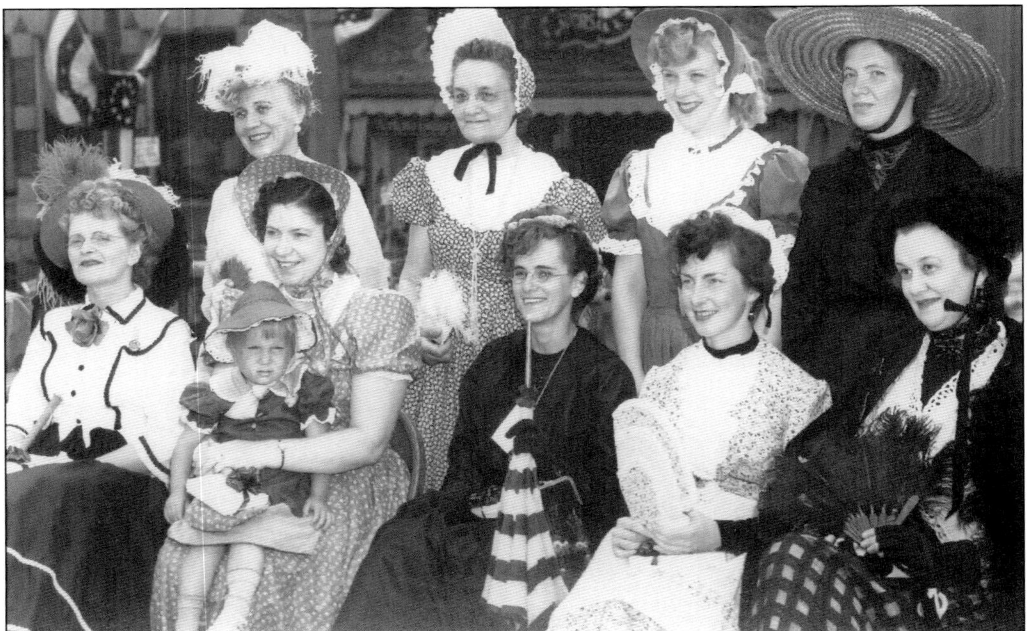

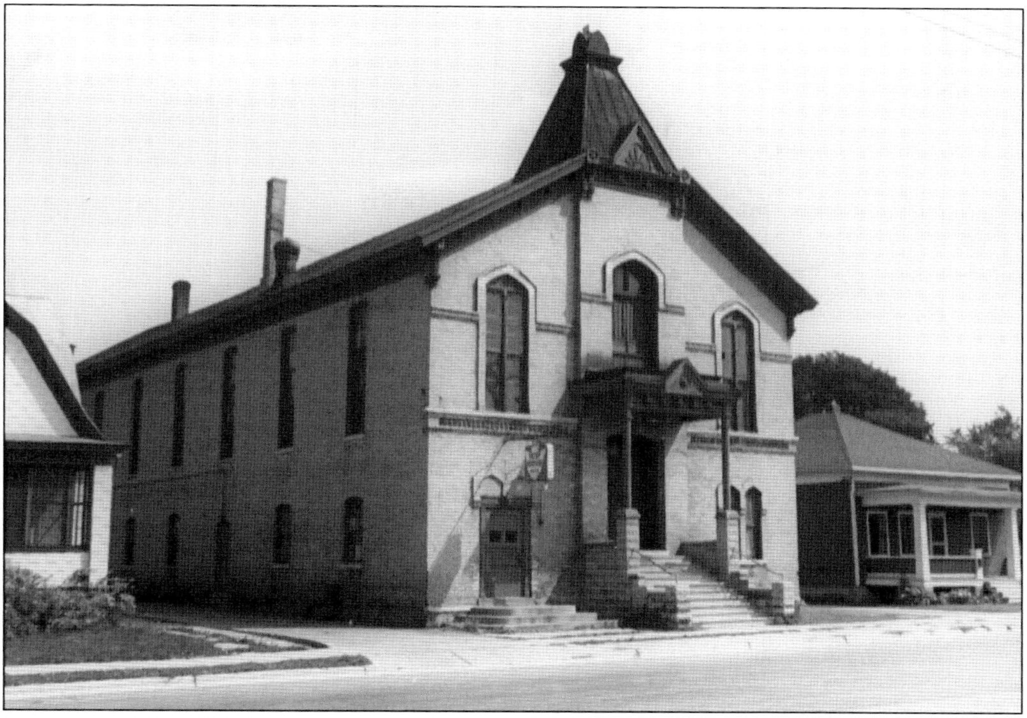

Germania Hall at 320 Chute Street was home to the Germania Benevolent Society in Menasha. The society had its beginnings on December 1, 1856, when nine men started the Concordia Society with the purpose of helping the sick and burying the departed. In 1862, a rival German organization was founded, the Menasha Turner Society. In 1888, the two societies merged under the name of German Unterstuetzungs Verein. In 1927, the name was changed to the Germania Benevolent Society. The building on Chute Street was built in the 1860s and razed in 1963.

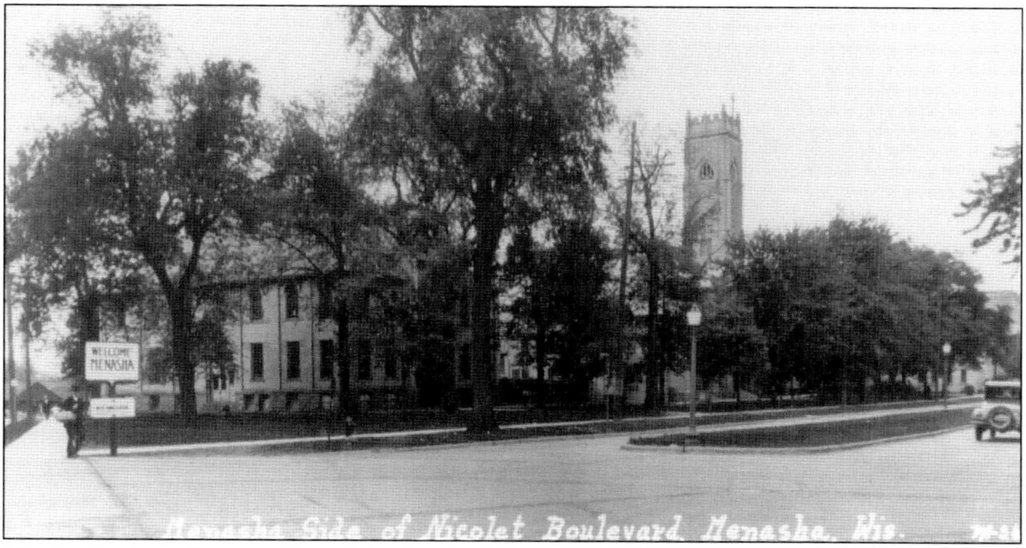

Nicolet Boulevard bisects Doty Island and separates Menasha from Neenah. In the 1800s, this picturesque thoroughfare was known as the Avenue, and it gained its new name during the Jean Nicolet monument celebration in 1906. But it wasn't that long ago that one could still stroll along the boulevard and encounter a paving stone embossed with that designation.

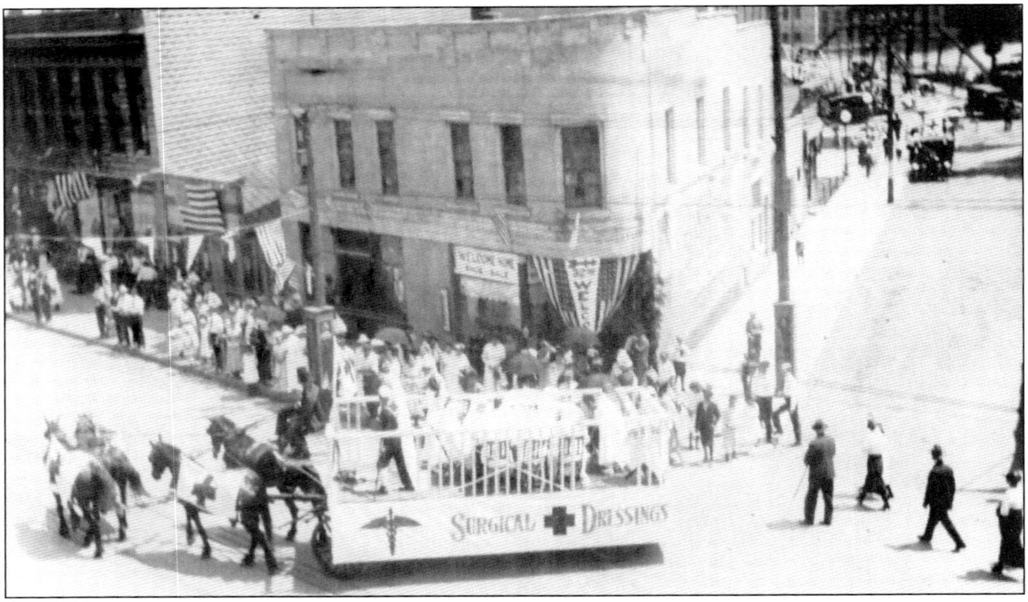

Welcoming home members of the 32nd Infantry Division in 1919, this World War I parade on Main Street passes in front of Henry Tuchscherer's shoe store. As with today's Labor Day sales, merging commerce with the events of the day, the sign announces the "Welcome Home" Shoe Sale.

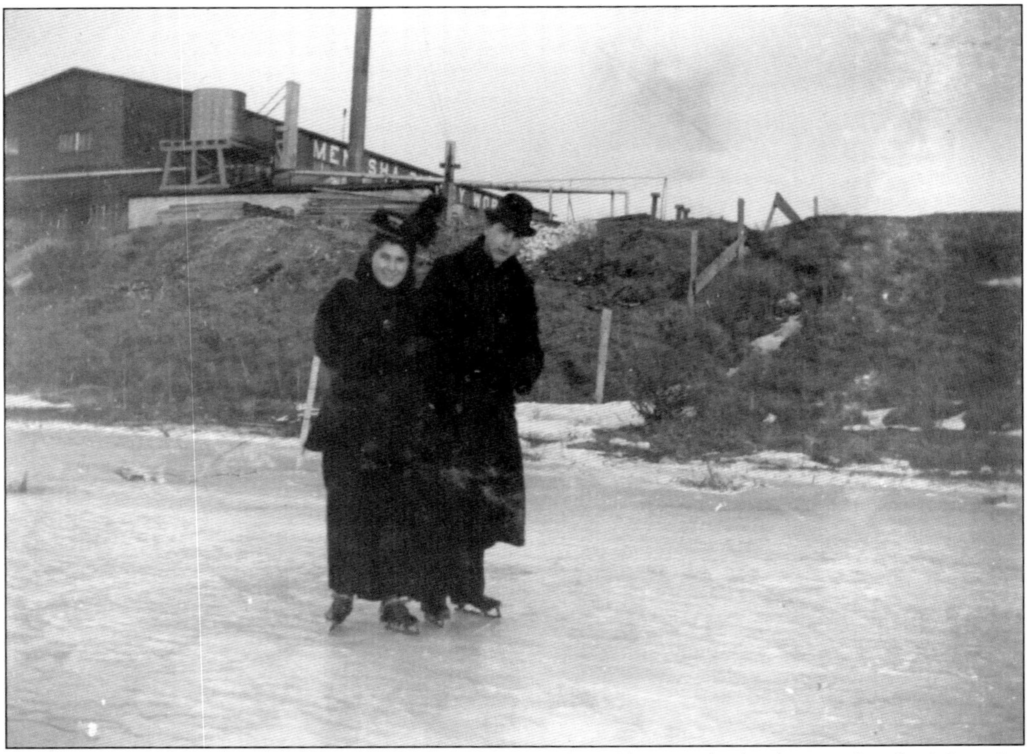

Skaters on Little Lake Butte des Morts enjoy a winter day of fun. In the background is the Menasha Wood Split Pulley Company, owned by P.V. Lawson Jr., once and future mayor of Menasha. Unlike so many Menasha businesses that located on the Fox River, Lawson's pulley company was situated on the lake, so it enjoyed a more convenient connection to the rail lines that passed nearby.

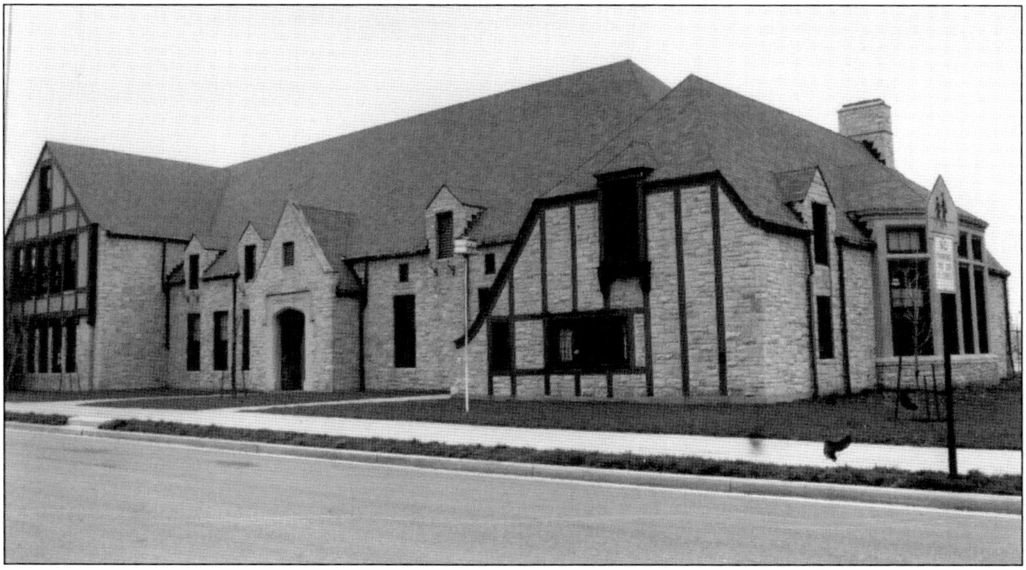

Jefferson Elementary School is an example of the Tudor/Elizabethan Revival movement of architecture, distinguished by its fine half-timbering, slate roof, and leaded windows. Built in 1932, this edifice is very similar to a structure in the Washington Street Historic District built around 1930; that building was erected as part of an effort instigated by Menasha Wooden Ware to create a business district in the "English style of architecture" to optimize use of the US 41 corridor running down Washington Street into Menasha. The Brin Building, completed in 1928, was also part of this initiative, but the rest of the business district was never realized.

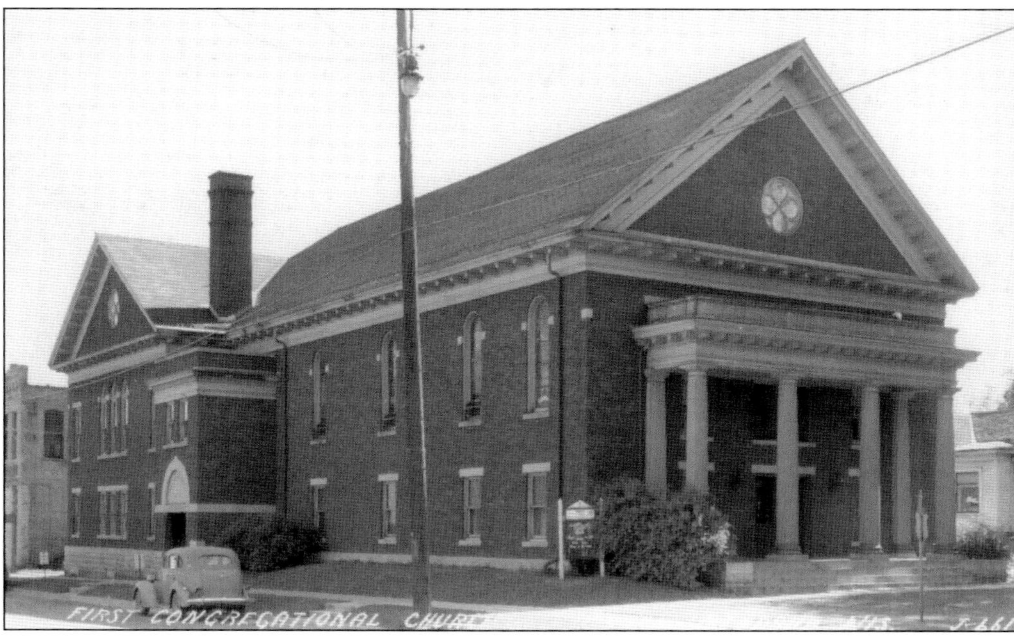

The first public religious services in Menasha were conducted by the Reverend O.P. Clinton, a Congregationalist missionary, in 1848. A church was built on this site in 1866; this church was constructed in the 1920s. In 1967, a new Congregational church was erected on Doty Island just over the city limits in Neenah near the old armory. This church now hosts an evangelical congregation.

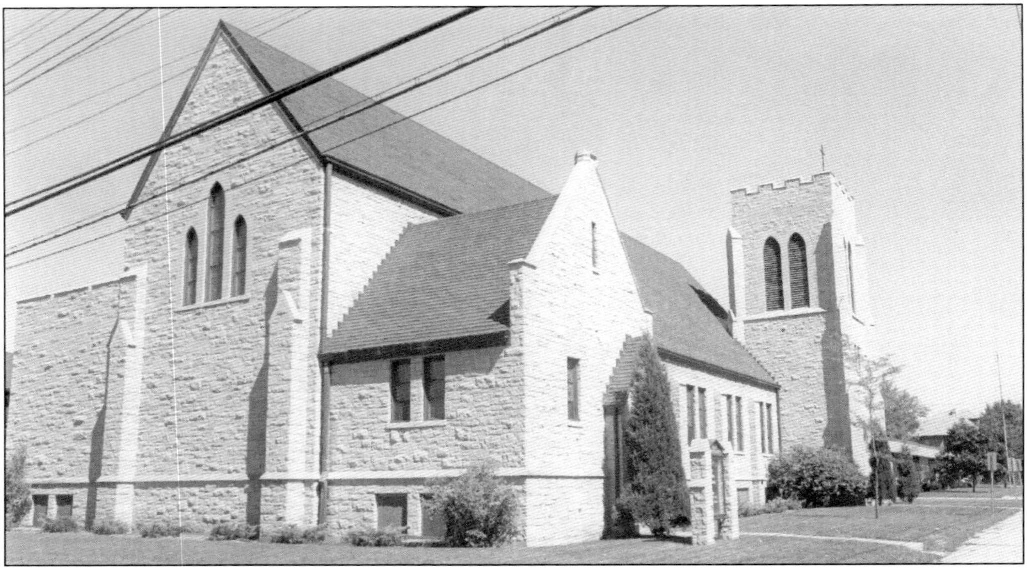

Trinity Lutheran Church was founded in 1857. Originally located on Chute Street between Tayco and Milwaukee Streets, the years brought enough growth to eventually include a school and community hall. In time, the congregation outgrew the property it had held for so many years, so this church was built on Broad Street in 1952.

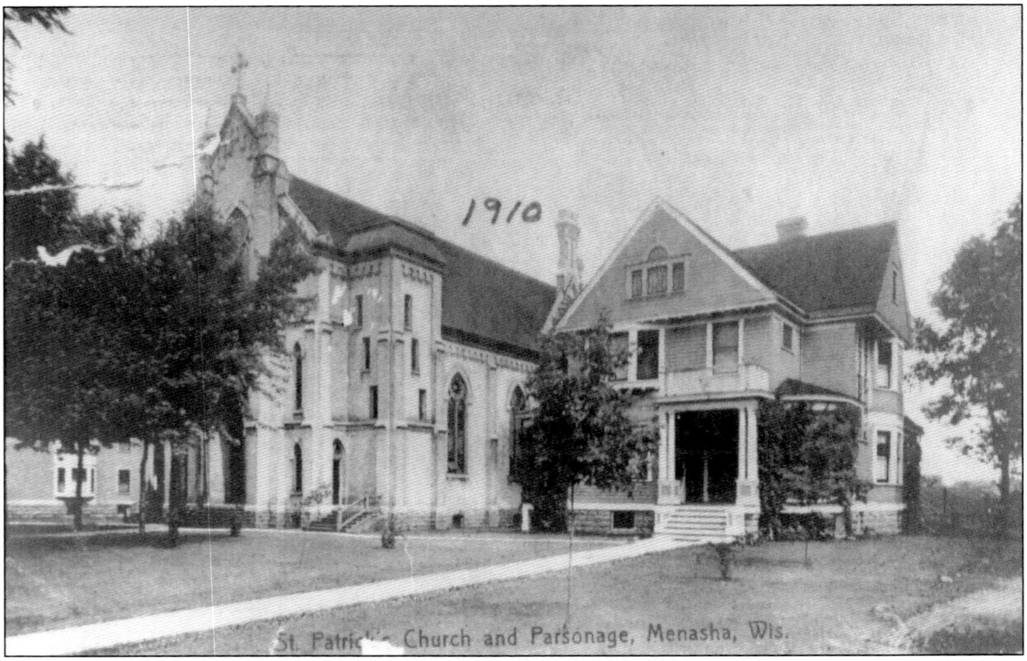

In 1848, the St. Malachy Mission was established to serve approximately 20 Catholic families at the Winnebago Rapids settlement. This parish later evolved into St. Charles Borremeo. Since the parishioners didn't own their church, they decided to build their own. The new church was dedicated and named St. Patrick's Congregation on July 5, 1883. The caption in this 1910 photograph states that the parsonage (better known as a rectory) is situated to the right of the church. The convent can be seen through the trees to the left of the church.

In 1867, German-speaking Catholics of Menasha separated from St. Charles' (now St. Patrick's) and organized a parish of their own: St. Mary's. On Ash Wednesday in 1883, fire destroyed the first St. Mary's church, devastating the parish. But somehow, within three days, their pastor rallied his parishioners to provide $14,000 towards a new church, and in November of the same year, the new church was dedicated. This church is a classic example of German Gothic architecture. It seats 1,000, and its spire towers nearly 200 feet.

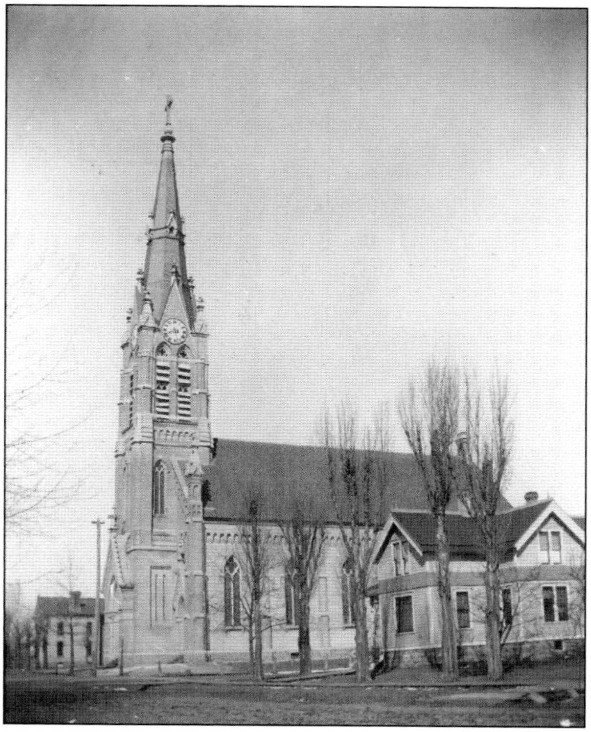

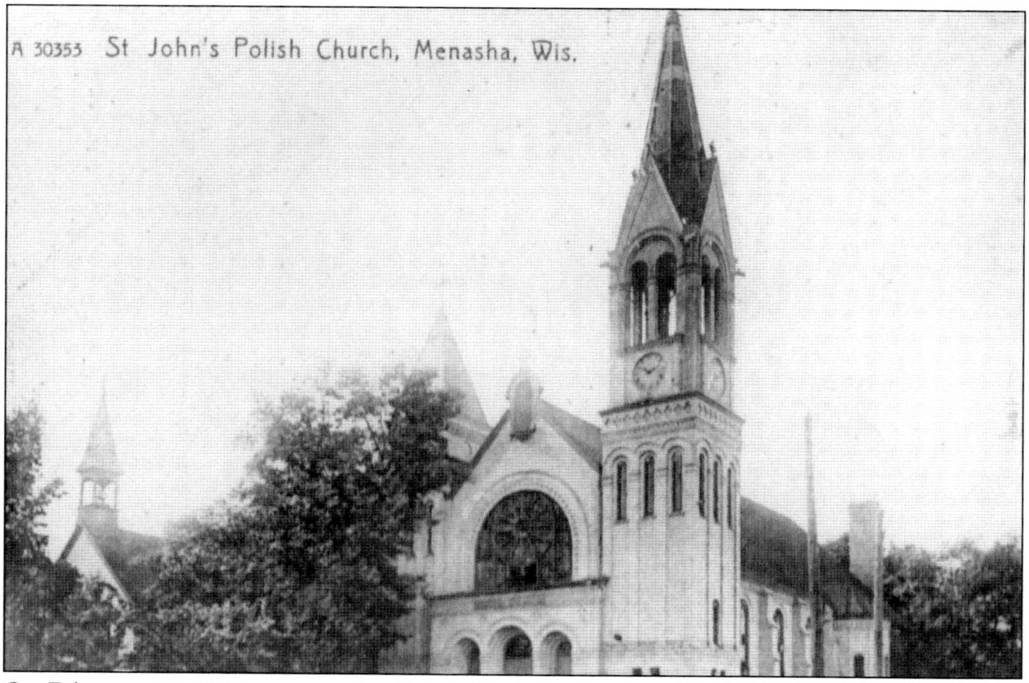

On February 25, 1888, seventy-five Polish Catholic families decided to break away from the German Catholic congregation at St. Mary's. The result was the formation of St. John's Polish Catholic Church and School in the Polander settlement. This building was erected in 1900 on the corner of Fifth and DePere Streets. The cost of the church was $16,000, and it is an example of the Romanesque Revival movement of architecture.

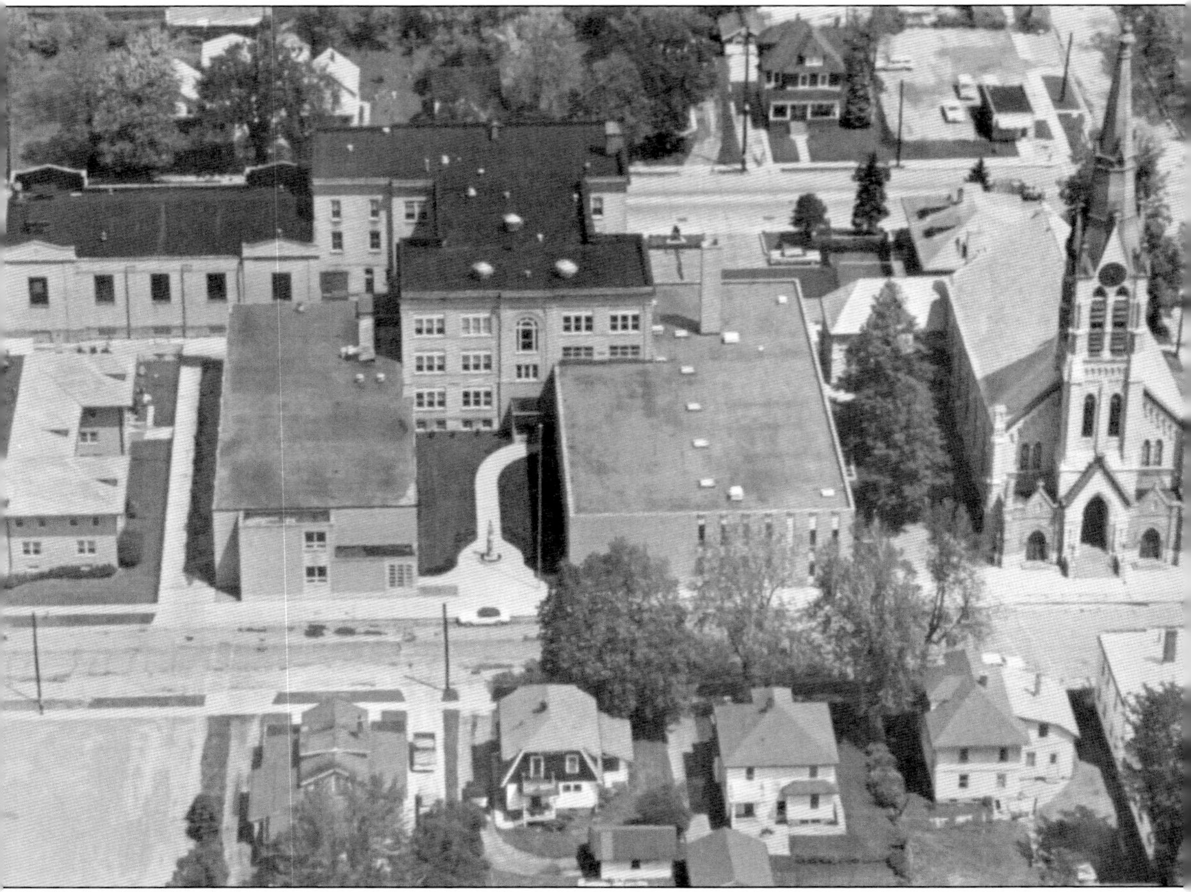

This aerial view shows the St. Mary's campus in 1967 with St. Mary's High School in the top center. Though the elementary school dates back to 1868, the high school was only established in 1928. Students were accepted from the three Catholic parishes in Menasha: St. Mary's, St. John's, and St. Patrick's, and the two parishes in Neenah, St. Gabriel's and St. Margaret Mary's. The elementary and high schools were housed in the same building for the next quarter century, with the high school largely occupying the third floor. The 1952 and 1962 additions to the left and right of the main building allowed the elementary grades to move out, giving the high school more classroom space. Eventually, time and technology limitations made the existing facilities outdated. In the fall of 1997, a new high school facility opened in Neenah. (Author's collection.)

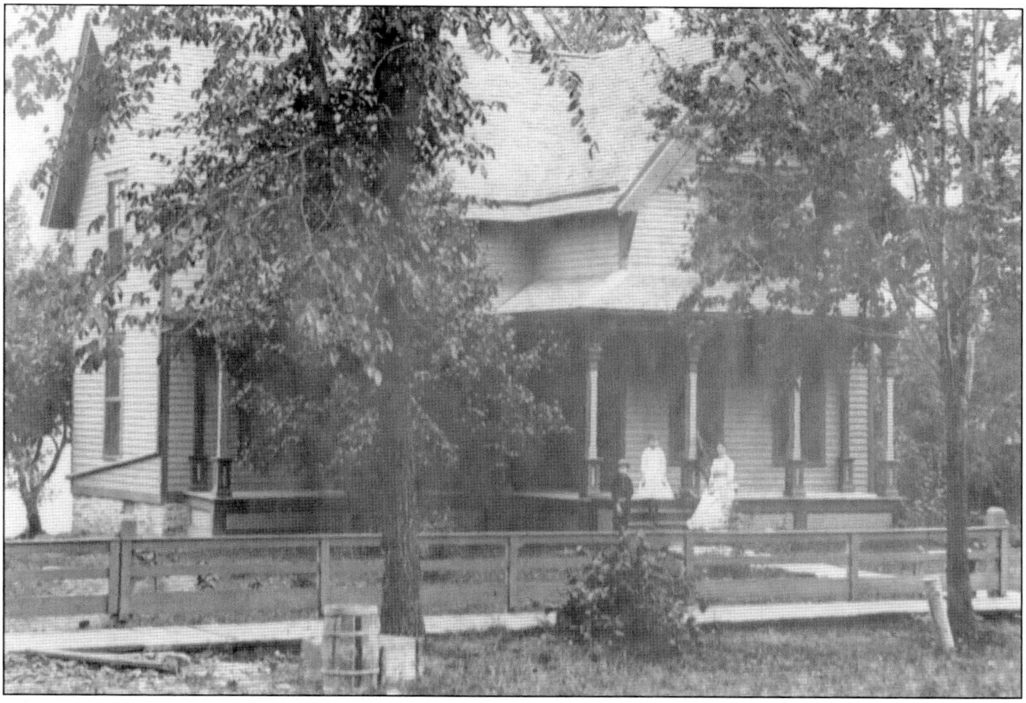

The P.J. Robertson home at 515 Broad Street, pictured here in 1890, reportedly cost $2,000 to construct. Notice the wooden sidewalks in front of the home. In 1896, Robertson and then-insurance agent George Banta went into business together, starting a fuel company. In 1898, P.J. Robertson became Menasha's city clerk.

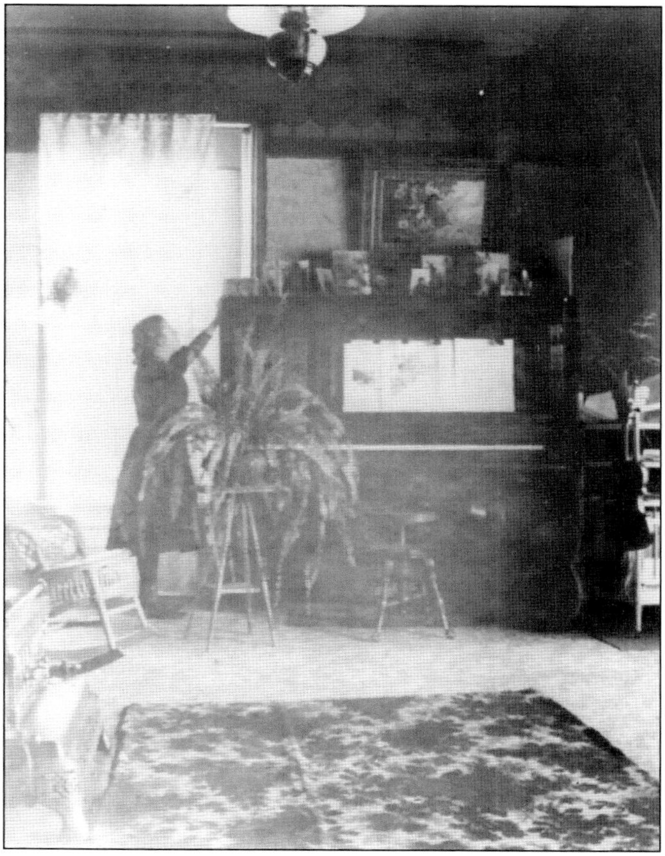

The piano was the centerpiece of the parlor, which was the cultural and entertainment center of the home during the days of old; usually someone in the family could play. With no radio or recorded music in the 19th and early 20th centuries, sheet music of the latest popular songs was the entertainment medium in the country's parlors. Records eventually replaced sheet music as the music industry's largest force.

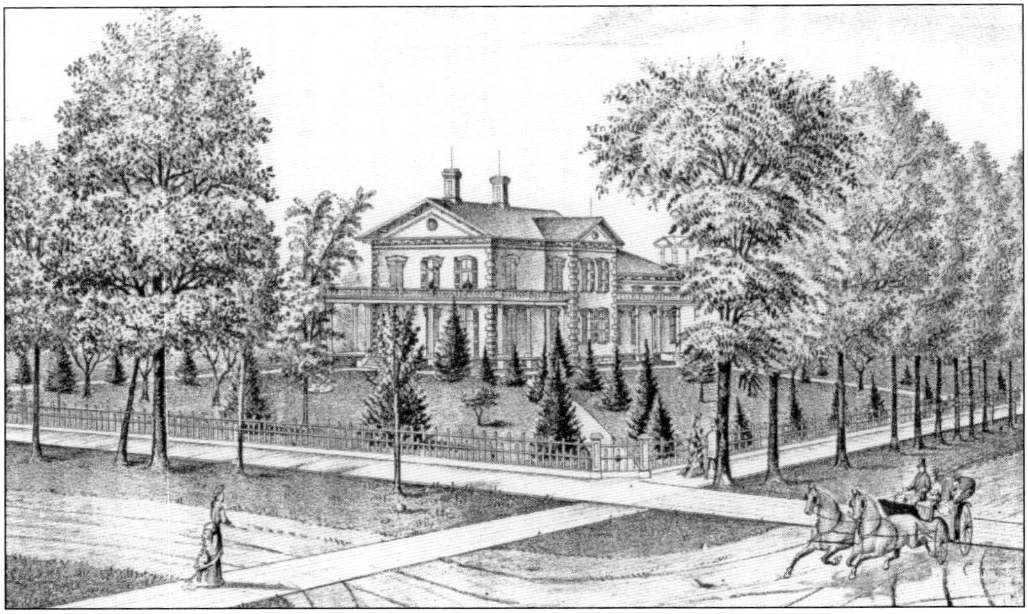

The Reuben M. Scott home was located on Racine Street at the site of the present-day post office between Broad and First Streets. R.M. Scott was an influential businessman and entrepreneur in Menasha history. This lithograph was featured in the 1880 *History of Winnebago County* by Richard J. Harney.

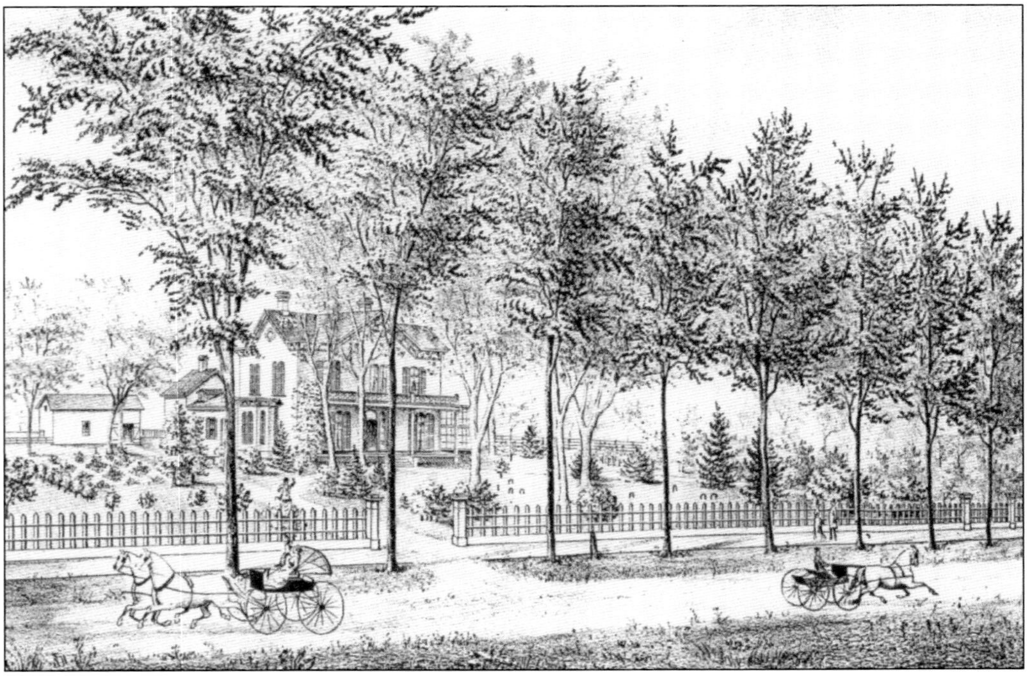

Elbridge Smith was one of the first settlers in Menasha, arriving in October 1848. He constructed the first frame building in Menasha on Canal Street, where he set up his law practice. Later, the first school in Menasha with teacher Hettie Frost was formed there; students were charged the tuition of one shilling per week. (Due to ongoing shortages of US coinage in some regions of the country, shillings continued to circulate well into the 19th century.)

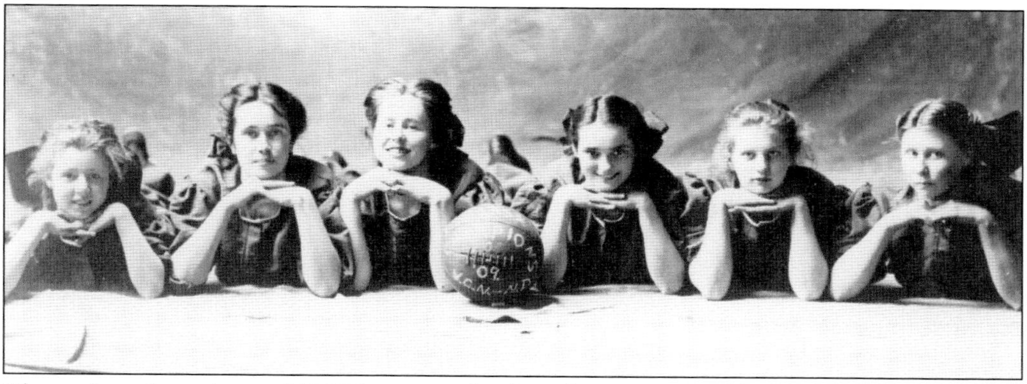

These class champions of 1909 have no idea how far women's athletics will progress in the coming years. They could never have imagined how commonplace it would become for their great-granddaughters to participate in sports and have opportunities beyond their wildest dreams, due to Title IX legislation. Title IX requires all schools receiving federal funds to offer equal opportunities based on gender, including in sports. The girls are dressed in the physical education uniform consisting of athletic bloomers, usually worn with stockings and often with a sailor middy blouse.

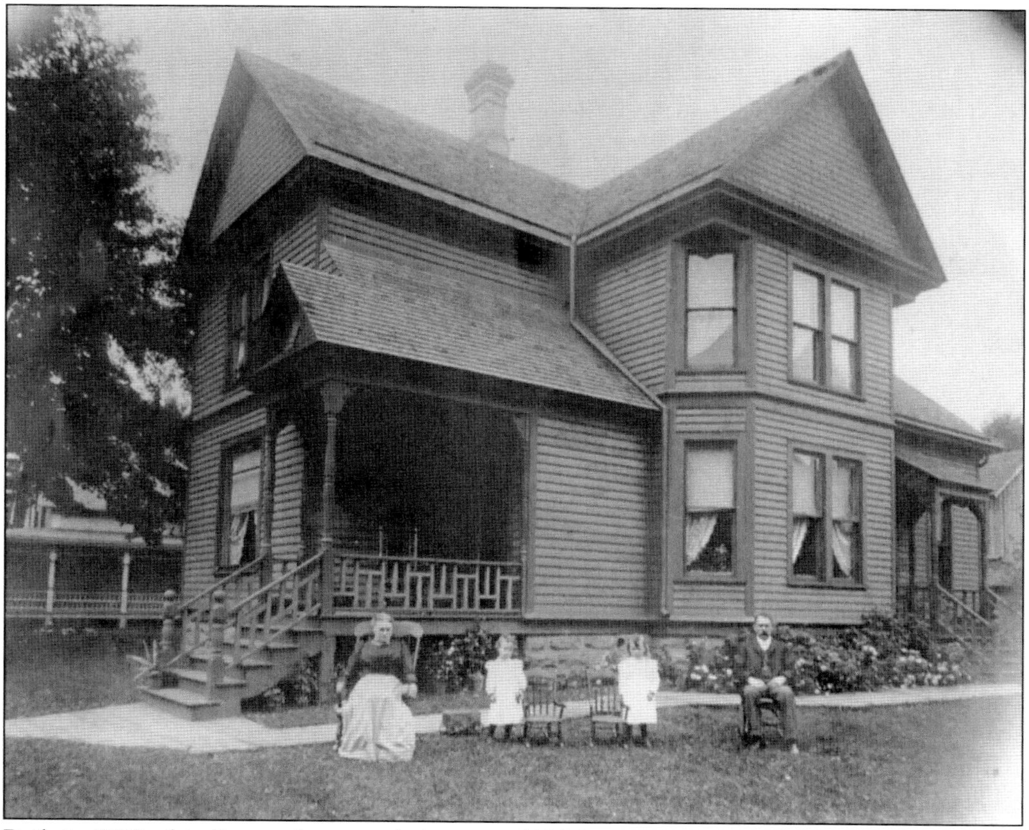

Built in 1900, this Queen Anne–style house at 319 Naymut Street was home to grocer Robert Ross Booth. Pictured here is his wife, Mary McKenna Booth, their twins Robert and Mary (born May 1895), and Booth himself. Queen Anne became an architectural fashion in the 1880s and 1890s, in tandem with the industrial revolution.

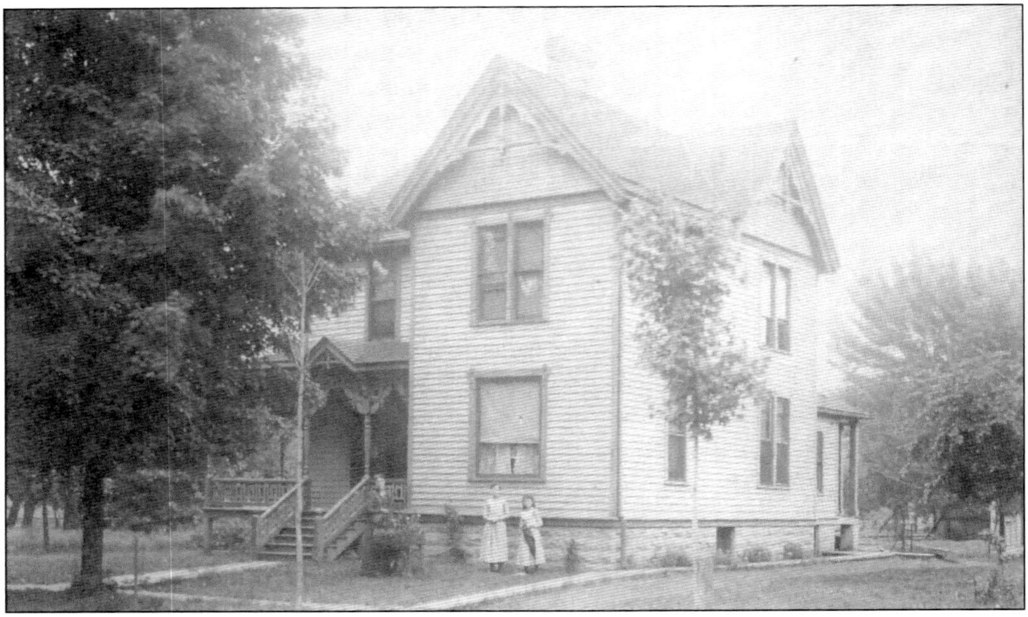

Tyler D. Phillips lived with his family at 435 Ahnaip Street. Phillips's business, listed as "furniture and undertaking" in the 1913 Menasha Telephone Directory, was located at 546 Water Street. While it might seem improbable to have a furniture store and undertaker joined in business today, it was quite common during this time, for who better to construct burial caskets than a skilled furniture maker?

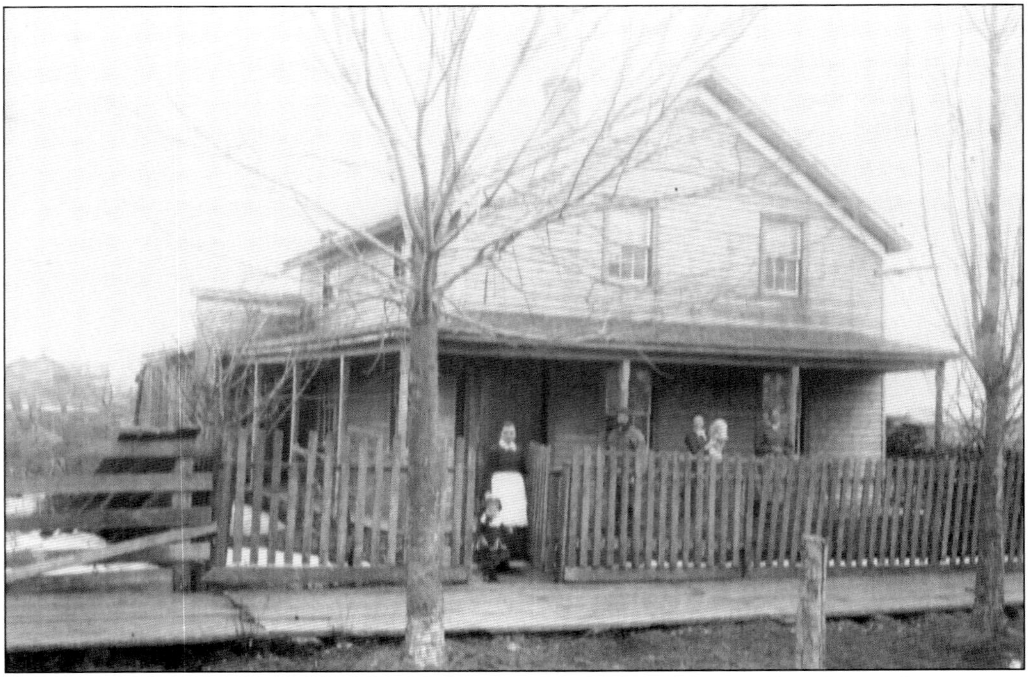

The home of David and Katherine Roessler was at 824 Broad Street. David Roessler came to Menasha in 1877 and became Menasha's town marshal. When he died in 1890 at the age of 34 from pneumonia, his obituary reflected that he "was particularly strong in his opposition to vagrants and many of them speak of him as 'the terror.' "

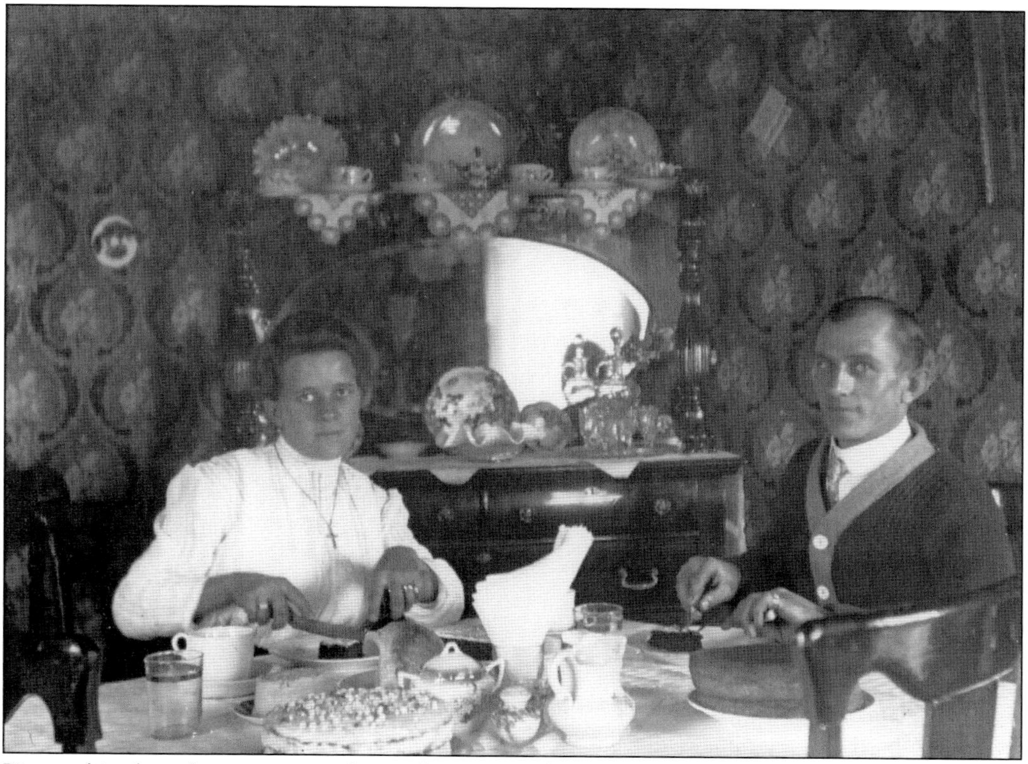

Pictured in their dining room at Seventh Street and Appleton Road are John and Frances Stolla, enjoying a festive dessert. John was a fireman at the Island Paper Company. He chose to be pictured in his sweater on this occasion, as it was, according to him, a "German tradition."

This home belonged to Elisha D. Smith, the founder of Menasha Wooden Ware and benefactor of Menasha. Located on the corner of Keyes and Park Streets and adjacent to the park that would later bear his name, the mansion was built in 1870 and razed in the 1940s.

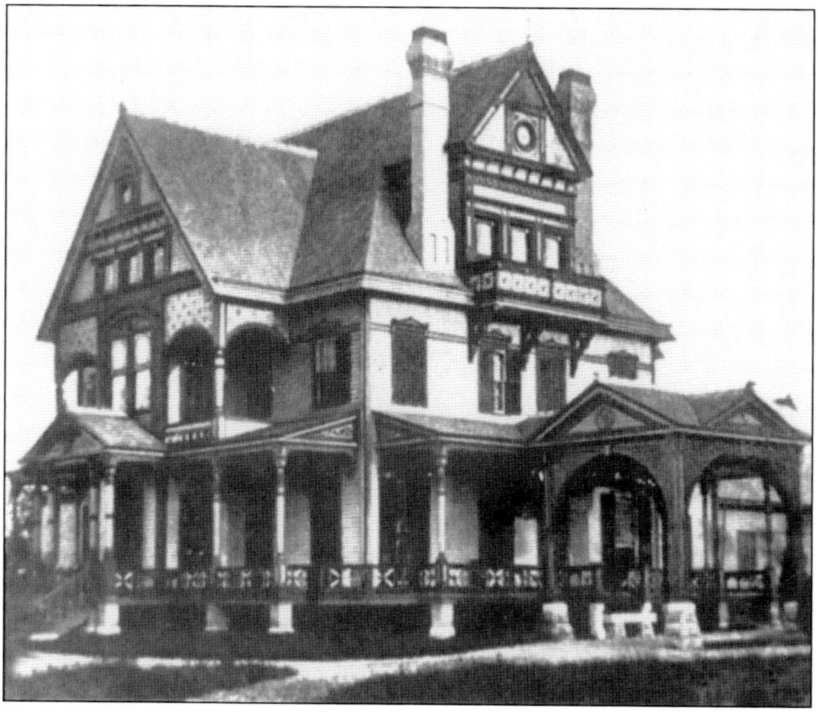

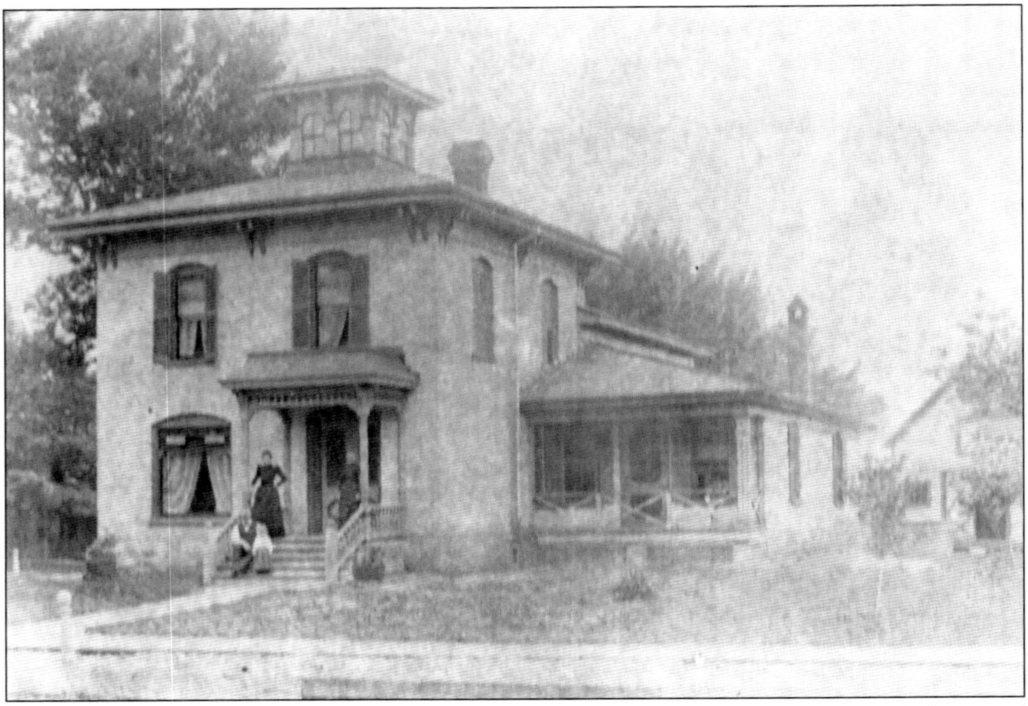

The Mitchell house, also known as the Rosch house, sits at the northwest corner of Chute and Tayco Streets. One of the oldest houses remaining in Menasha, it is of Italianate Renaissance design. The house was built in 1854 by John Mitchell, owner of a door, sash, and blind factory. In 1890, the structure was purchased by John Rosch, a local druggist and one-time mayor of Menasha.

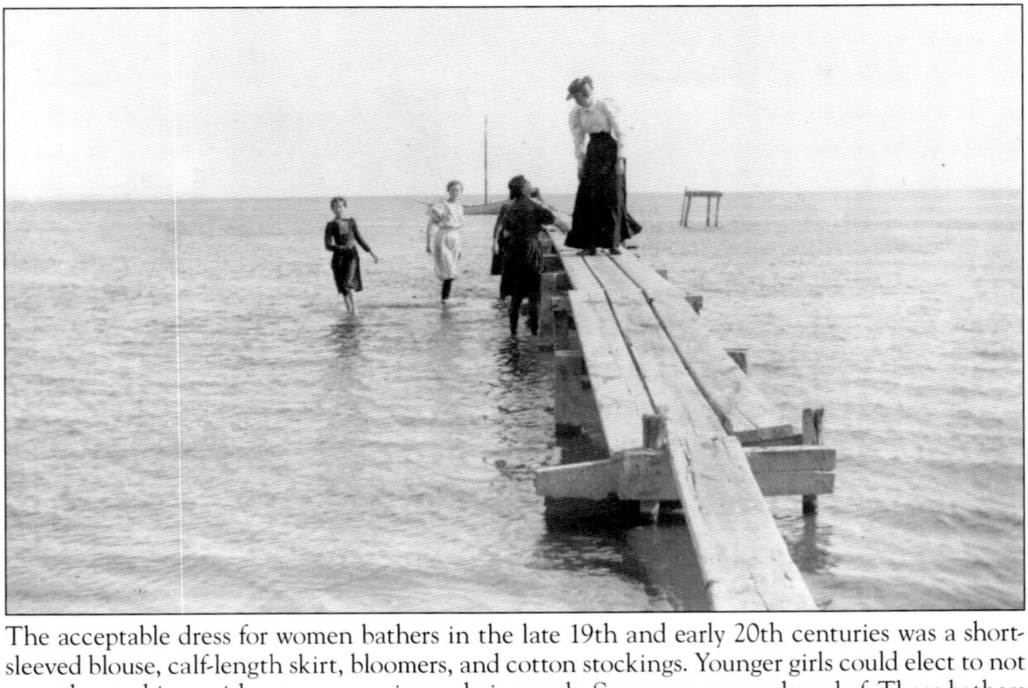

The acceptable dress for women bathers in the late 19th and early 20th centuries was a short-sleeved blouse, calf-length skirt, bloomers, and cotton stockings. Younger girls could elect to not wear the stockings without compromise to their morals. Sunscreen was unheard of. These bathers were at Brighton or Waverly Beach.

Five

City Fathers, Local Heroes, and More

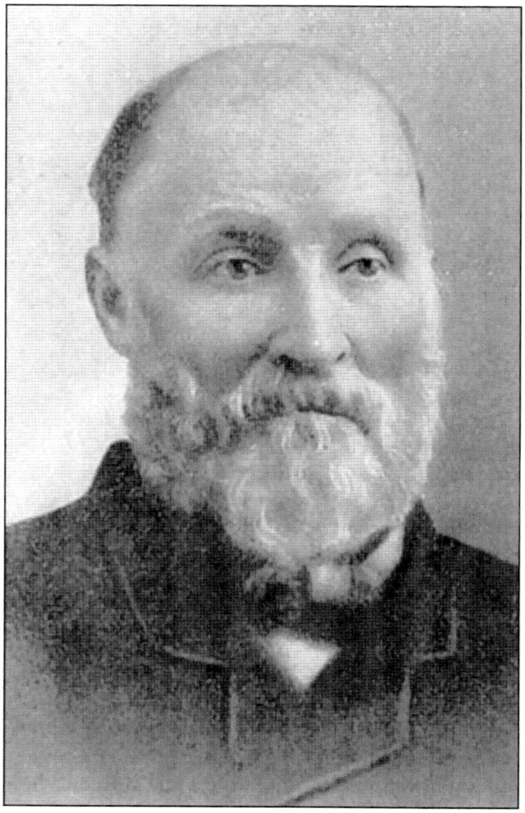

Considered the father of Menasha, Curtis Reed arrived in the area in 1848 and became the right-hand man of Gov. James Doty, invested in real estate, and negotiated water rights that culminated in the first dam in Menasha. Reed went on to build a sawmill, a gristmill, and a steamboat and became a leader of the city. He served five terms as the first president of the village board, and in his late 70s, he became the mayor for two terms. When he died in 1895, a few days before his 80th birthday, he was serving his second term as the city postmaster.

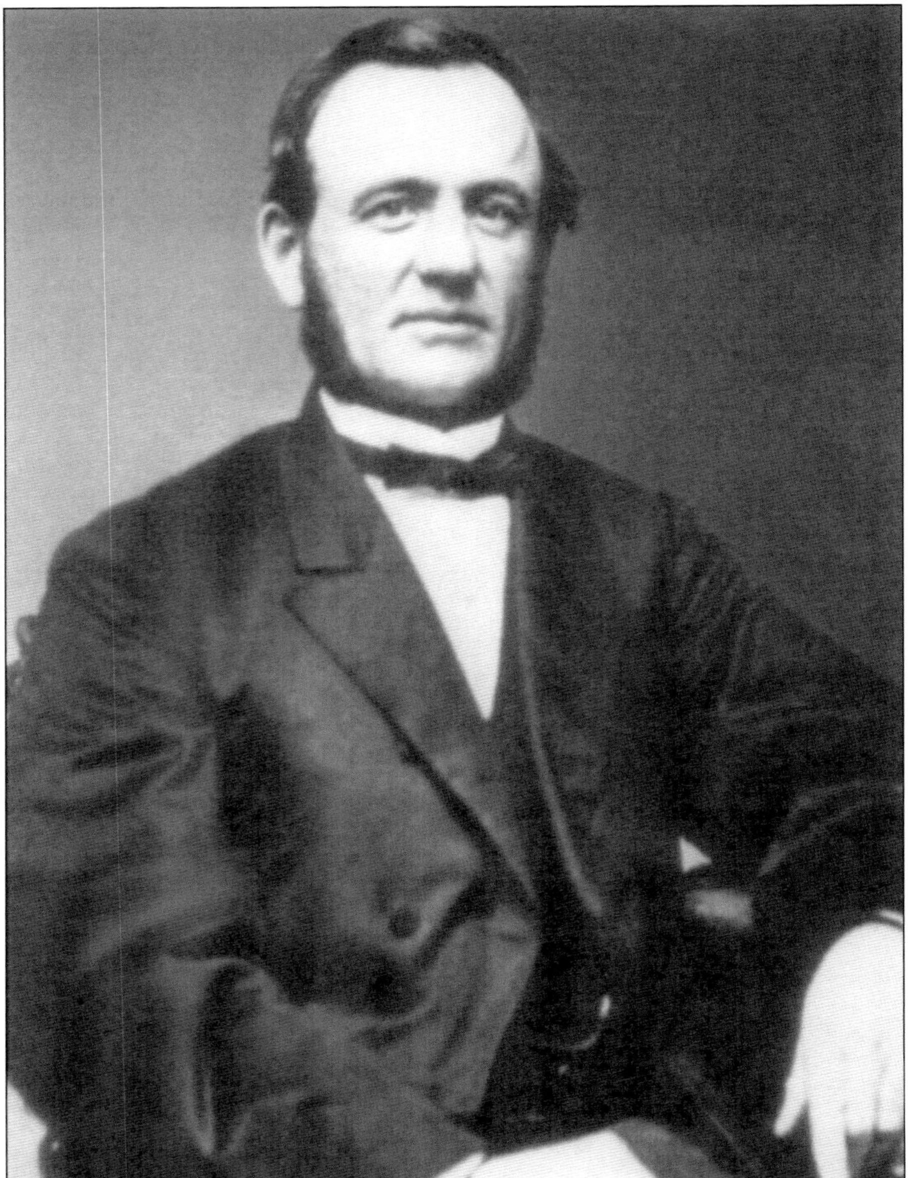

In 1852, Elisha D. Smith bought a pail factory for $1,200. Under Smith's leadership, the venture survived the Panic of 1857, and by 1871, it had become the largest woodenware maker in the Midwest, with 250 employees manufacturing products ranging from pails to tubs, churns, measures, butter tubs, and clothespins. In 1894, the founder's son Charles R. Smith merged a broom handle and barrel factory that he had founded with the Menasha Wooden Ware Company, creating the world's largest manufacturer of turned woodenware. By 1899, when the company founder died at age 72, Menasha Wooden Ware had annual revenues of $1 million and 1,000 people on the company payroll. Elisha D. Smith was a benefactor to the city, obtaining land on Doty Island in an effort to entice Milwaukee's Downer College to relocate to Menasha. When that effort failed, Smith donated the land to the city, and it became Smith Park. He also endowed a public lending library that bears his name to this day. He was so revered, his funeral procession extended for over a mile in length.

The Reverend O.P. Clinton was born on November 22, 1808, in Ferrisburg, Vermont. Clinton first visited the area in December 1845, and in March 1846, he moved his family from Lake Mills, Wisconsin, to Winnebago Rapids (later renamed Neenah). At the time, Reverend Clinton represented the American Home Missionary Society and worked as a missionary in northern Wisconsin. Reverend Clinton organized a Congregational Church in 1847 and moved to Menasha in 1848. On September 4, 1862, he enlisted and served as a chaplain for the 21st Wisconsin Infantry Regiment in the Civil War. He died in Menasha on June 19, 1890.

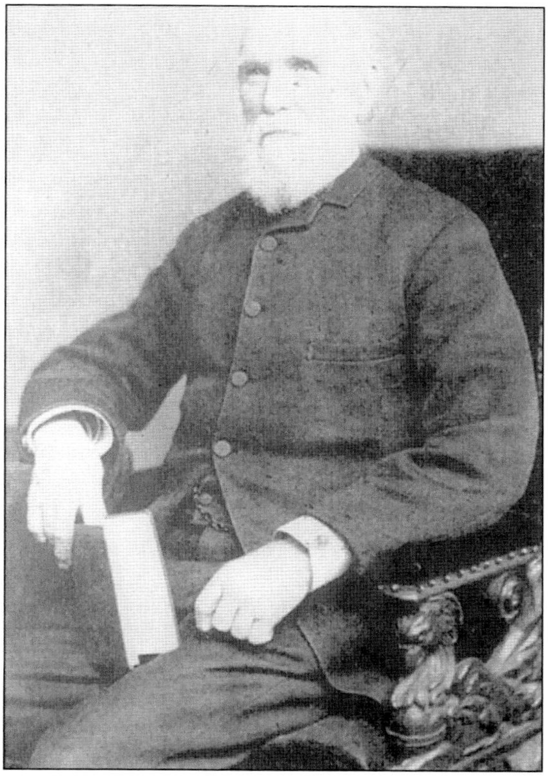

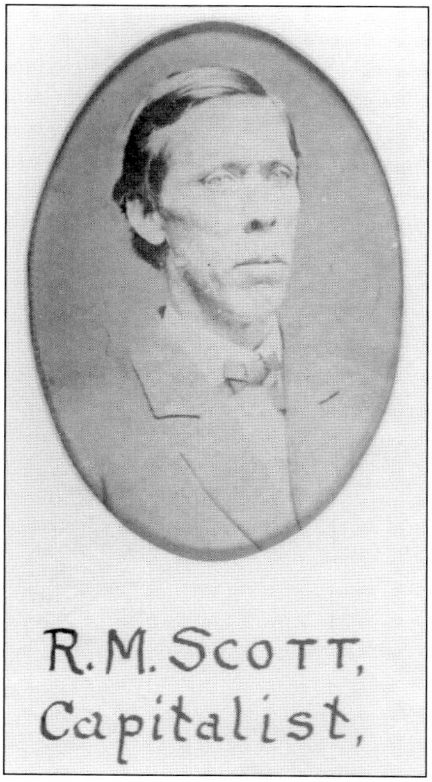

Reuben M. Scott attended the winter schools back home in Quebec, Canada, and assisted his father on the farm during the summers. When he was 18, Scott found work on farms in New York and Vermont before going to Wisconsin in 1848. He ventured largely into real estate for a time until 1860, when he and a partner, a Mr. Fisher, purchased the Star Flouring Mill in Menasha. In 1869, he built the National Hotel, which was considered the grandest structure in the city at that time. Scott invested heavily in city property, farmland, and manufacturing companies and employed many men for lumbering. He also built, on contract, the first 64 miles of the Wisconsin Central railroad in 121 days, a feat never before accomplished in the state. Scott died July 5, 1890.

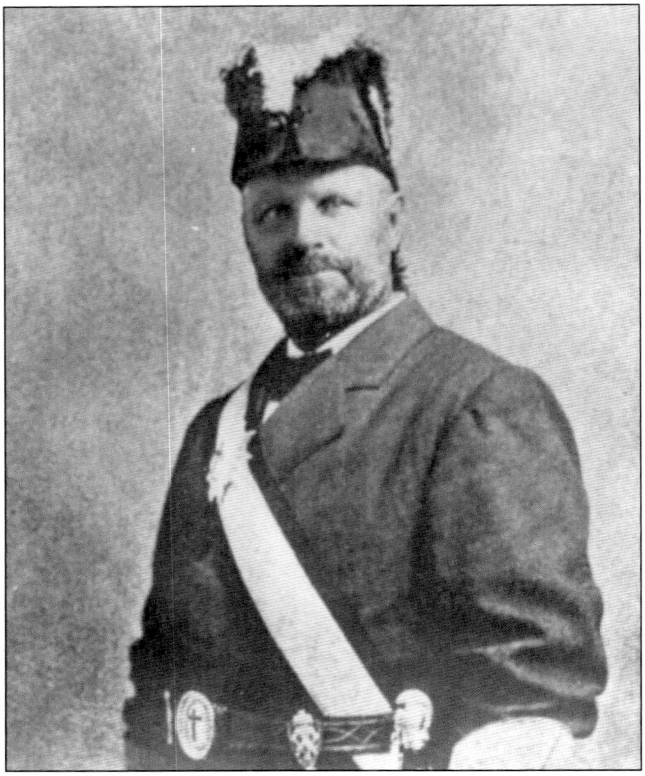

Publius Virgilius "P.V." Lawson Sr. arrived in Menasha in 1856, buying into a sash factory and planing mill with W.H. Hart. Selling it off three years later, he entered into a business arrangement with Andrew J. Webster involving a spoke and hub factory. This lasted until 1880, when he parted ways with Webster and entered a partnership with John Strange in a sawmill and lumberyard. Lawson Sr. was active in local politics as trustee, a school board member, and as mayor for four consecutive one-year terms. He died in 1881.

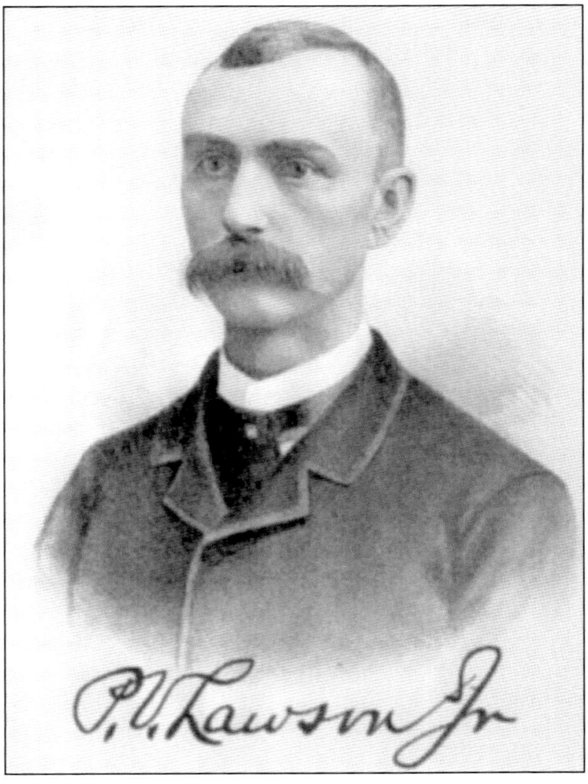

P.V. Lawson Jr. was brought to Menasha as a two-year-old by his father. A lawyer by trade, he left law after practicing for 11 years to establish the Menasha Wood Split Pulley Company in 1888. Like his father, Lawson Jr. was active in politics as well, elected mayor from 1886 to 1889 and again in 1893 and 1896. A great orator, he presided over many association and fraternal gatherings, lecturing on natural history topics such as geology, paleontology, and archaeology. A prolific writer, Lawson Jr. contributed to many scientific journals, magazines, and newspapers and wrote critically received histories of Winnebago County and treatises on American Indians. He died in 1920.

One of Menasha's earliest pioneers, Samuel S. Roby arrived in town in 1850. At different times, Roby served as treasurer of Menasha from 1856 to 1866, as well as clerk, trustee, and assessor for the village and, later, city. Concurrently, he engaged in business pursuits, owning a well-regarded grocery and dry goods business.

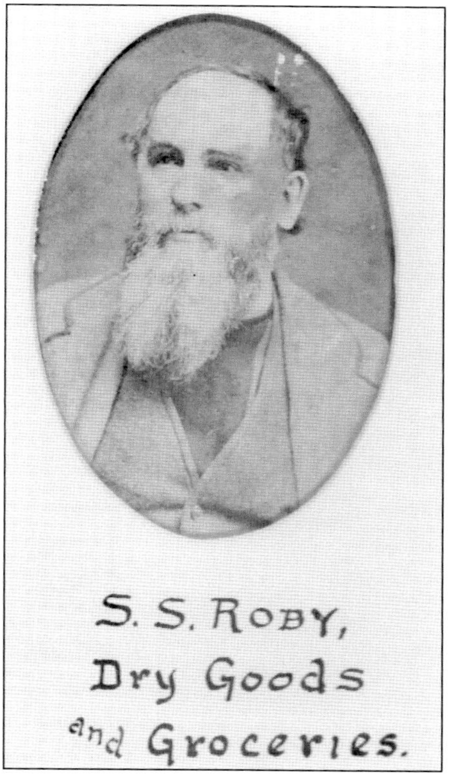

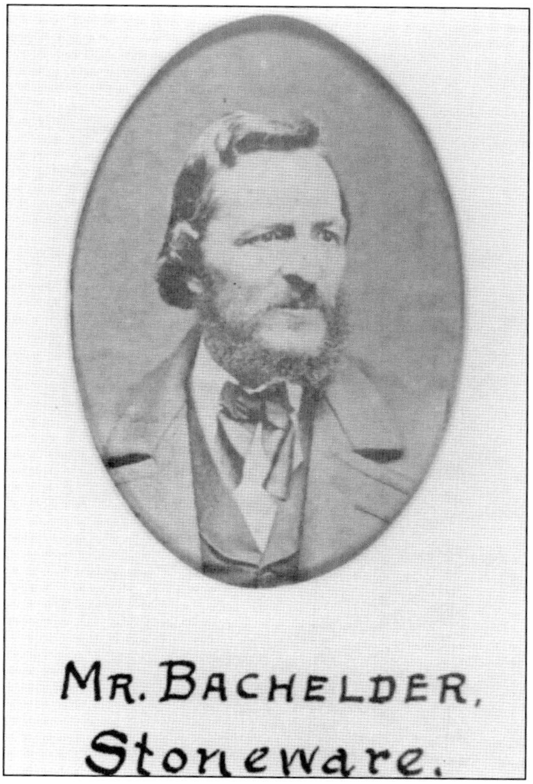

Carlton Bachelder was born near Concord, New Hampshire, in 1829. His father owned and operated a pottery in Exeter, Maine, and Bachelder learned the trade during his youth. At the age of 18, in August 1847, he came to Wisconsin to join his father and lived on a farm in the town of Taycheedah in Fond du Lac County. In 1850, he moved to Menasha, where he began a pottery business and continued in the wholesale business of stoneware.

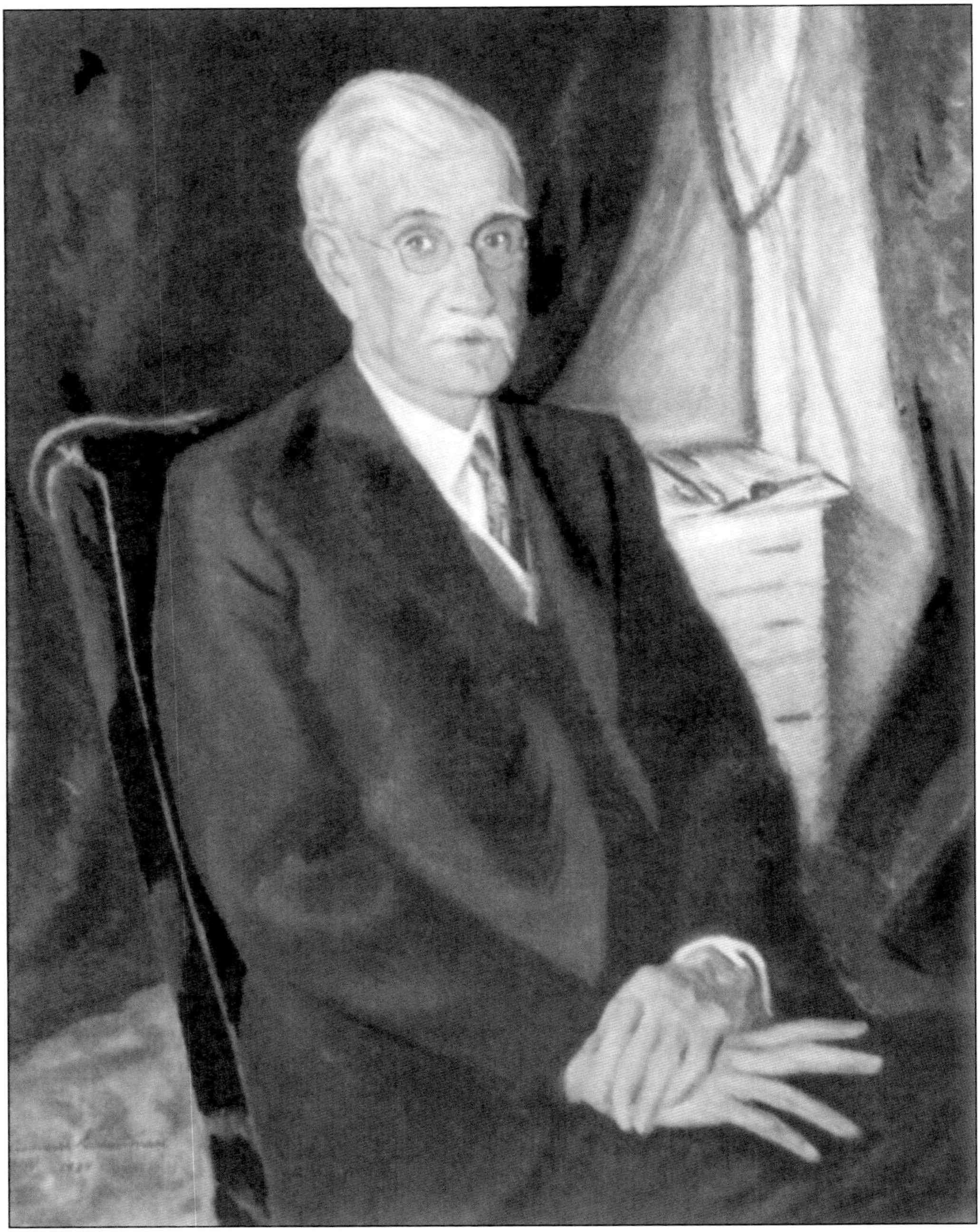

Arriving in Wisconsin as an agent for the Phenix Insurance Company of Brooklyn, New York, George Banta Sr. settled in Menasha in 1886. His chief hobby was running a small printing business out of a backyard shed. On Washington's Birthday in 1901, he arrived home to find his printing shed in flames. Moving to temporary quarters on Main Street until he could rebuild at home, he gained so much work at his new location that he decided to make it his chief business. The George Banta Company was incorporated in September 1901, and it became a major printer of fraternity and sorority magazines. In time, the company became a publisher of textbooks, as well as *Encyclopedia Brittanica* and *The Proceedings of the US Naval Institute*. Banta Sr. was also a two-term mayor of Menasha before his printing career took off. He died in 1935.

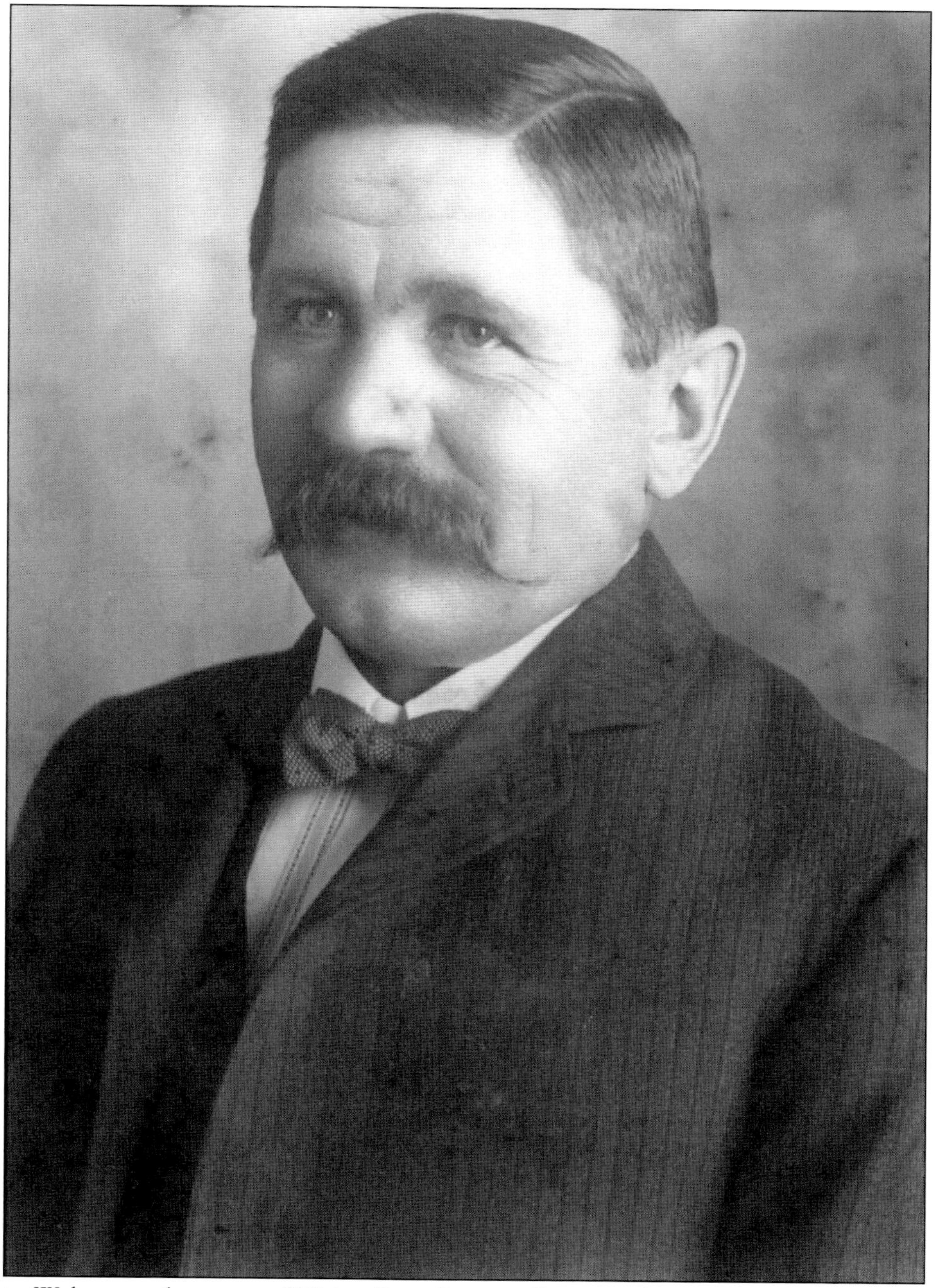

Christ Walter was the owner of Walter Bros. Brewing Company, brewer of Gold Label and Gem beers. While not as celebrated as the Busch (Budweiser), Uehlein (Schlitz), or Pabst families in the 1950s, the extended Walter family were the largest brewers in America, operating breweries in Menasha, Eau Claire, Appleton, and West Bend, Wisconsin, as well as in Pueblo and Trinidad, Colorado. Unable to match the marketing and sales budgets of the big national breweries, the Walter breweries closed one after another in the 1950s, 1960s, and 1970s. The last one to survive was Walter Brewing in Eau Claire, which lasted until 1989. Christ Walter's brewery was the first to close its operations in 1956, but he enjoyed a separate political career in Menasha, becoming the Third Ward representative in the city council and, later, president of the Board of Aldermen.

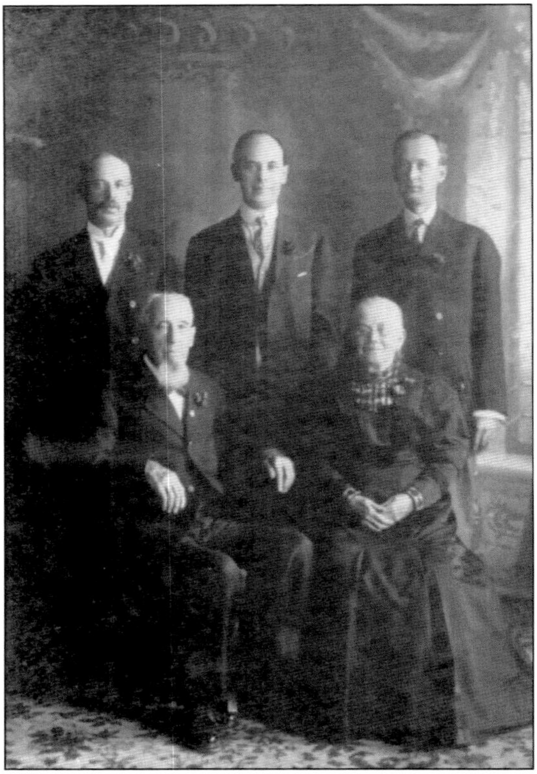

The Tuchscherer family was known throughout the Twin Cities for their businesses: dry goods and shoes and a department store, for which they had partnered with the Schlegals at Milwaukee and Main Streets. Their shoe store was a fixture downtown for well over 90 years. Pictured from left to right are (first row) Jacob and Regina Tuchscherer; (second row) Adam, Henry, and Thomas Tuchscherer. Henry was the owner of the Tuchscherer Shoe Store.

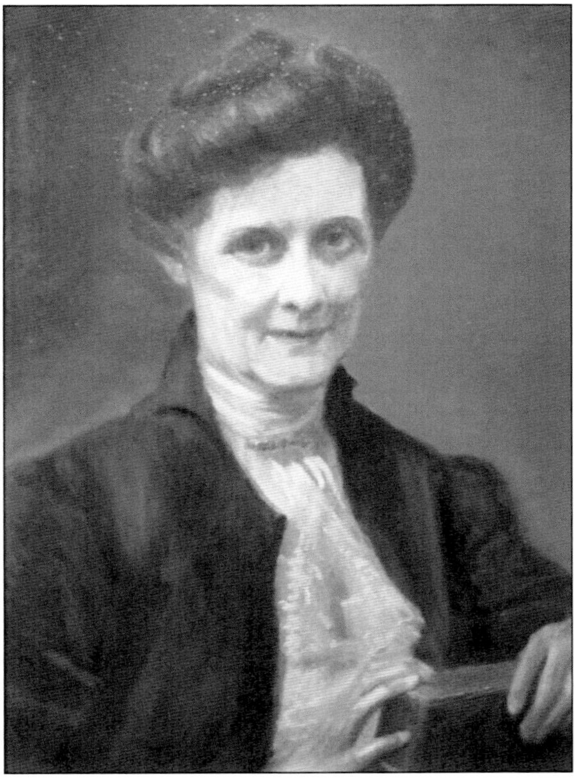

Lucy Lee Pleasants became Menasha's first librarian when the Menasha Free Library Association was formed in 1896 and located on the second floor of the Tuchscherer and Schlegal department store. As the effort progressed and the now-familiar Elisha D. Smith Public Library was built, Pleasants became the library's head librarian and managed it until her retirement in 1919. She was also an author and poet. She published *Old Virginia Days and Ways: Reminiscences of Sally McCarty Pleasants* in 1916, as well as the long-form poem "Plutarch's Lives." In 1930 and 1931, a children's room was built as an addition to the library and dedicated to her. (Courtesy of the Menasha Public Library.)

John Rosch, local druggist and mayor of Menasha in 1887, was the first person in Menasha to operate a soda fountain. A political man, Rosch served several times as a delegate to the Democratic National Convention and entertained three-time presidential candidate William Jennings Bryan at his distinctive home on Tayco Street.

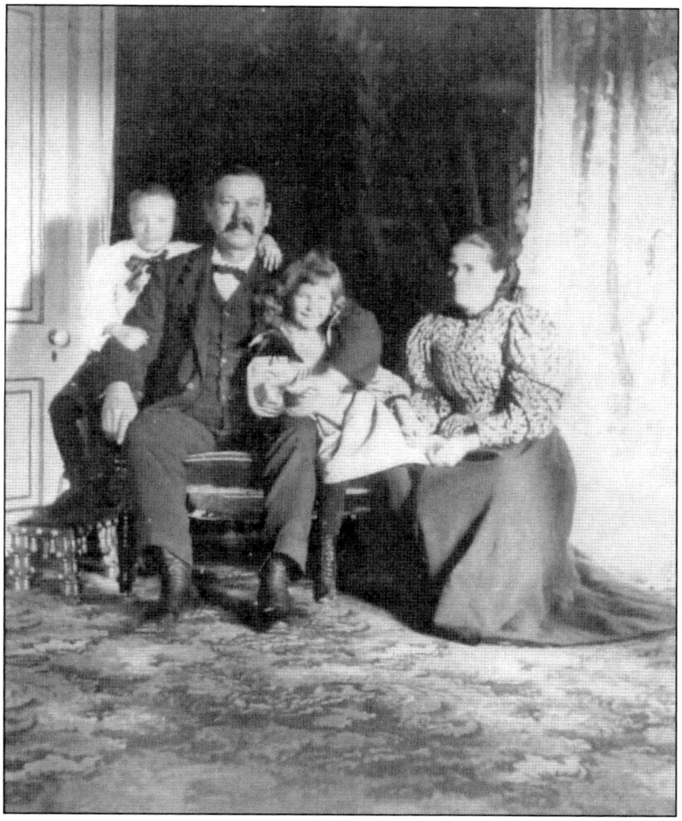

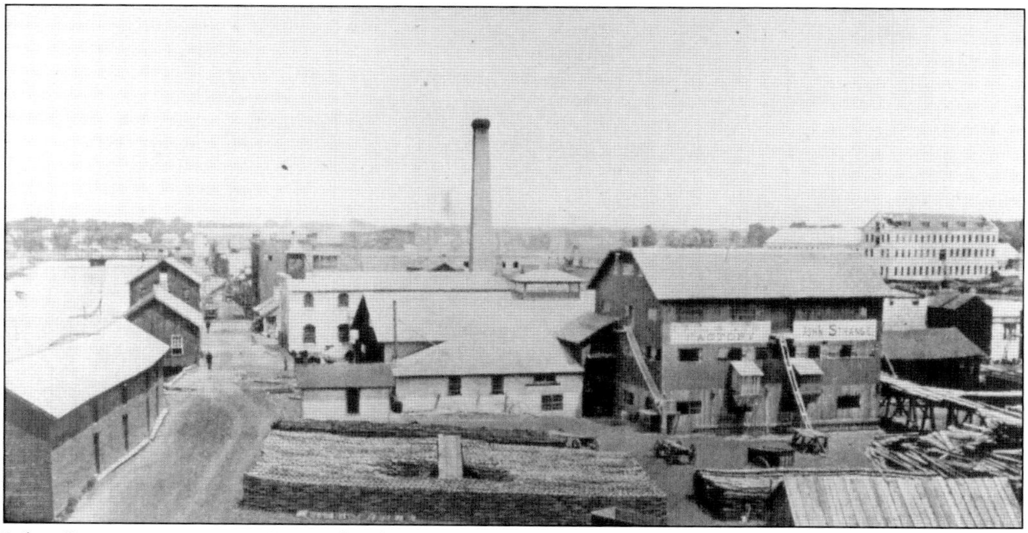

John Strange grew up in Menasha from the first year of his life, settling on Doty Island with his parents in 1852. Around 1884, he built a sawmill and pail factory. By 1891, Strange had converted his plant to a wrapping paper mill. The John Strange Paper Company merged with the Menasha Corporation in 1969. Strange was elected lieutenant governor of Wisconsin in 1908 and served one term. He was a strident supporter of Prohibition, and during World War I, he likened American brewers to our opponent in the war, saying, "The worst of all our German enemies, the most treacherous, the most menacing are Pabst, Schlitz, Blatz, and Miller."

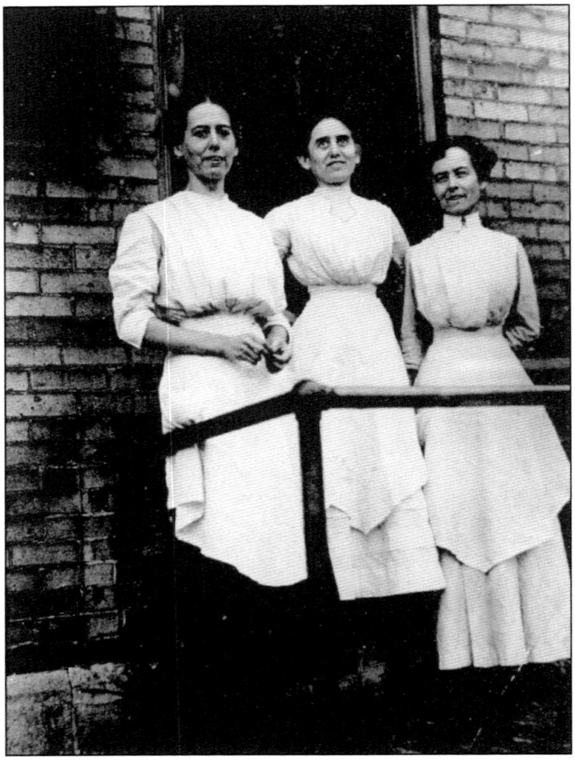

The Kemmeter sisters—from left to right, Mary, Louise, and Elizabeth—were accomplished seamstresses who had a dressmaking and hemstitching business at 31 Mill Street, later moving it to their residence on Second Street. In a world that existed before ready-to-wear or off-the-rack fashions were commonplace, a skilled dressmaker was always in demand.

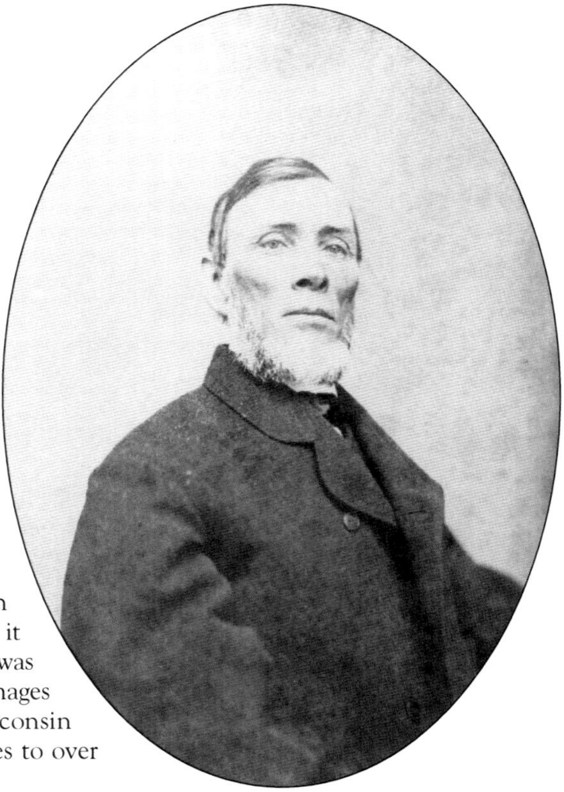

Amos D. Page, one of Menasha's early settlers, founded the Page farm outside Menasha in 1849. Page was born in 1818 in Maine, when it was still a part of Massachusetts. In 1886, he was one of many farmers in the area awarded damages due to improvements in the Fox and Wisconsin Rivers. His award was $760, which equates to over $18,000 in 2010.

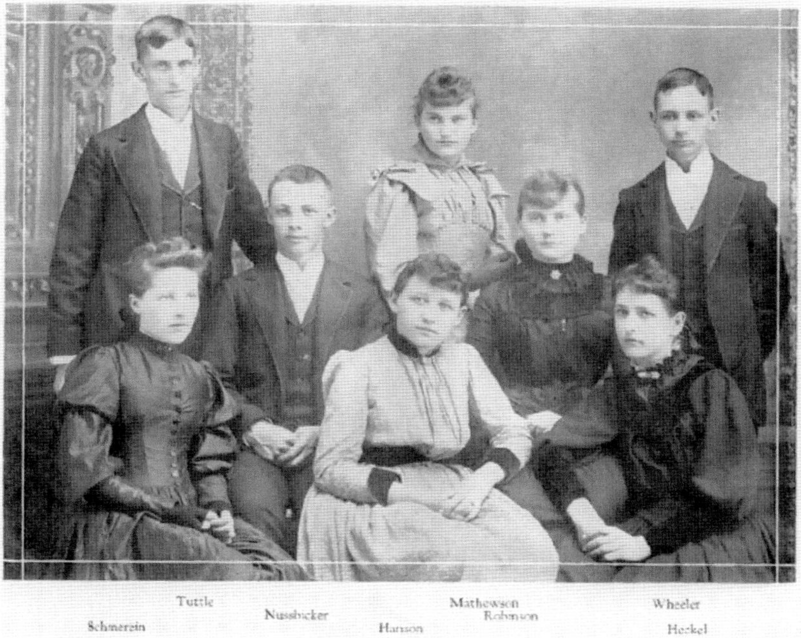

CLASS OF 1890

The eight members of the 1890 graduating class were all afforded the opportunity to speak at the commencement program, as audiences in the 19th century expected it. Orators were the celebrities of the day, and oration provided an important source of entertainment in a world without radio, television, or movies. Speeches, debates, and sermons often attracted large crowds, and every occasion seemed to require one or more speeches. Judging from the topics, these students' orations were not the traditional graduation addresses of today. A Latin phrase on the program's back cover, "Per aspera ad astra," translates as, "Through hardships to the stars."

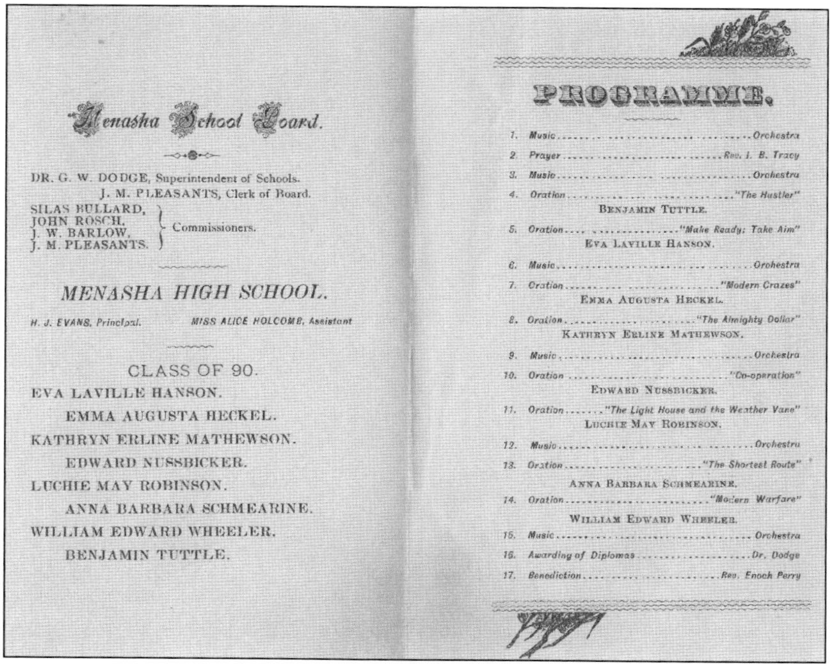

Menasha School Board.

DR. G. W. DODGE, Superintendent of Schools.
J. M. PLEASANTS, Clerk of Board.

SILAS BULLARD,
JOHN ROSCH,
J. W. BARLOW,
J. M. PLEASANTS. } Commissioners.

MENASHA HIGH SCHOOL.

H. J. EVANS, Principal. MISS ALICE HOLCOMB, Assistant

CLASS OF 90.

EVA LAVILLE HANSON.
EMMA AUGUSTA HECKEL.
KATHRYN ERLINE MATHEWSON.
EDWARD NUSSBICKER.
LUCHIE MAY ROBINSON.
ANNA BARBARA SCHMEARINE.
WILLIAM EDWARD WHEELER.
BENJAMIN TUTTLE.

PROGRAMME.

1. Music........................Orchestra
2. Prayer........................Rev. I. B. Tracy
3. Music........................Orchestra
4. Oration........................"The Hustler"
BENJAMIN TUTTLE.
5. Oration........................"Make Ready: Take Aim"
EVA LAVILLE HANSON.
6. Music........................Orchestra
7. Oration........................"Modern Crazes"
EMMA AUGUSTA HECKEL.
8. Oration........................"The Almighty Dollar"
KATHRYN ERLINE MATHEWSON.
9. Music........................Orchestra
10. Oration........................"Co-operation"
EDWARD NUSSBICKER.
11. Oration......."The Light House and the Weather Vane"
LUCHIE MAY ROBINSON.
12. Music........................Orchestra
13. Oration........................"The Shortest Route"
ANNA BARBARA SCHMEARINE.
14. Oration........................"Modern Warfare"
WILLIAM EDWARD WHEELER.
15. Music........................Orchestra
16. Awarding of Diplomas........................Dr. Dodge
17. Benediction........................Rev. Enoch Perry

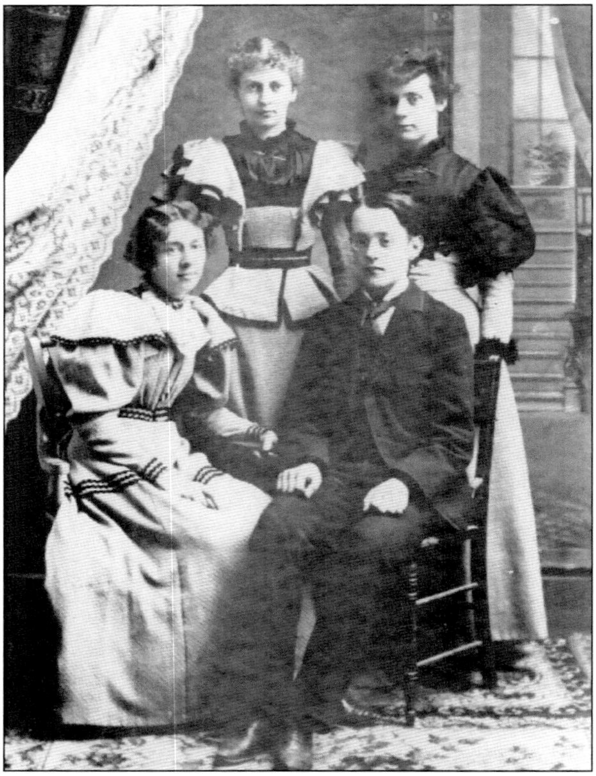

Pictured is the Menasha High School graduating class of 1895; from left to right, they are (first row) Katherine Paul and Richard Tunnicliffe; (second row) Carolyn Bullard and Cora Belle Wheeler. Tunnicliffe became a professor of music at Bowling Green, Ohio, and Wheeler became a nurse in Los Angeles. The other two ladies married and became housewives.

The seventh grade of the Fourth Ward School, located on the 700 block of First Street, poses for its class picture in this undated photograph. Hopefully, it was the visiting photographer who misspelled the town's name on the slate in front of the class. The school no longer stands.

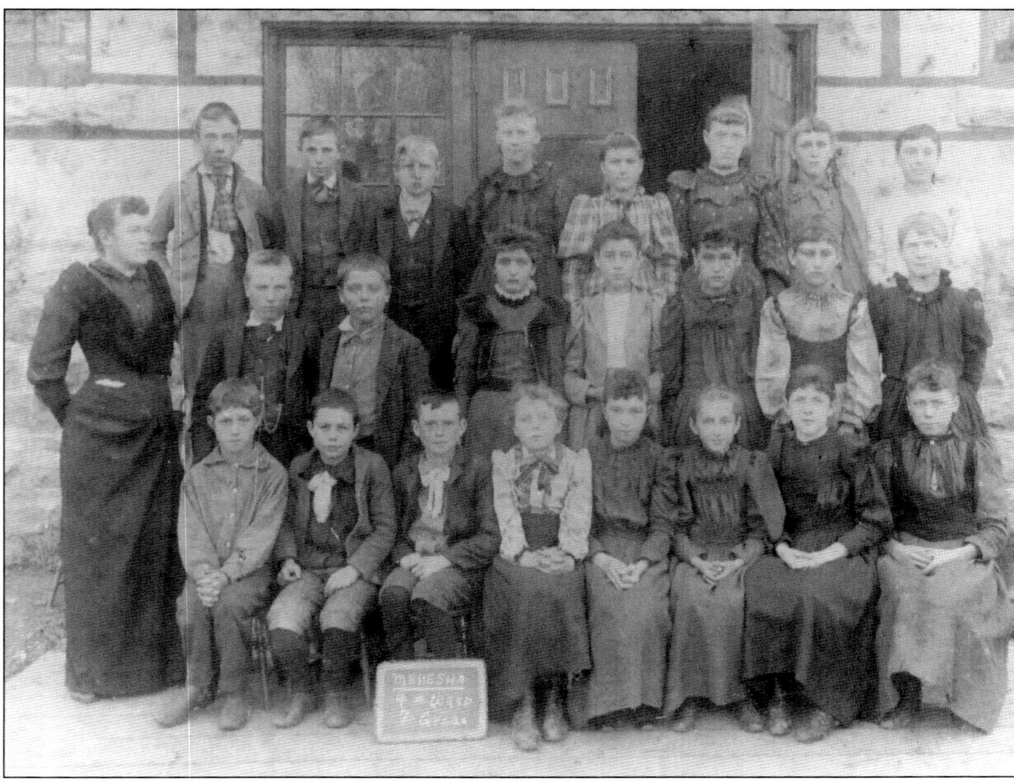

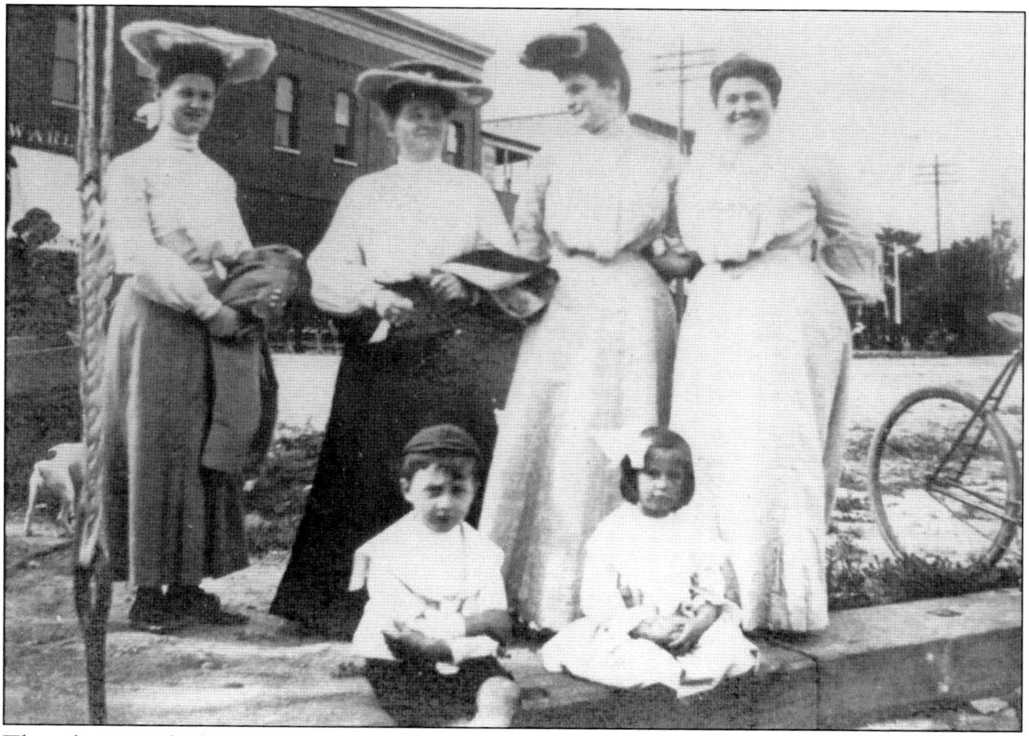

This photograph shows Loescher's Hardware in the background, standing at the end of Racine Street by the Fox River. Pictured from left to right are (first row) Clarence Loescher and Marcella Schneider; (second row) two unidentified women, Lou Schneider, and Barbara Loescher.

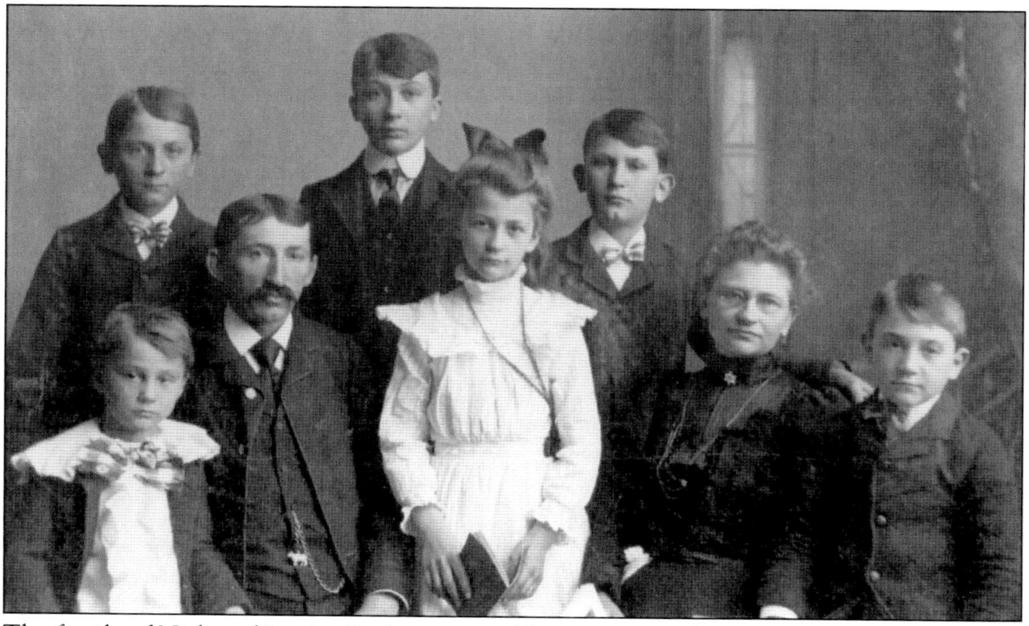

The family of Nick and Louisa Beck is pictured here sometime between 1900 and 1909. They are, from left to right, (first row) Ben, Nick Sr., Rose, Louisa, and Nick Jr.; (second row) William, Frank, and Alexander. Nick Beck ran the City Meat Market on Main Street, just east of Milwaukee Street, known as one of the most respected butcher shops in Menasha.

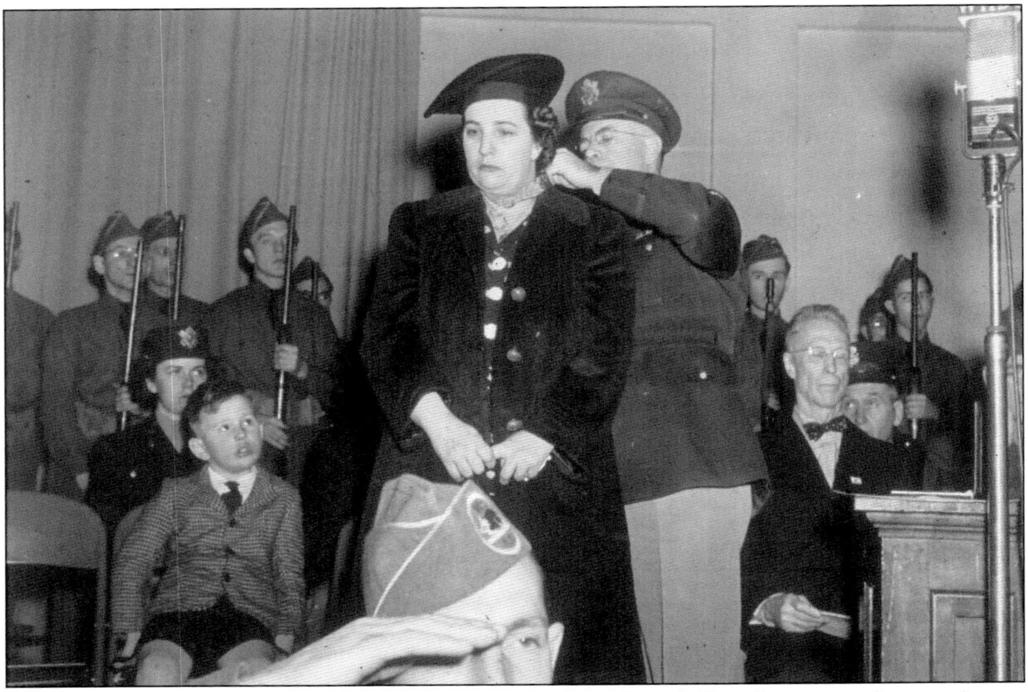

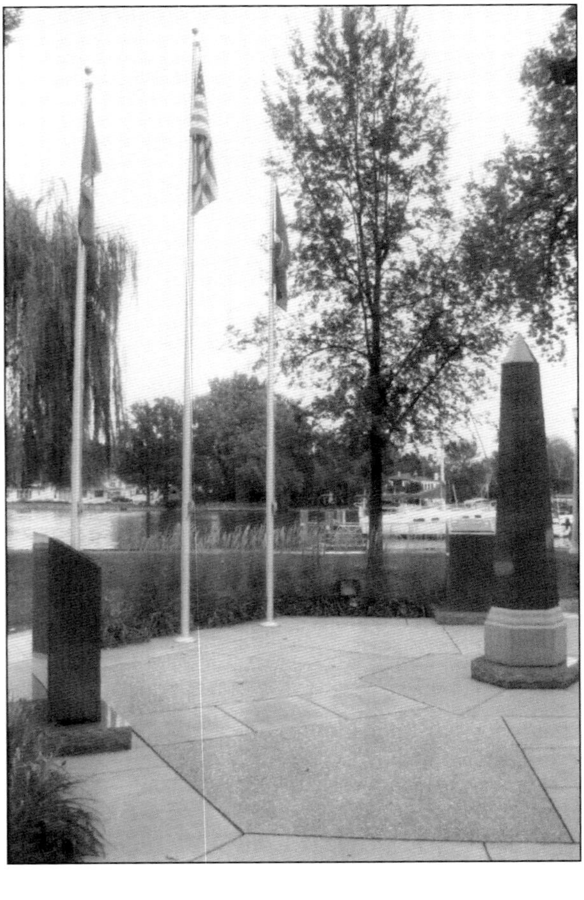

Elmer J. Burr Jr. was posthumously awarded the Medal of Honor for service during World War II in New Guinea as a member of Company I, 3rd Battalion, 127th Infantry, 32nd Division, Wisconsin National Guard. On December 24, 1942, Burr Jr. covered a grenade with his body to save the lives of his comrades. Though he died of his wounds the following day, he was awarded the Medal of Honor on October 11, 1943. This photograph shows his wife, Lucille, receiving the medal on behalf of her husband. (Courtesy of Neenah Public Library.)

On April 25, 1967, as a Specialist Four in Company C, 1st Battalion, 35th Infantry Regiment, 25th Infantry Division in Vietnam, Ken Stumpf rescued three wounded comrades despite heavy fire and single-handedly disabled an enemy bunker. He was awarded the Medal of Honor for his actions during the battle. He served 29 years with the US Army before retiring in 1994. He and Elmer Burr are honored on the Isle of Valor (pictured) at Smith Park. (Courtesy of hmdb.org and photographer Keith L.)

Six

City Services

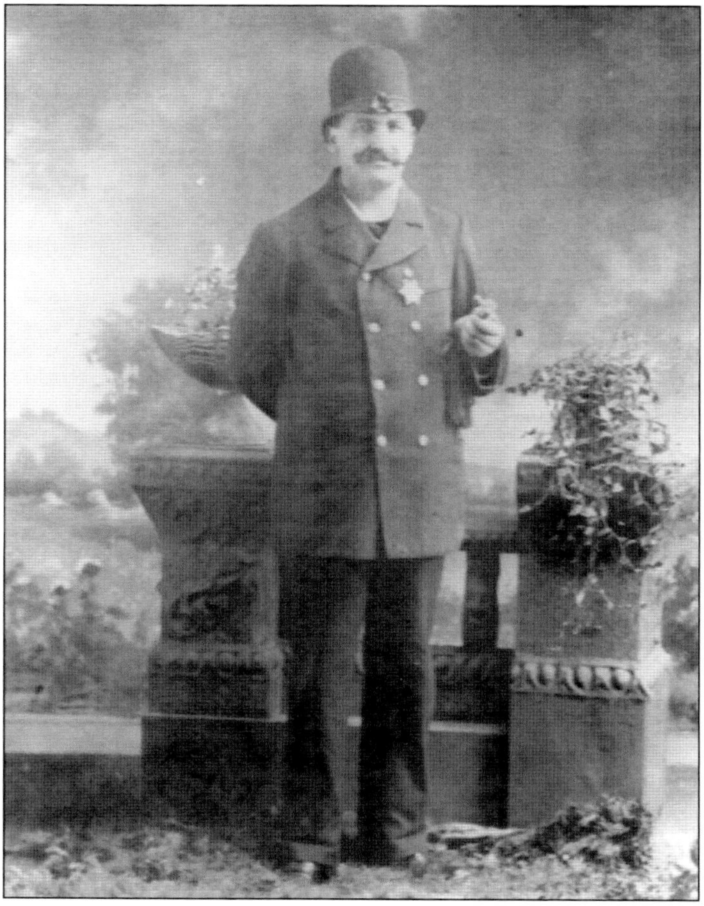

Officer John Schreibeis is pictured here in 1890. Born in Two Rivers in 1861, he arrived in Menasha in 1881. He served as a police officer for four years before leaving the force and entering the grocery business. Schreibeis also became instrumental in local politics, serving as Fourth Ward member of the board of education and as a member of the Board of Parks Commissioners.

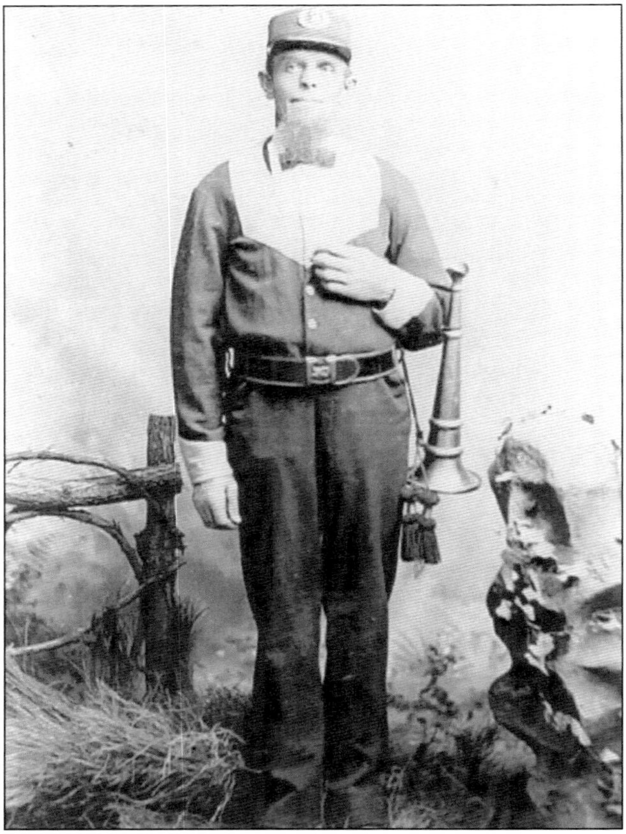

Early Menasha fireman John Schubert poses in this 1884 photograph. Draped over his left arm is a speaking horn, or trumpet, the forerunner of today's bullhorn. It allowed the relay of orders to the firefighters. Horns used in the field were typically made of tin, brass, or silver, but they were also sometimes given out as awards; some were ornamented with gold or semiprecious stones.

In this 1898 photograph, a crowd gathers at the laying of the cornerstone of the Elisha D. Smith Public Library. Before Smith's and librarian Lucy Lee Pleasants's vision was fulfilled, a freestanding public library for Menasha had been just a dream. At the time, the library consisted of limited volumes in a few rooms on the second floor of the Tuchscherer & Schlegel Department Store. (Courtesy of Menasha Public Library.)

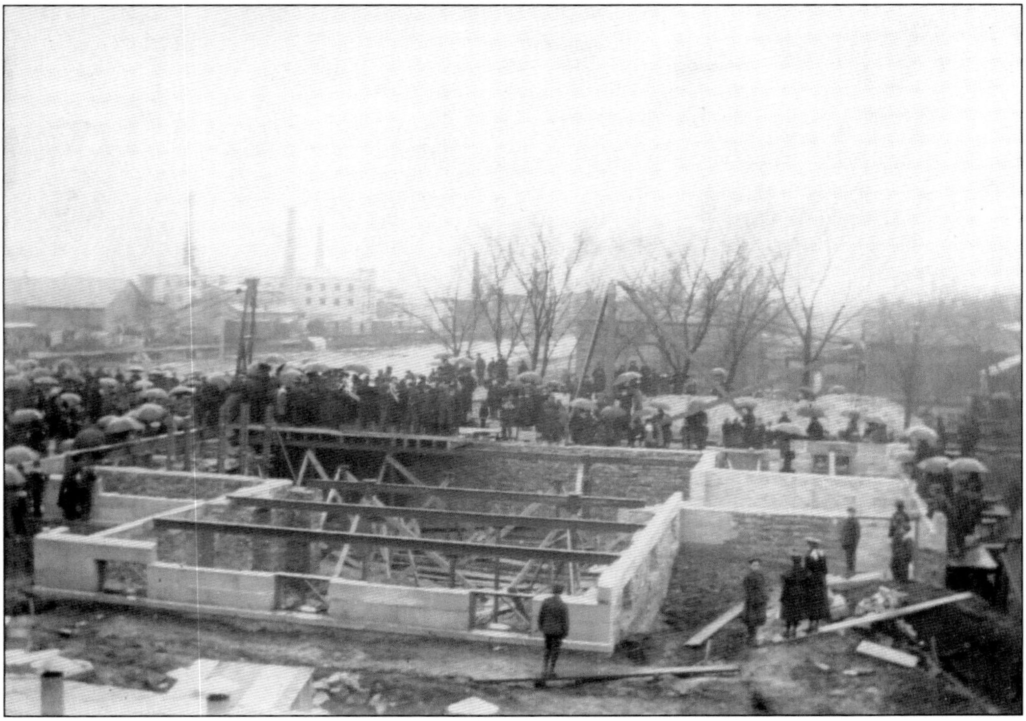

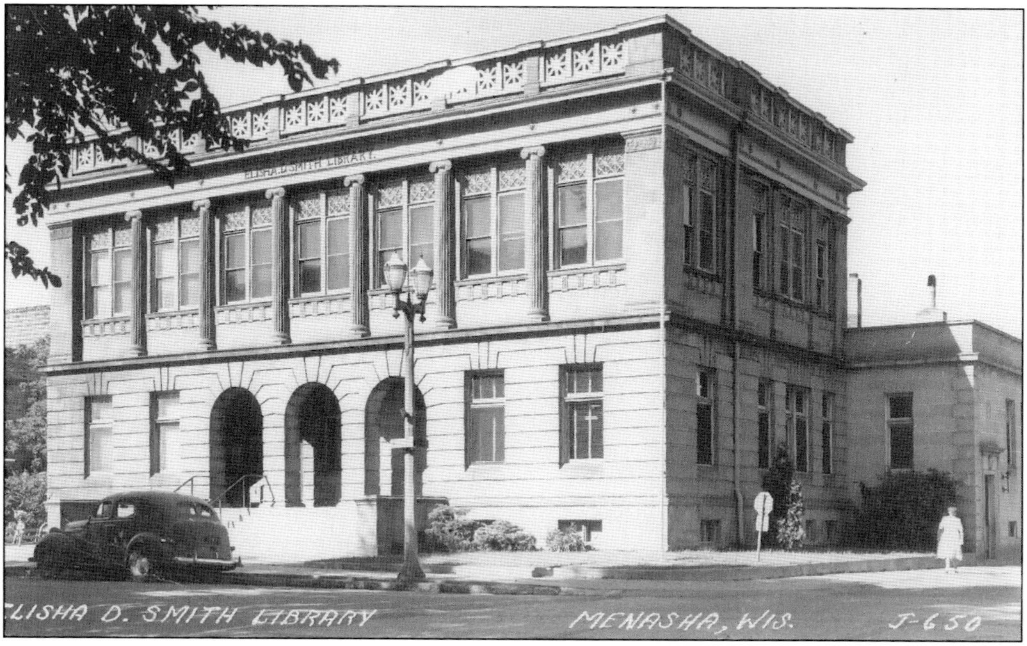

The Elisha D. Smith Library was designed by Van Ryn & de Gelleke Architects of Milwaukee in the Neoclassical style. Dedicated on October 21, 1898, the building was funded with a $20,000 gift by Smith, who was president of Menasha Wooden Ware. The *Library Journal* of that era reports that the mayor was presented the keys to the library by Smith in a brief speech.

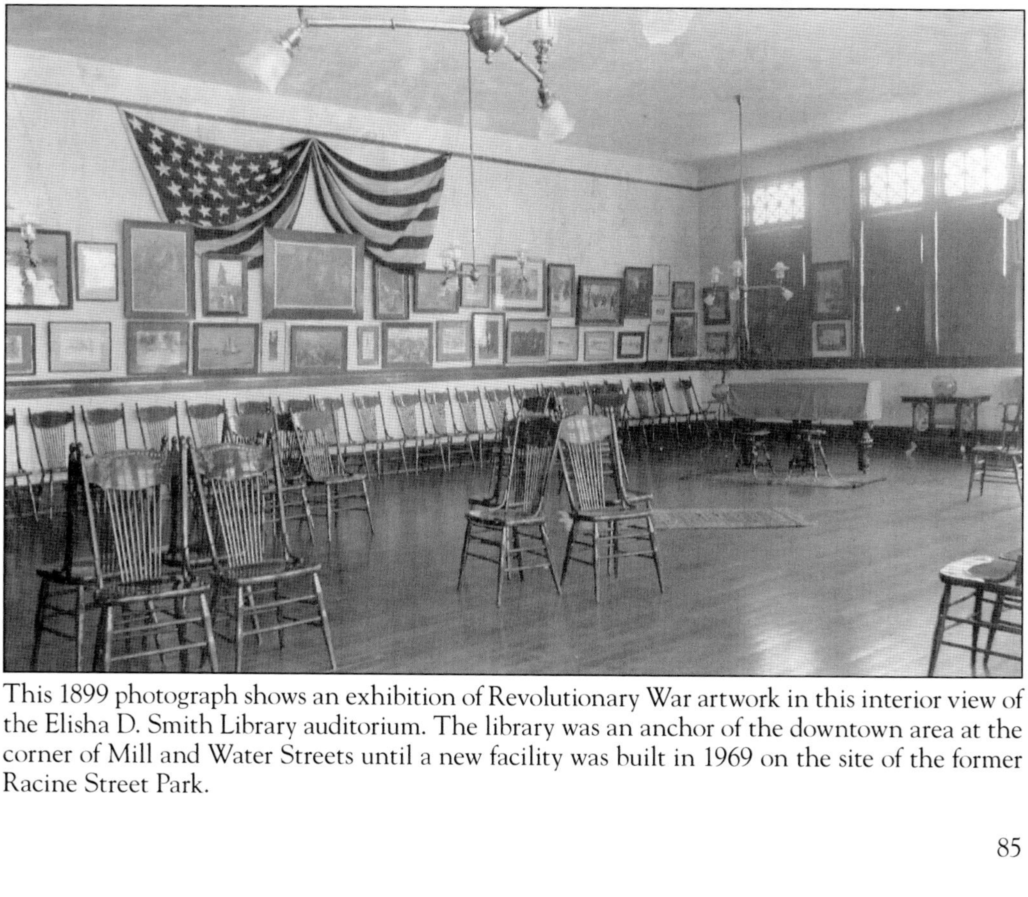

This 1899 photograph shows an exhibition of Revolutionary War artwork in this interior view of the Elisha D. Smith Library auditorium. The library was an anchor of the downtown area at the corner of Mill and Water Streets until a new facility was built in 1969 on the site of the former Racine Street Park.

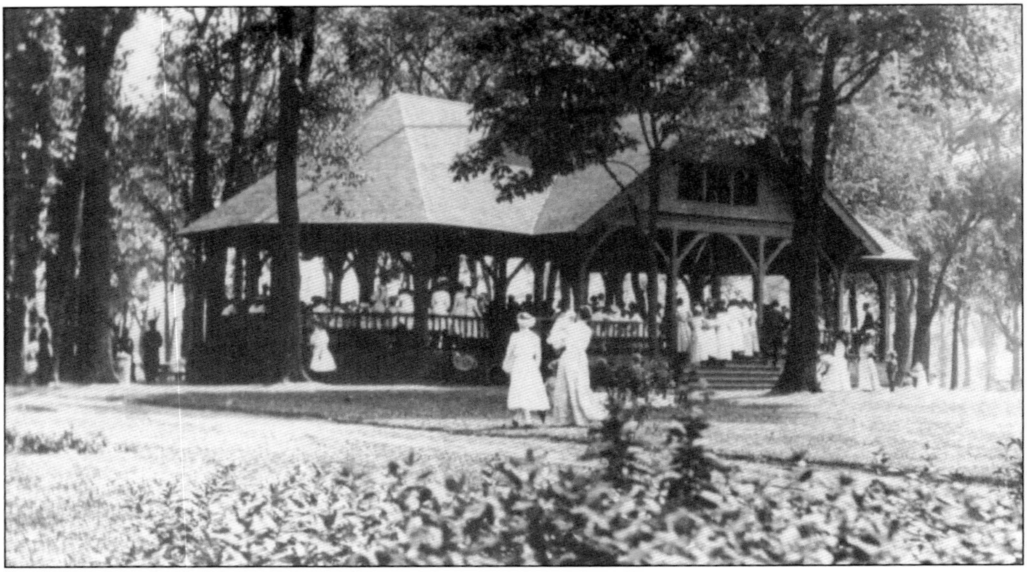

Along with the land to create Smith Park, Menasha Wooden Ware founder Elisha D. Smith had this pavilion constructed to encourage use of the park. Smith, a pious man, stipulated that there be a strict ban on alcohol, circuses, gambling, sports, and dangerous machinery at the park. Of course, this ban also included Sundays, save for religious activities and temperance meetings.

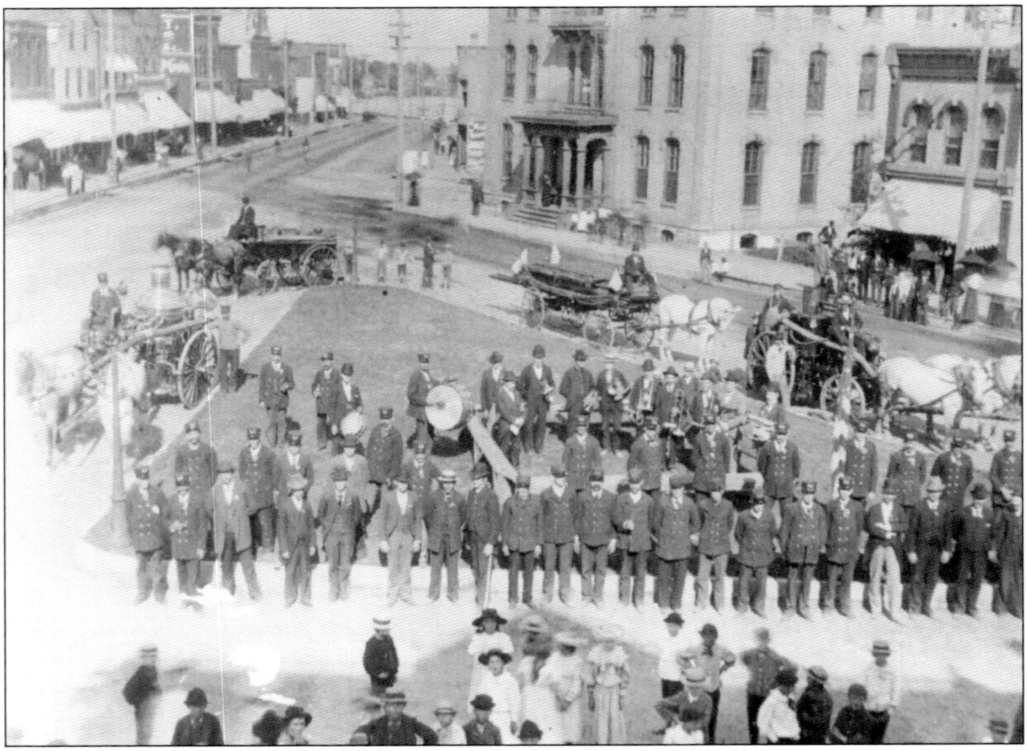

The Menasha Fire Department Band plays city square as the entire department turns out in full regalia in 1900. Photographs reflect the changing style of the city square, in front of the Bank of Menasha corner, over time. At this time, it was a triangular piece of ground. Later, it became a circle surrounded by flowers and centered with a flagpole.

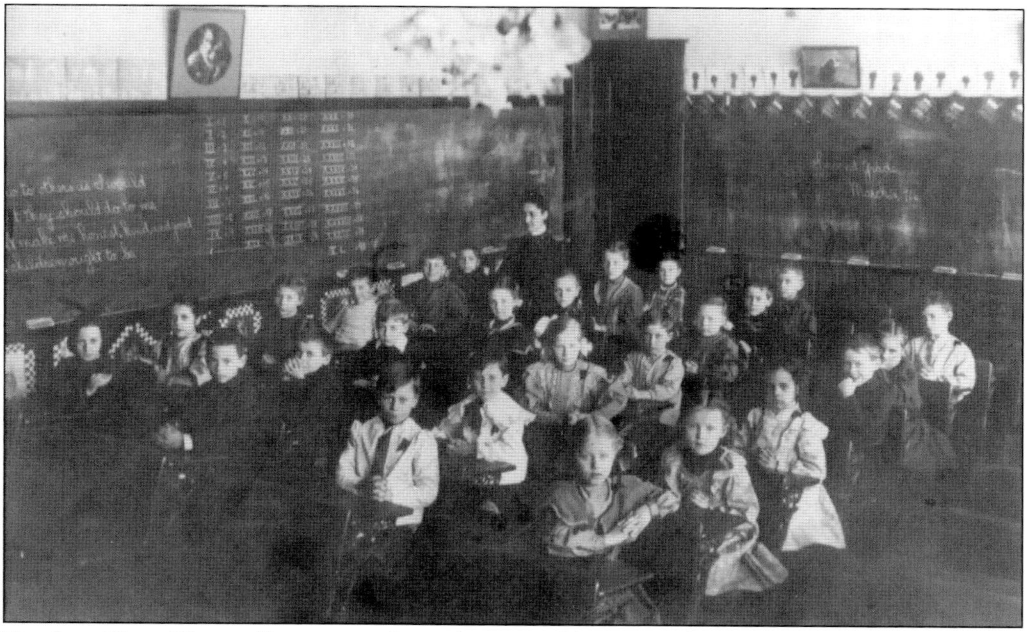

Teacher Clara Christofferson stands at the rear of her second grade classroom in this 1906 photograph. Lessons include Roman numerals and the Golden Rule, as evidenced on the blackboard. Educational reform in the latter 19th century dictated that larger schools replace the traditional one-room common school. To make it easier and faster for one teacher to instruct many students, there had to be as few differences between the children as possible. Since the most conspicuous difference was age, children were grouped on this basis, and each group had a separate room.

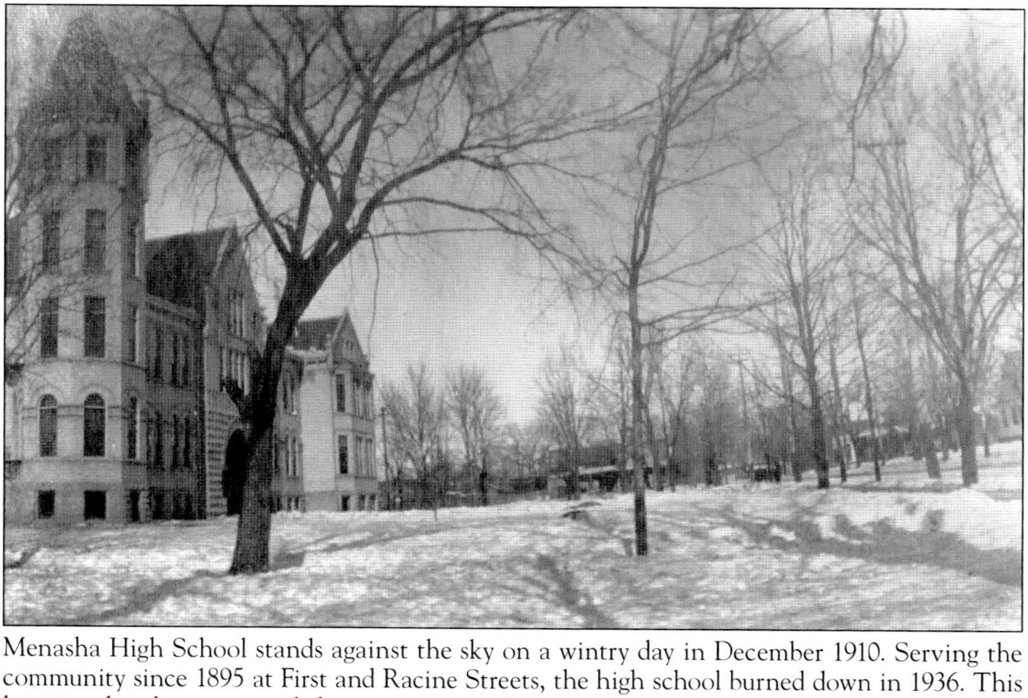

Menasha High School stands against the sky on a wintry day in December 1910. Serving the community since 1895 at First and Racine Streets, the high school burned down in 1936. This location then became a park for many years and, later, the site of a new public library and police and fire departments.

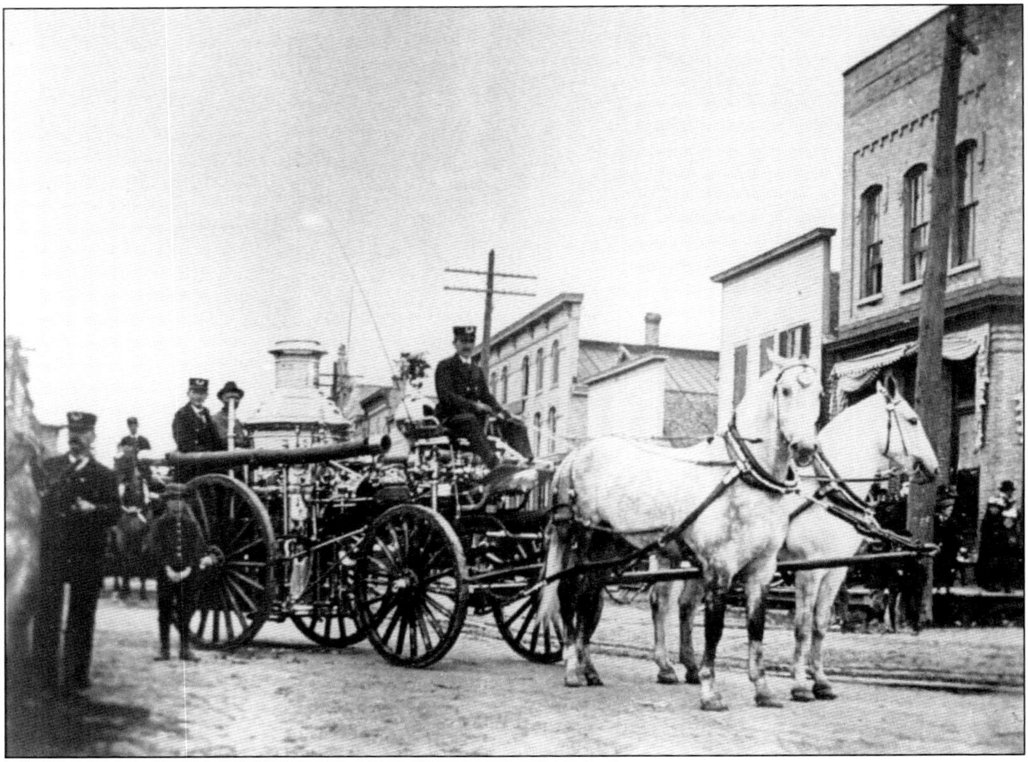

Members of the Menasha Fire Company pose near Racine and Main Streets with their steam pumper, most likely in the 1890s. The W.W. Pankratz Fuel and Ice Company on Kaukauna Street furnished the horses for the fire department and took care of sprinkling the streets. The heavy vertical fast-firing boilers were effective in fighting fires but were eventually phased out in the 1920s with the advent of motorized vehicles.

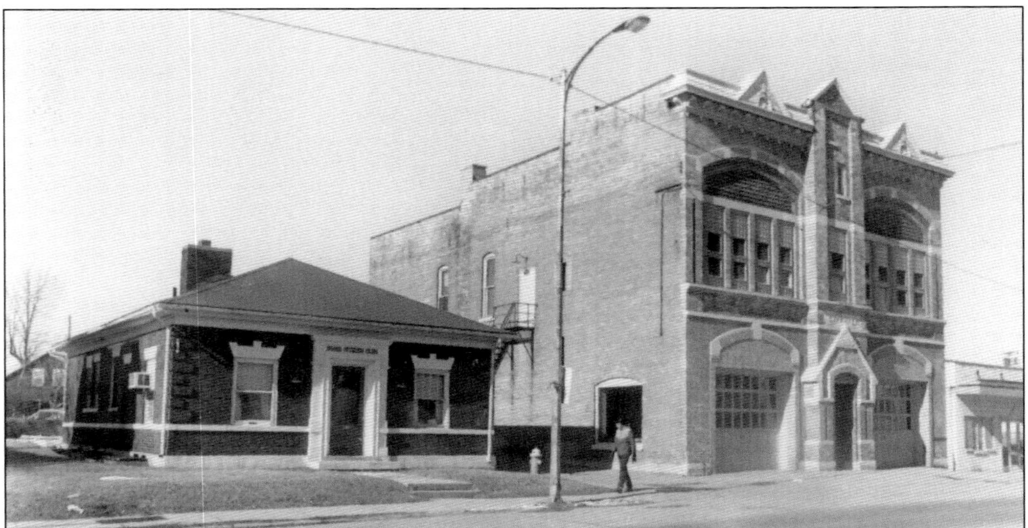

The smaller of the two buildings pictured here was originally the police station and later became the senior citizens center. The old city hall and fire station next door would last until 1986. To the right of the fire station are the last remnants of the Gibson Chevrolet dealership.

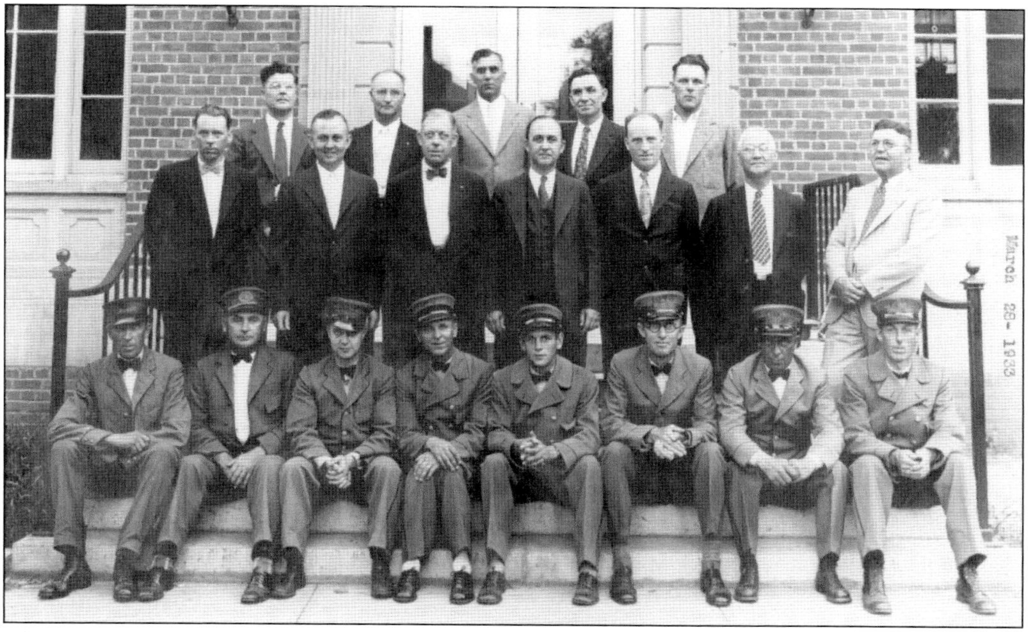

The staff of the Menasha Post Office poses in this 1933 photograph, shortly after the building's completion. In 1931, about $120,000 was allotted for a new building, and it was constructed on the site of the former Reuben M. Scott residence at 84 Racine Street. Postmaster L.J. Ellinger leans against the railing in the middle row to the right. This building is an example of Georgian Period revival, inspired from the classical forms of 18th-century Colonial American architecture.

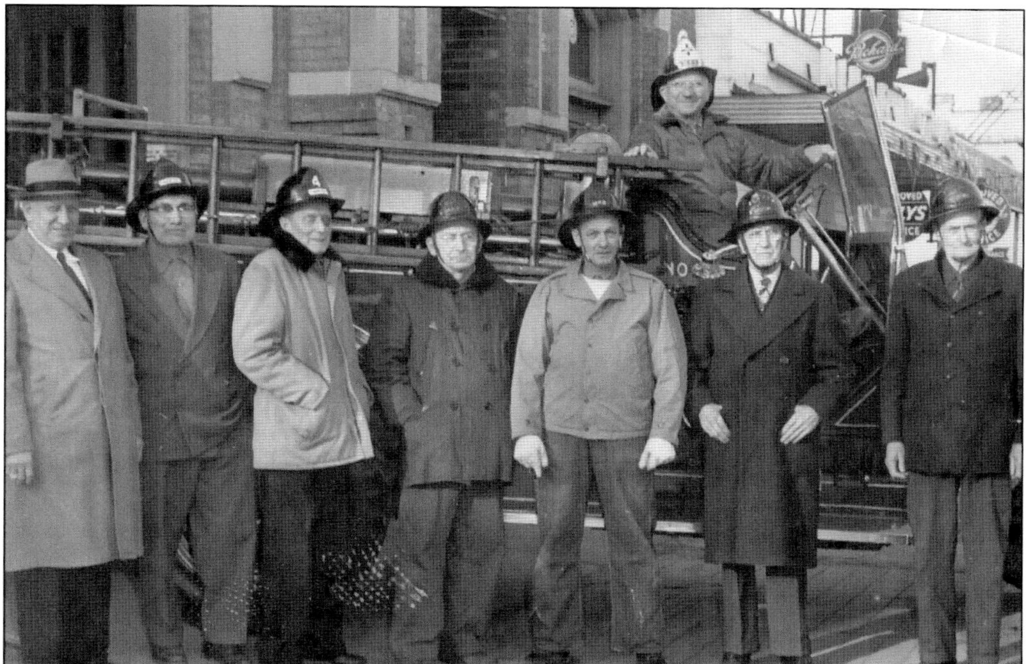

Old meets new in this c. 1940 photograph showcasing veterans of the Menasha Fire Department at the old city hall station on Main Street. Jack Dombrowski sits behind the wheel. The Packard dealership next door would later evolve into Gibson Chevrolet.

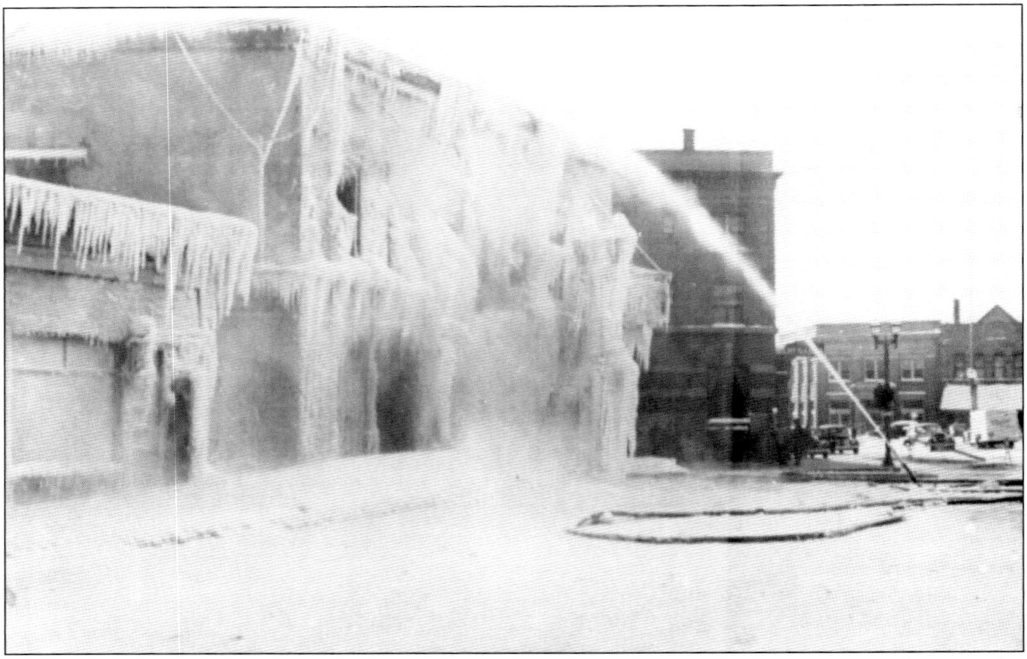

The Tuchscherer shoe store caught fire in the early morning of January 18, 1940. This was the oldest brick building left in Menasha at the time, and the weather-challenged firefighters battled the blaze for four hours. Damage was estimated at $40,000. The temperature was 21 below when the four residents of the upstairs apartments were roused at 5:00 a.m. and fled to safety. After the fire, Walker's Barber Shop, located next door, did not reopen for business; however, the Tuchscherer shoe store was rebuilt and remained in business for another 40-plus years, selling shoes in its Art Moderne–style building.

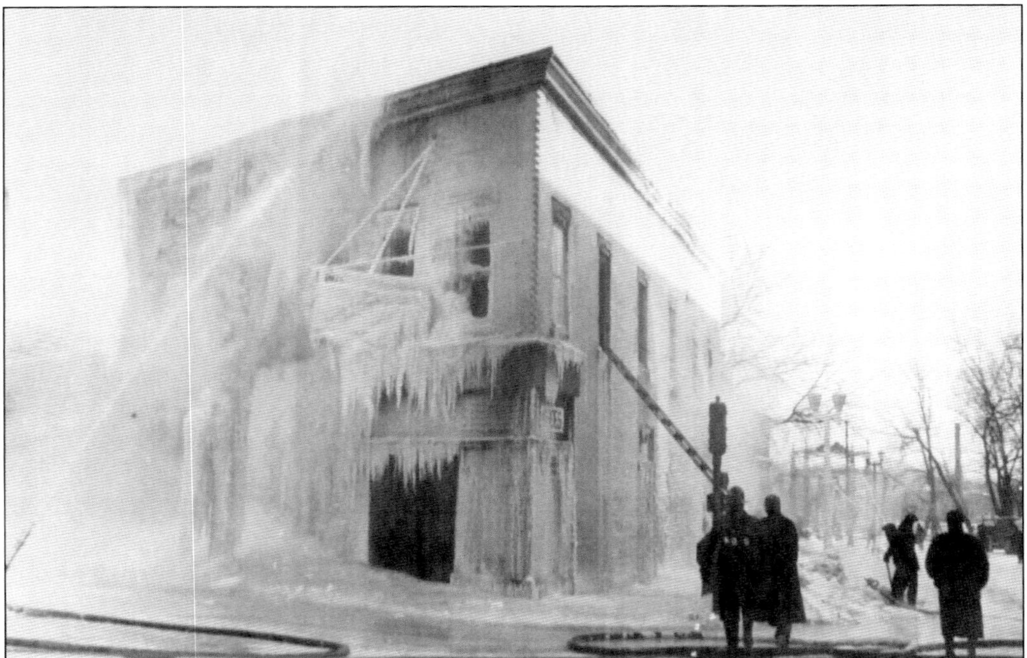

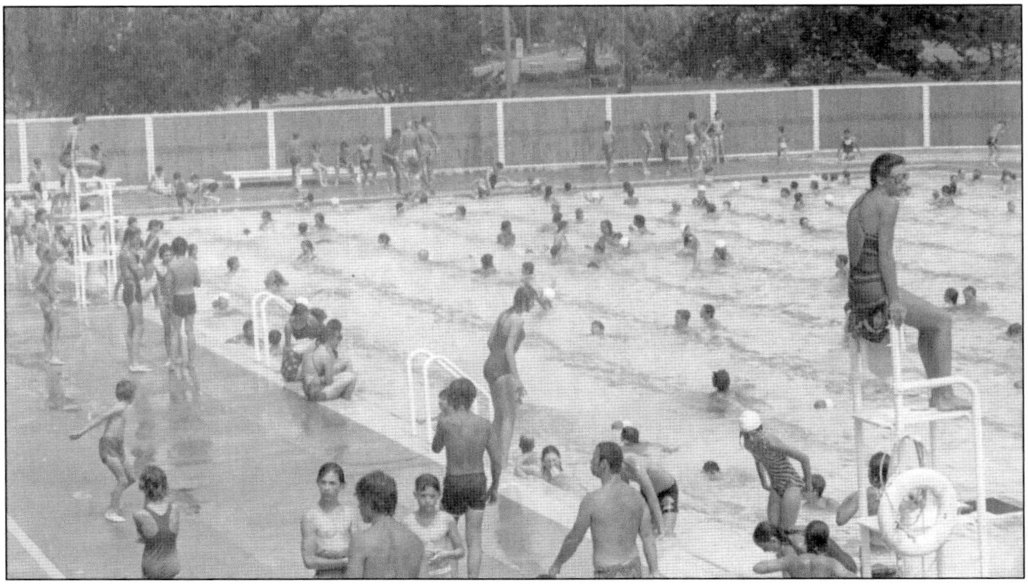

Memorial Day in 1958 saw the dedication of the municipal swimming pool. Located in Jefferson Park, the facility was designed by the Stanley Engineering Company of Muscatine, Iowa, in collaboration with the Menasha Citizens Advisory Committee, chaired by Ralph Risley. Before completion of the pool, organized swimming had been offered at Smith Park adjacent to the Memorial Building.

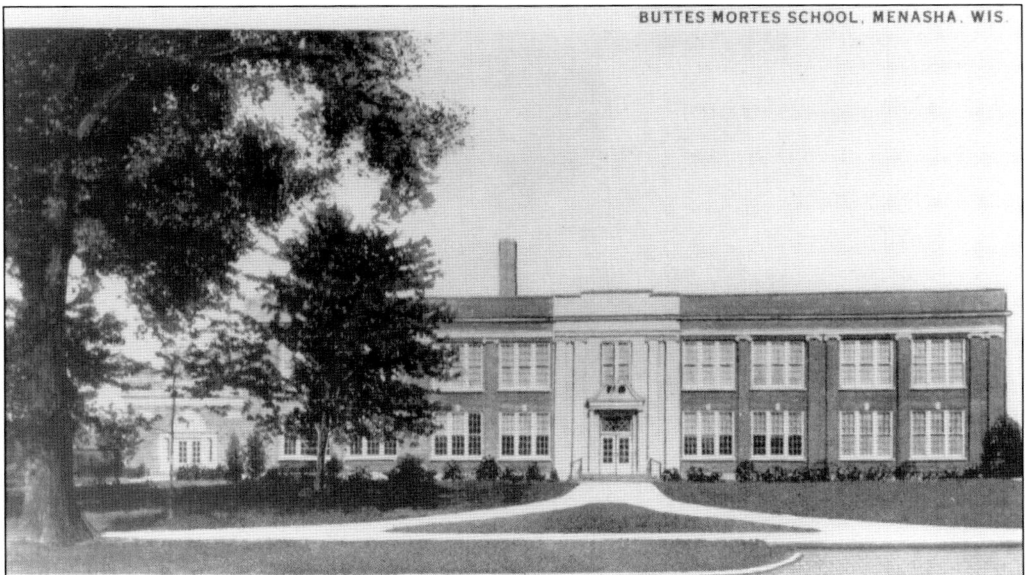

Completed in 1928 for the Second Ward at a cost of $125,000, Butte des Morts School was originally built as an elementary school. Designed by Charles G. Reynolds, it was constructed by the Held Company of Minneapolis in the Neoclassical style. It later became a junior high school and now serves as an elementary school once again.

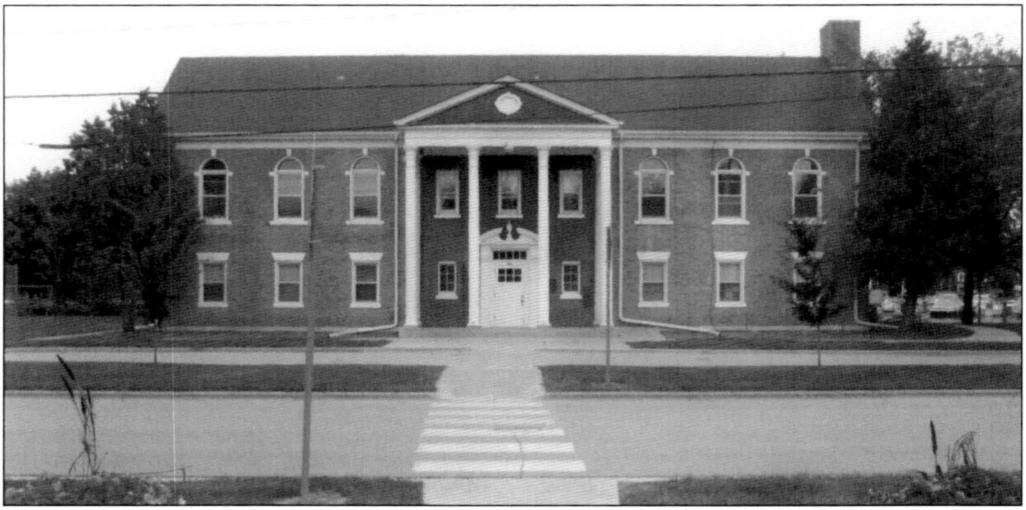

In 1928, the Soldiers and Sailors Memorial Building was constructed at a cost of $35,000. Present home to the Menasha Historical Society and located on Keyes Street across from Smith Park, the "Mem" was the place to be for park dances for many years. The building also provided changing rooms for swimmers, game rooms for teens, and other park activities and classes. (Courtesy of hmdb.org and photographer Keith L.)

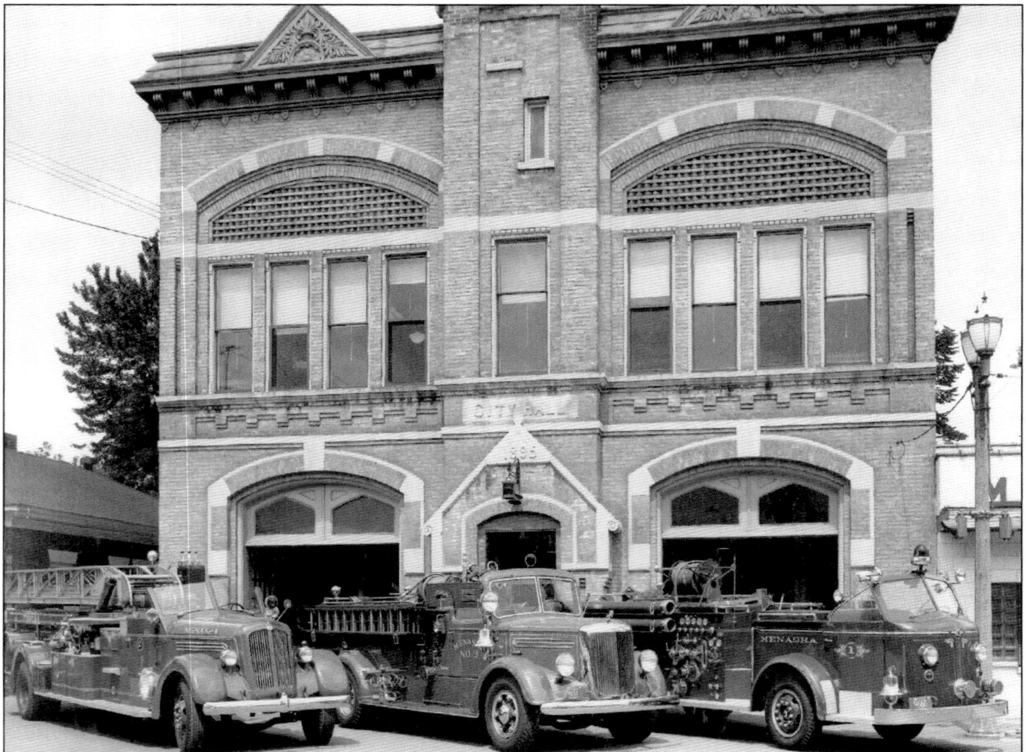

The city hall and fire station was built in 1885 and located on Main Street. The fire department occupied the lower level, and the city offices were on the second floor. This building was torn down in the 1980s. Originally, horses were stabled to the right of the building before motorized fire trucks became commonplace.

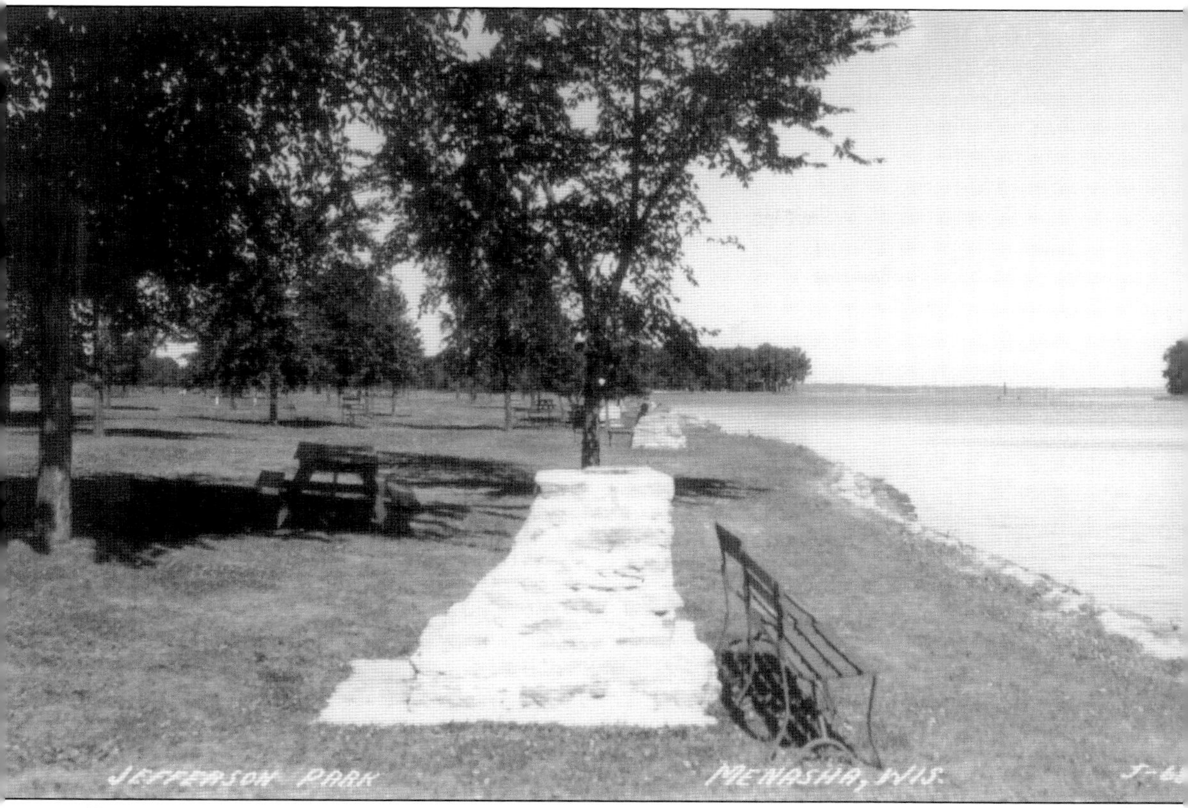

Jefferson Park, one of the jewels of the Menasha Recreation Department, was built in 1932 and 1933 as a project of the Works Project Administration (WPA). Jefferson Park had the advantage of its proximity to Lake Winnebago and the Fox River to provide a striking park facility envied to this day. Jefferson Elementary School, located at the intersection of Second and Ice Streets, is adjacent to the park. Completed in 1931 at a cost of $125,000, it had been built at the behest of the city council in order to provide local employment during the Great Depression. Its unusual styling is categorized as Tudor/Elizabethan Revival.

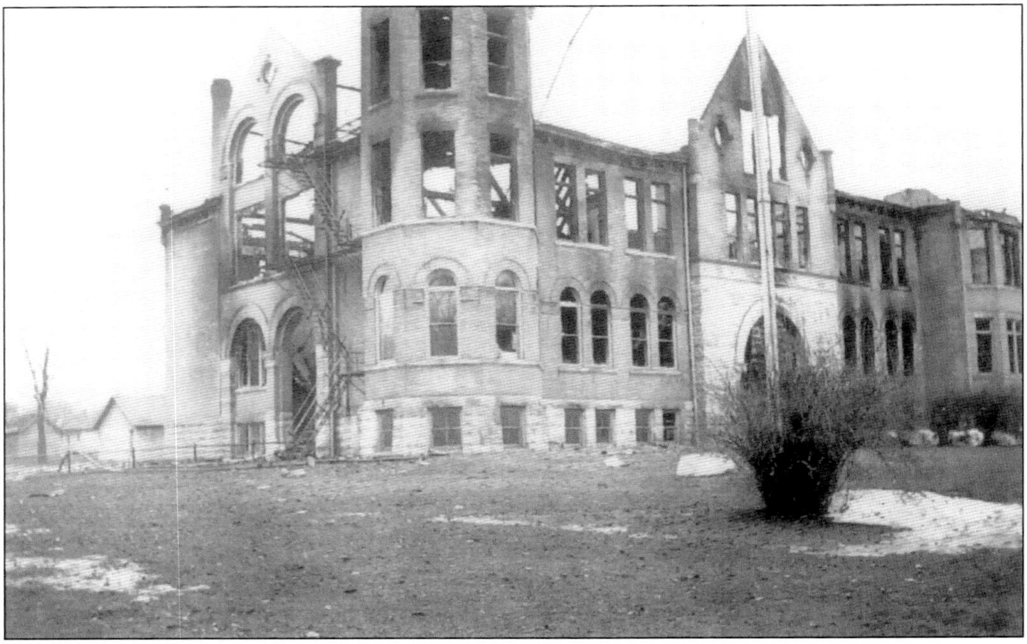

In 1935, a new high school building was proposed at a cost of $270,000 in federal grant money. In March 1936, Menasha High School burned down, and the need for a new school was immediate. The fire's exact origin is unknown, but it was thought to have started in the machine shop. To keep the school year going, classes were distributed among the remaining schools and other public buildings until the new high school could be completed in 1938. Once the old school was razed, the land became Racine Street Park until the new Elisha D. Smith Library opened in 1969, followed by the combination police/fire station in 1979.

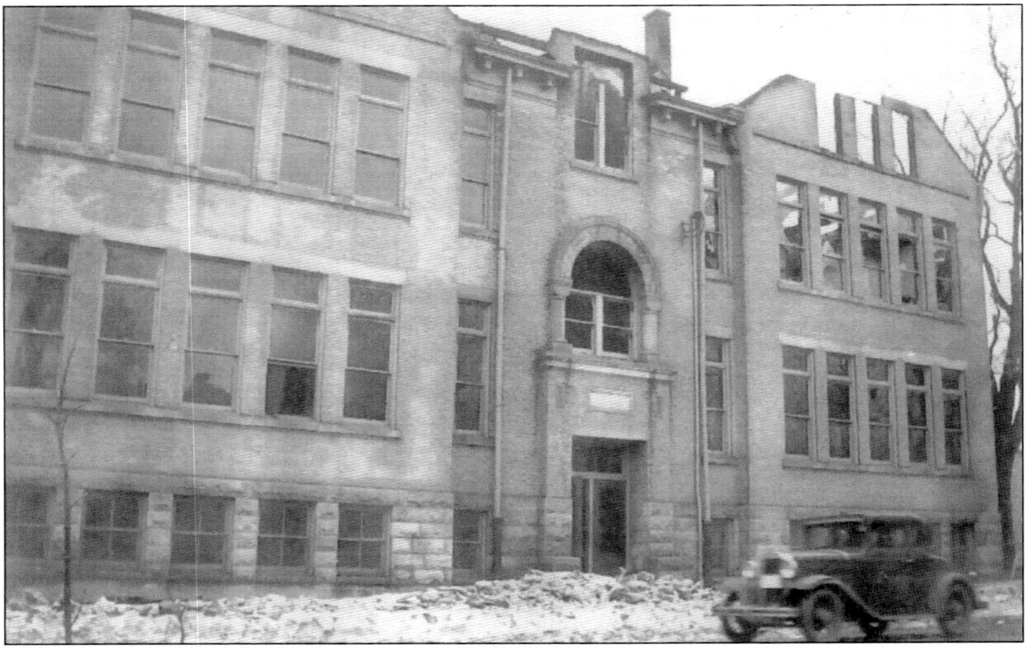

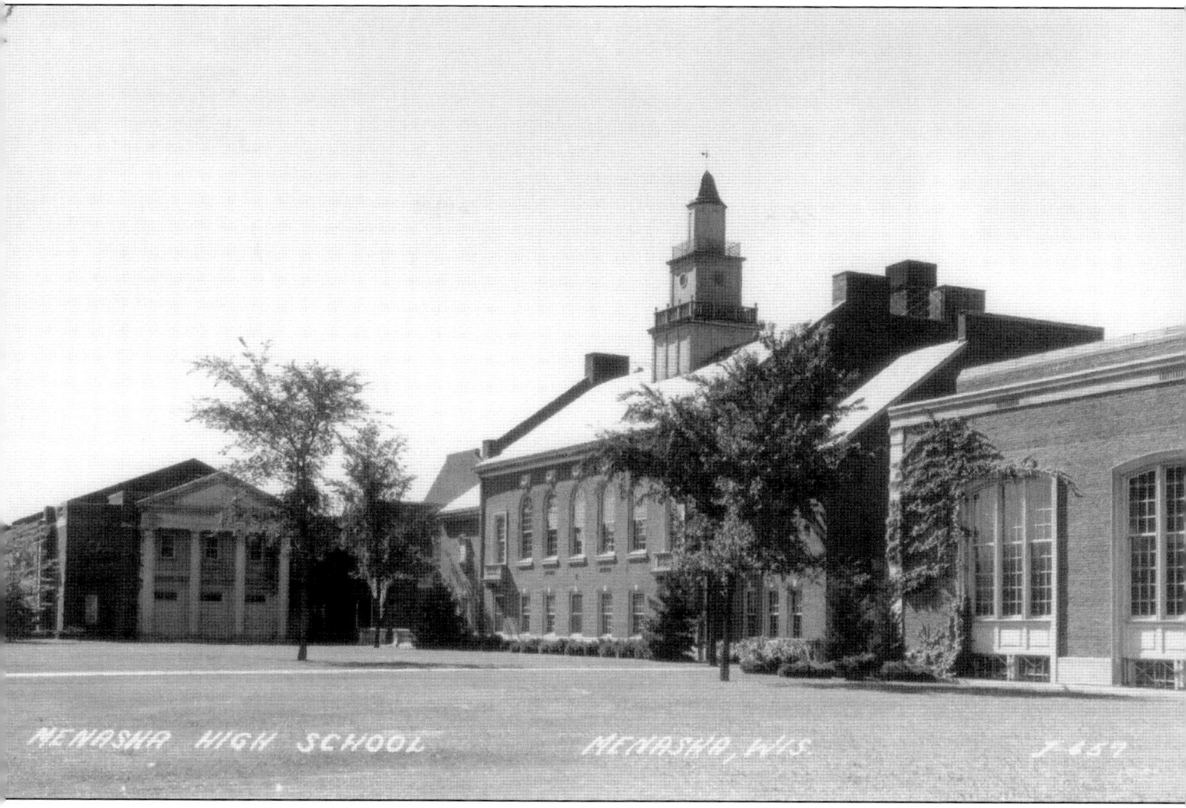

The new Menasha High School at Seventh and Racine Streets was completed in 1938 as a WPA project to serve as a junior and senior high and vocational school. Costing $600,000 and employing 197 workers on its construction, the school exhibited a style known as Colonial Revivalism, incorporating Georgian detail with a Neoclassical auditorium. (Author's collection.)

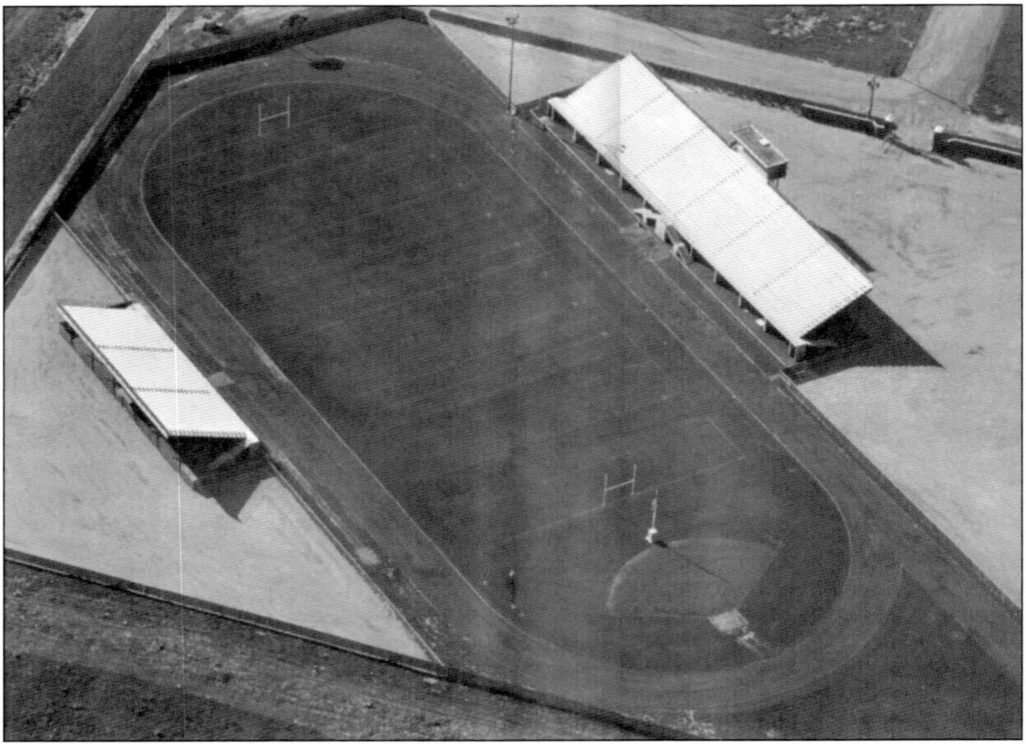

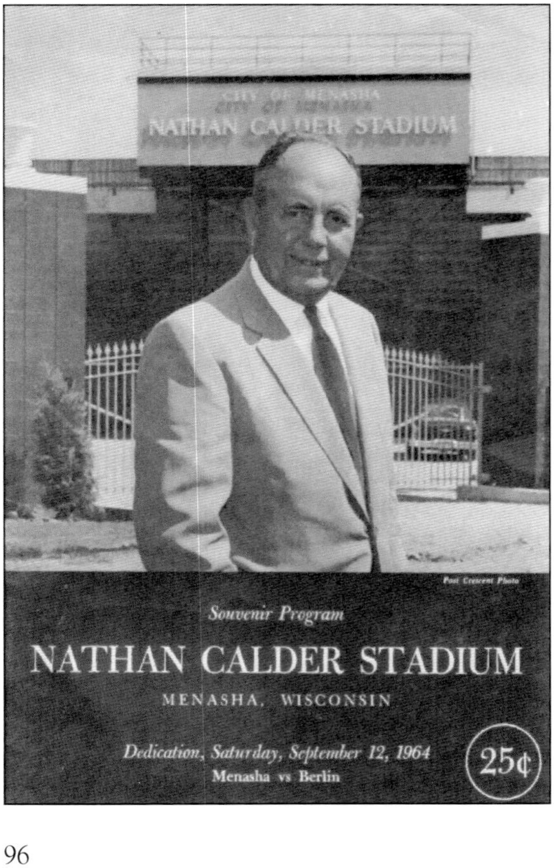

Nathan Calder Stadium, located at 600 Eleventh Street, was first proposed in 1947 by George Banta Jr. upon Coach Calder's retirement. Coach Calder had been an institution at Menasha High since the 1920s. In 1964, the effort finally saw fruition, and the stadium was dedicated on September 12 of that year at the Menasha vs. Berlin football game. Over the years, the facility has been an excellent site for football games, track meets, and other outdoor sporting events for both the Menasha School District and St. Mary Central High School. (Both, author's collection.)

Seven

Businesses

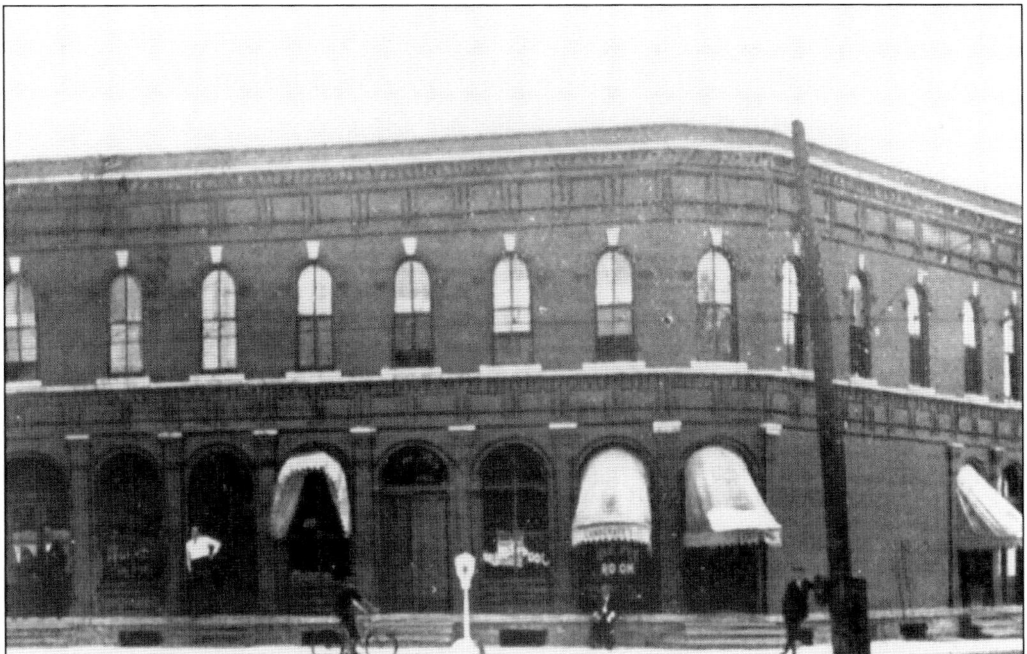

The Landgraf Hotel was built in 1871 at the intersection of Tayco and Main Streets. Later, the Brin Theater was built here in 1928. In its prime, the hotel had 30 rooms and was lit by gas and heated by steam. The hotel sent free buses to meet all trains; they also offered a billiards room and a grocery.

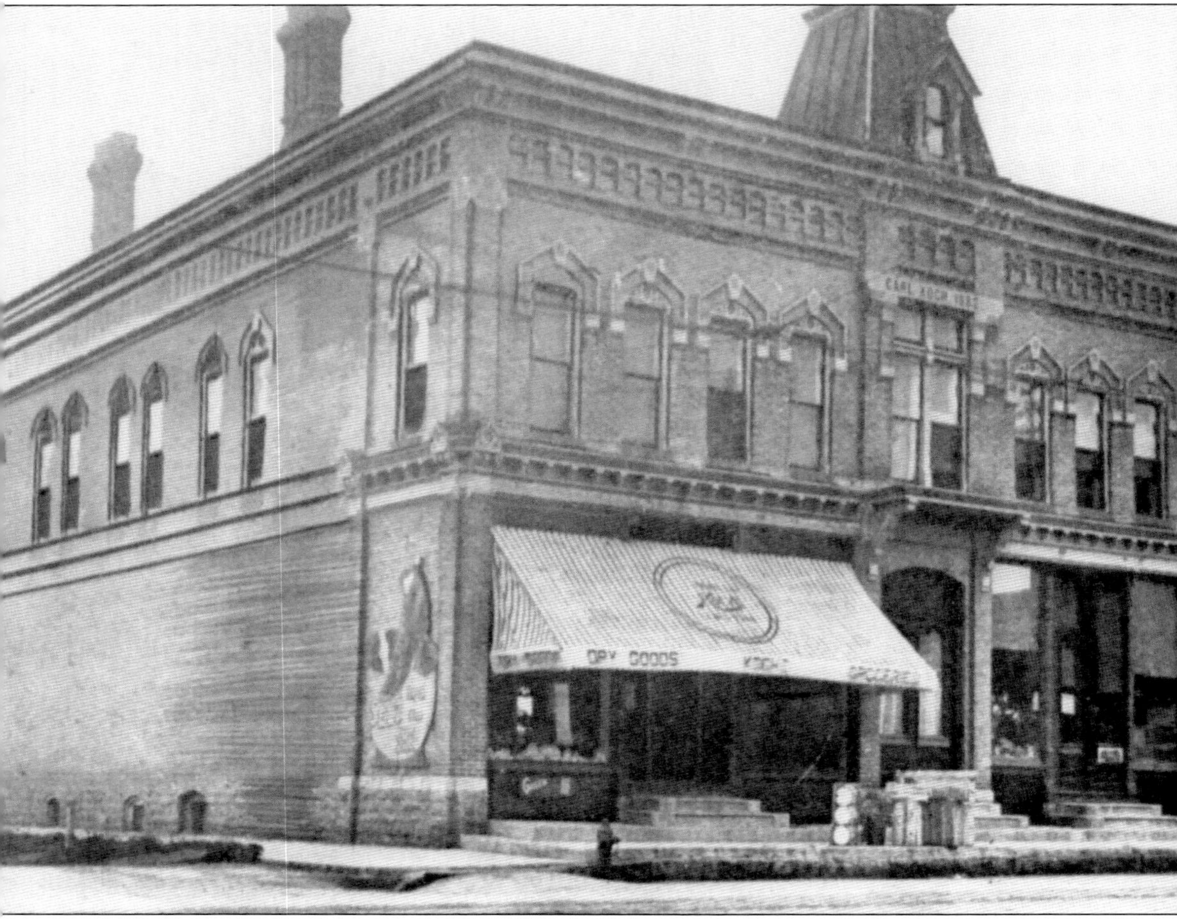

The Koch building was located on the corner of Tayco and Water Streets. The building was constructed in 1882 by Carl Koch, who operated a general store in the lower left half of the building. A lunch and sample room was located in the other half, and the building contained apartments on the second floor. The size of the Koch building reflects the importance of the farm trade that accessed the Butte des Morts Bridge at the time. Soon after it was built, the bridge burned and was never reconstructed. As a result, trade in the Tayco Street area languished until the early 20th century.

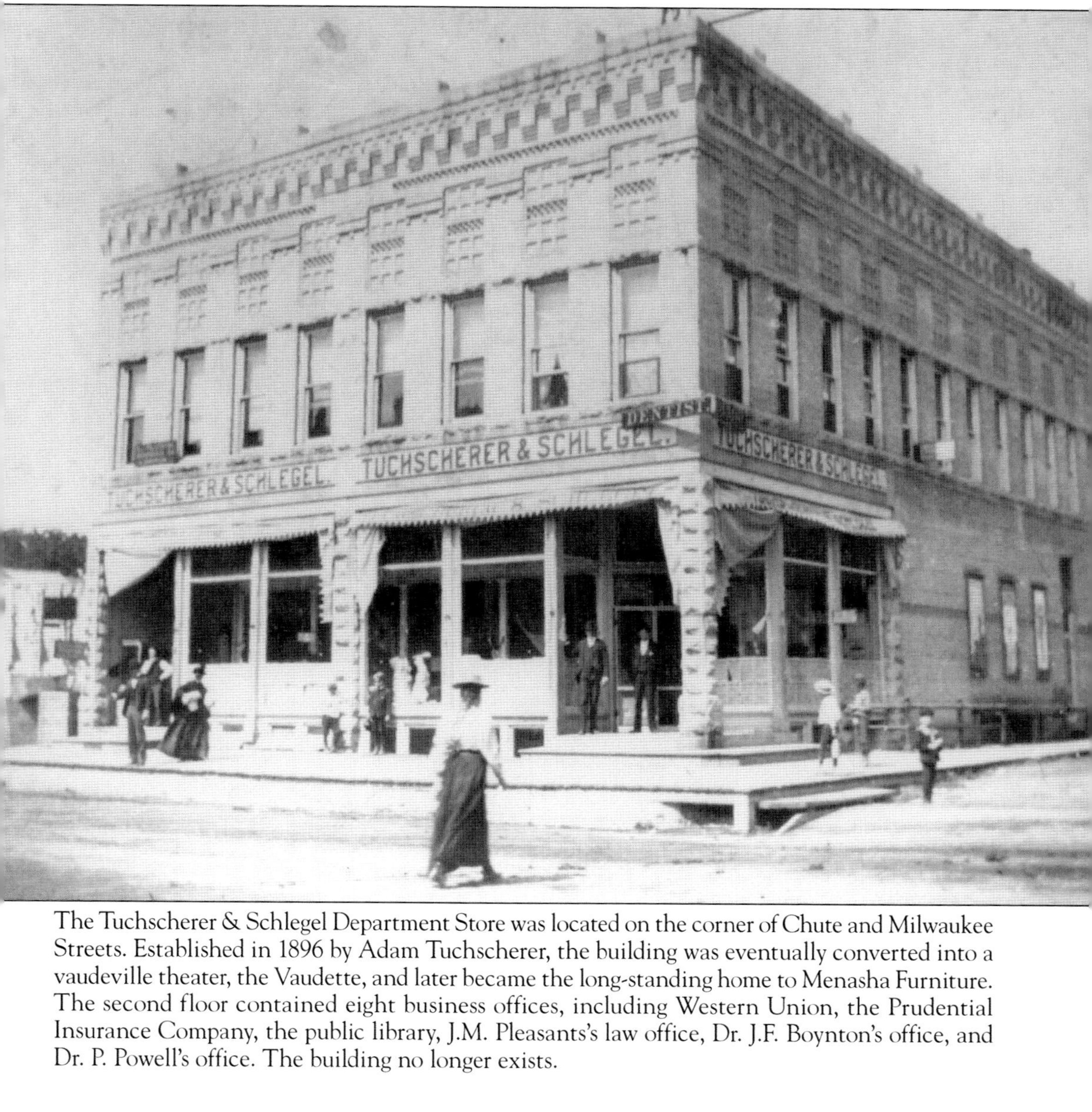

The Tuchscherer & Schlegel Department Store was located on the corner of Chute and Milwaukee Streets. Established in 1896 by Adam Tuchscherer, the building was eventually converted into a vaudeville theater, the Vaudette, and later became the long-standing home to Menasha Furniture. The second floor contained eight business offices, including Western Union, the Prudential Insurance Company, the public library, J.M. Pleasants's law office, Dr. J.F. Boynton's office, and Dr. P. Powell's office. The building no longer exists.

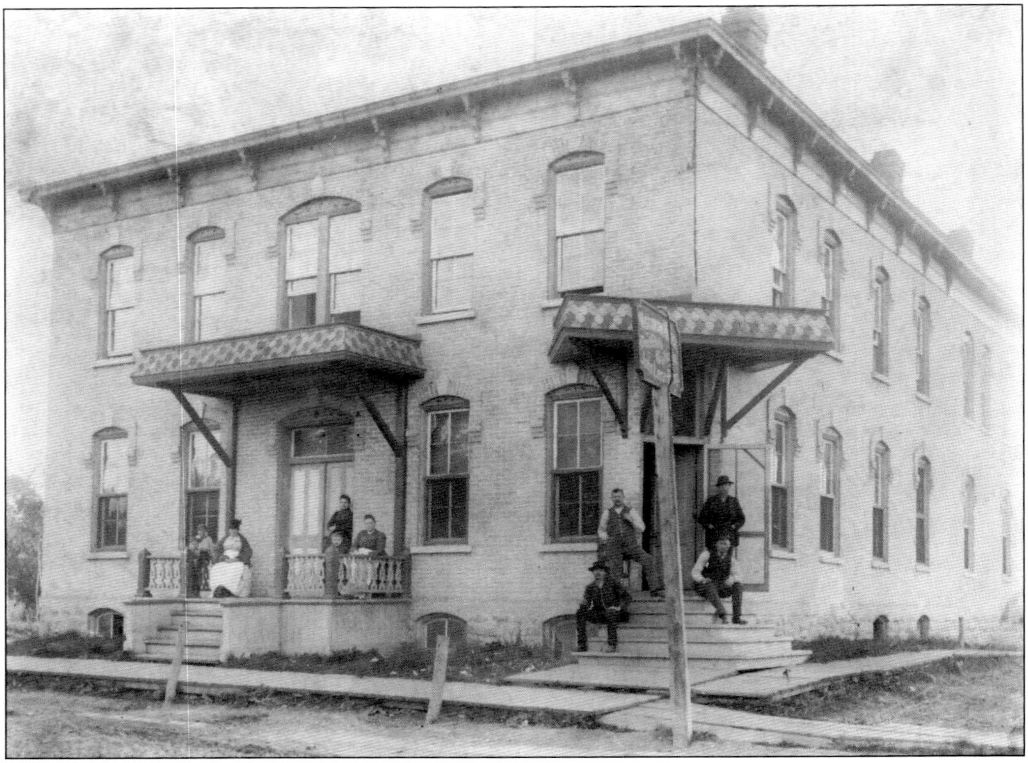

The Hotel Lenz had many incarnations. Starting business as the Wisconsin House in 1871 by John Lenz Jr., this facility at the corner of Third and Racine Streets had a beer garden in the springs and summers, catering to a German clientele. The sign on the street in the image above announces that this is a German guesthouse. Situated on the streetcar line and close to the Soo Line depot, this lodging enjoyed access to transportation others did not. The streetcar tracks came up Third Street and turned down Racine Street on the way to downtown. The building was demolished in 1978, but by then, it was known as the Schumacher Hotel.

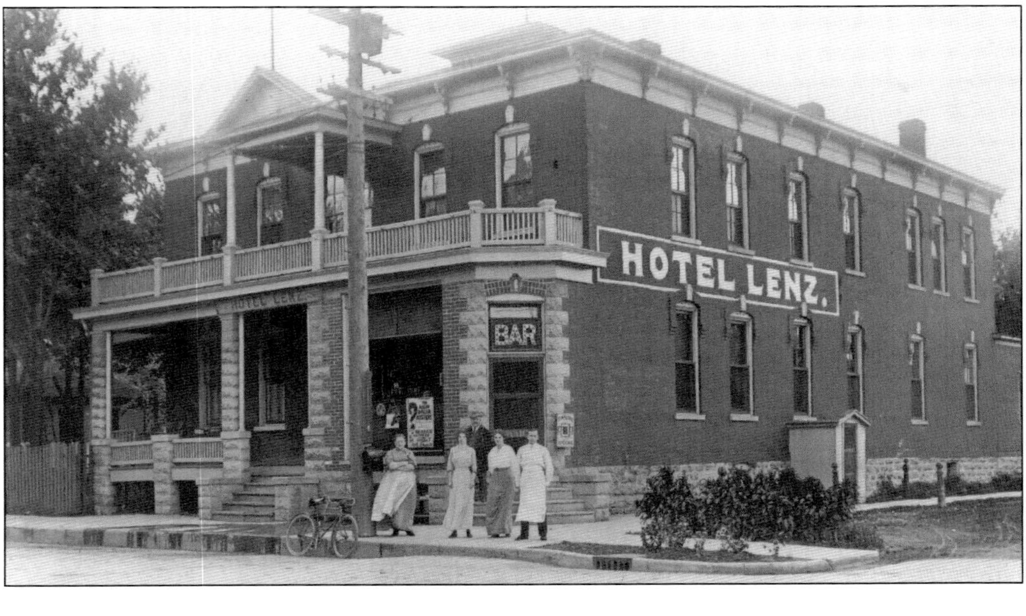

The National Hotel was built in 1869 by Reuben M. Scott and managed by John Roberts. Later, Roberts established Roberts Resort on Doty Island. The hotel had 42 steam-heated rooms that rented for $2 per day. Reportedly the center for social life within the city for its time, the National burned down in 1901, and the Hotel Menasha was built on the site four years later.

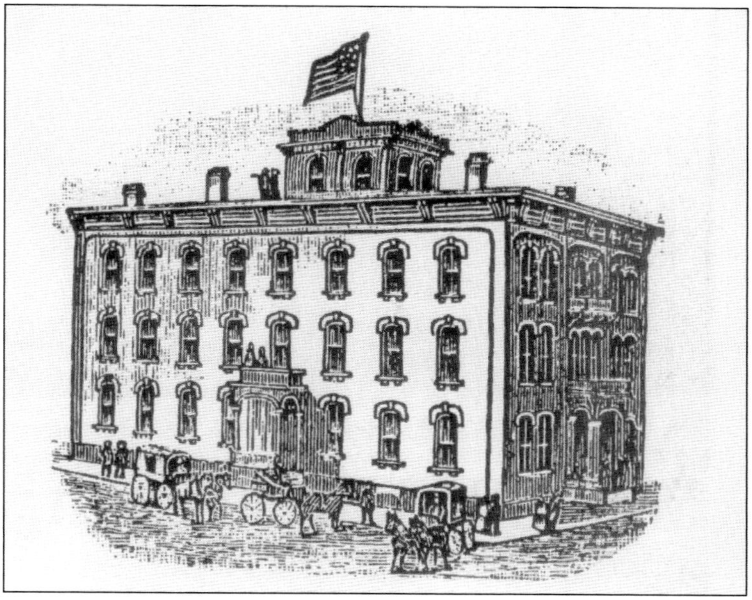

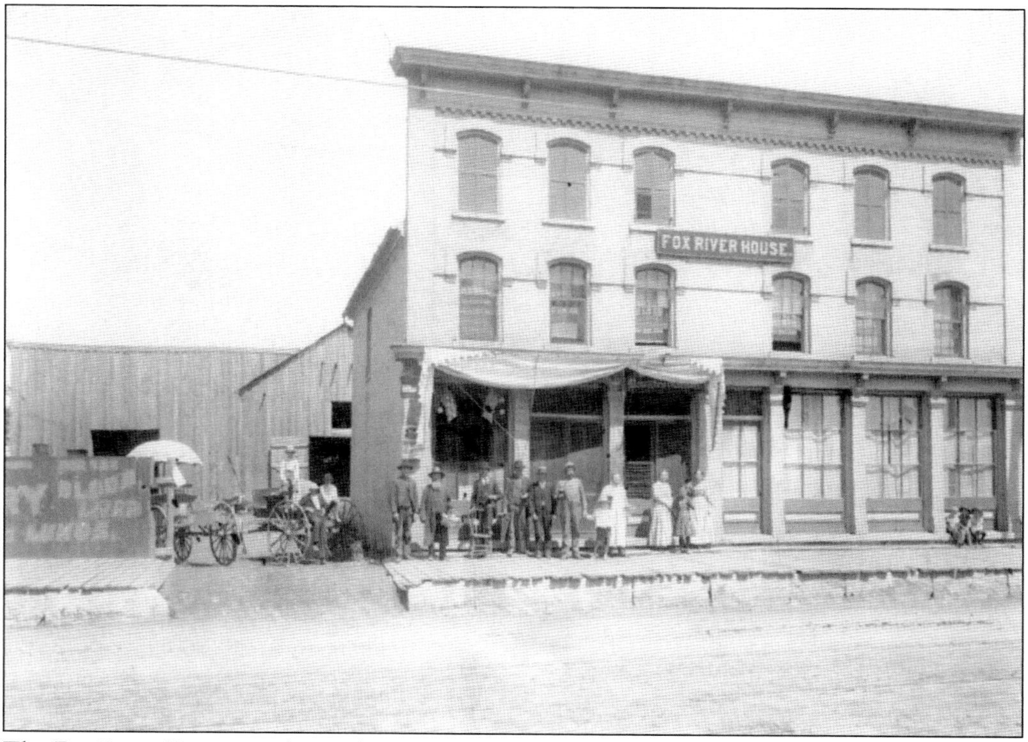

The Fox River House was located on the north side of Main, just west of Racine Street. Owned and managed by Mike Mielke, this hotel catered to farmers coming to town to mill their wheat. As with the Hotel Lenz, the sign above the door labels the inn as a German *gasthaus*.

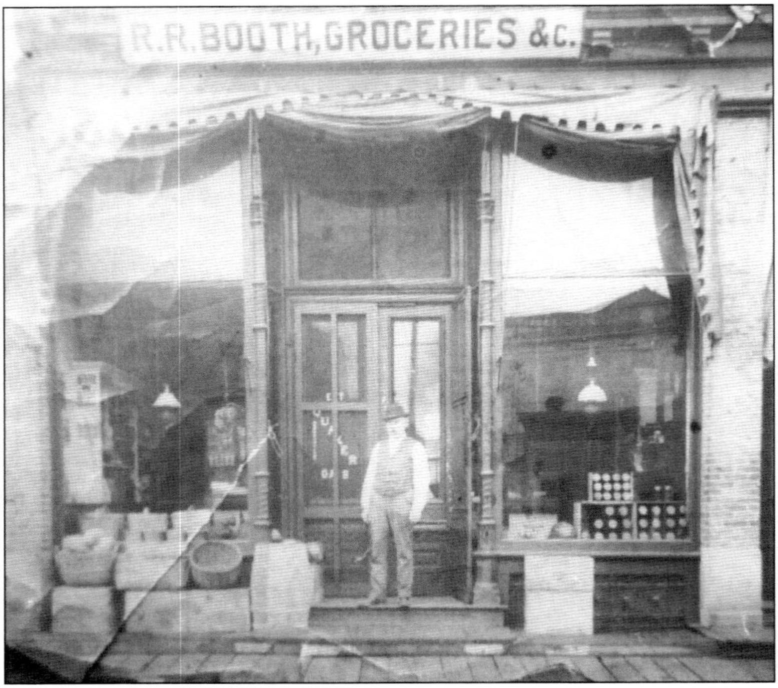

Robert Ross Booth, pictured here at 204 Main Street, dealt in staple and family groceries, provisions, and canned goods. Booth, a native of Ireland, immigrated to America in 1866; he initially lived in Massachusetts for three years before moving to Madison, where he worked as a spinner until 1880. (Spinning was a textile job weaving yarn for various fabrics and flax for linen.)

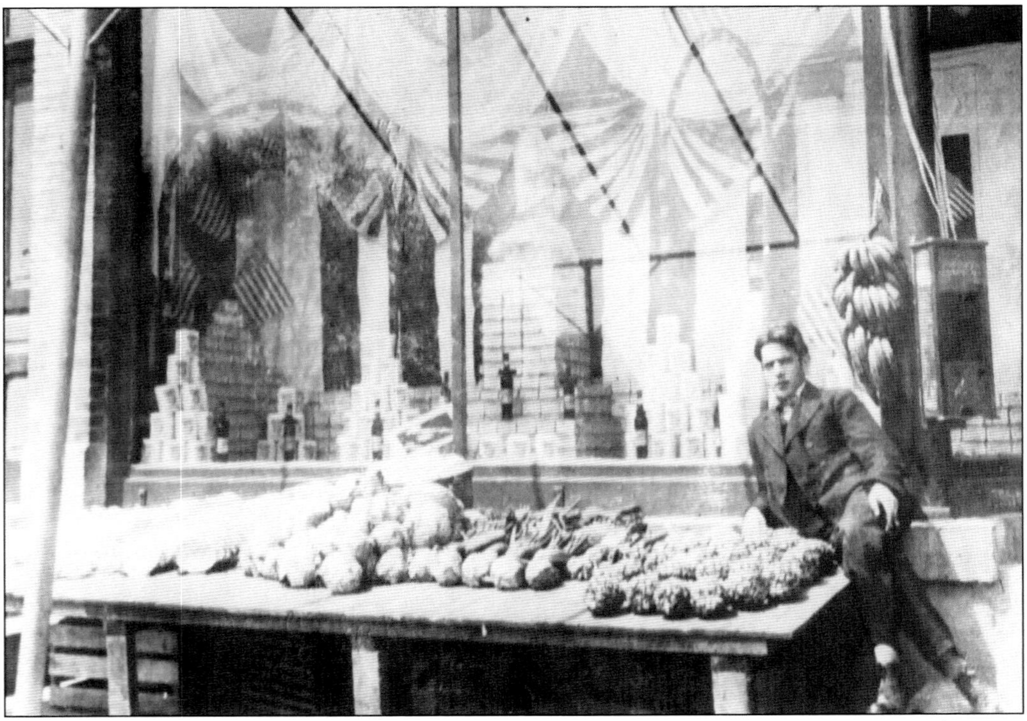

Joseph Luka ran this grocery at the corner of Broad and Appleton Streets. He was also vice president and treasurer of the Menasha Wholesale Company. With his wife, Emma, and their child, he lived farther down from the shop on Broad Street. This 1914 photograph shows the display of fresh vegetables and fruits Luka used to entice customers inside; these products, including bananas and pineapples, must have seemed quite exotic to some residents.

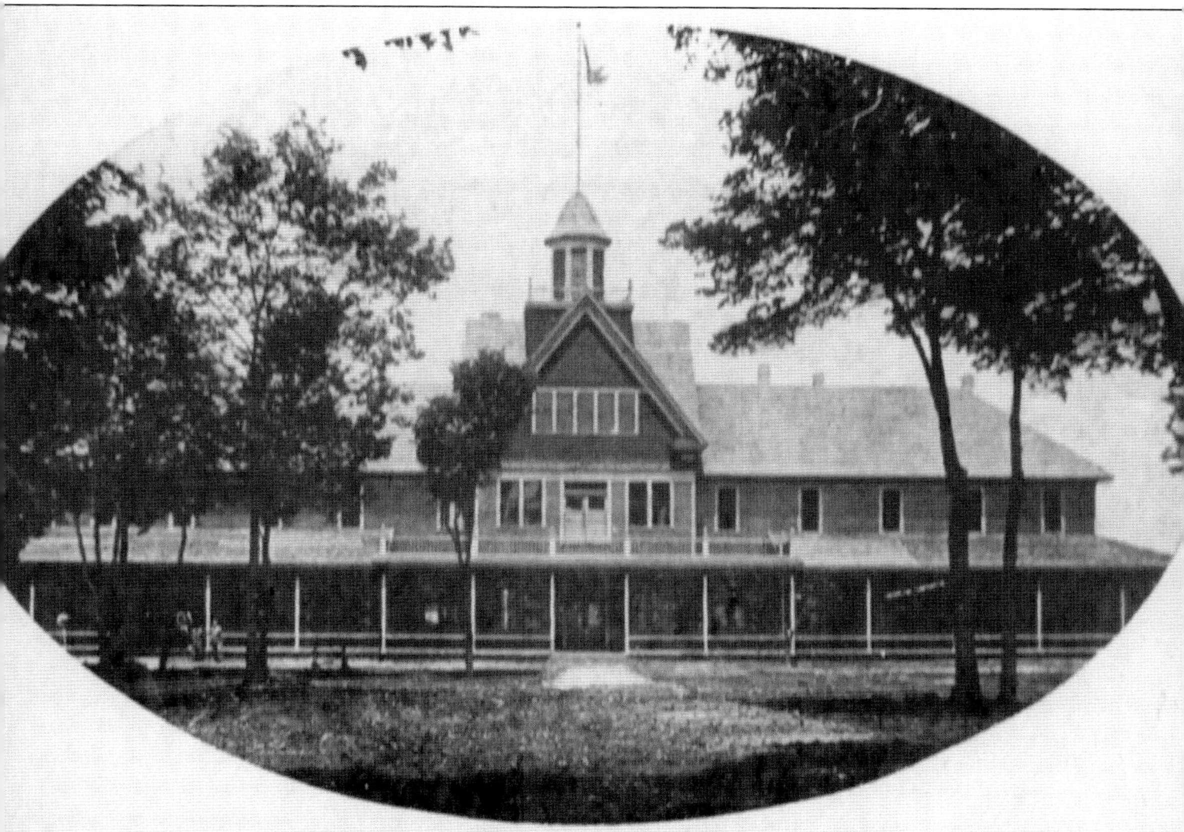

BRIGHTON BEACH HOTEL, MENASHA, WIS.

Between Menasha and Waverly Beach to the east was Brighton Beach, situated at the end of Third Street. In various stages of development since 1886, a hotel was finally built here in 1899, positioned 300 yards back from the Lake Winnebago shoreline. A saloon and meeting rooms were on the first floor, and the second floor was reserved for guest rooms. Popular as a venue for picnics, concerts, and other outdoor activities, and despite two renovations in 1913 and 1926, this spot was sold into private use after struggling for years in the shadow of the more successful Waverly Beach. Brighton found it difficult to compete with Waverly's amusements, which included a roller coaster. The Brighton Beach Hotel was torn down in 1927, and a private home was constructed on the grounds. In later years, the acreage was sold to a religious order of sisters for use as a retirement facility.

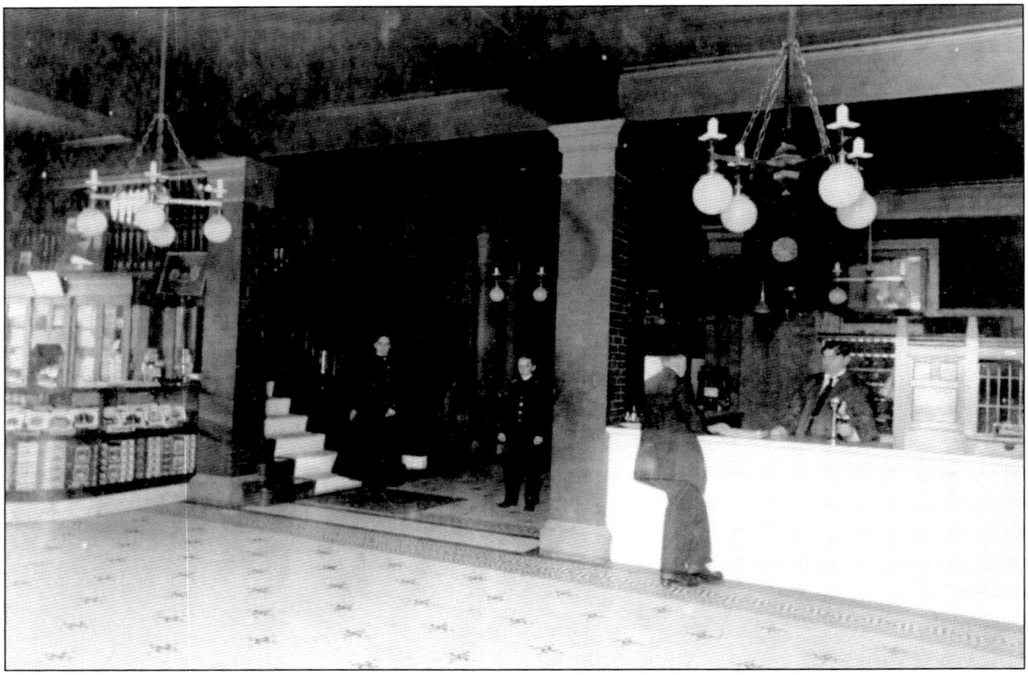

This 1905 interior view of the Hotel Menasha, captured shortly after its opening, shows the main lobby and desk area. The bellmen are poised at the stairs, ready to service any of the clientele coming in from the various train stations. Tom Fitzgibbon was the desk clerk, and Billy Guenter was the bartender in the hotel bar. Prominently placed on the floor are the spittoons for patrons' use. Notice the absence of bar stools, which are commonplace today. Most hotel bars existed largely to cater to business travelers, though many high-end local political deals may have been settled within these walls.

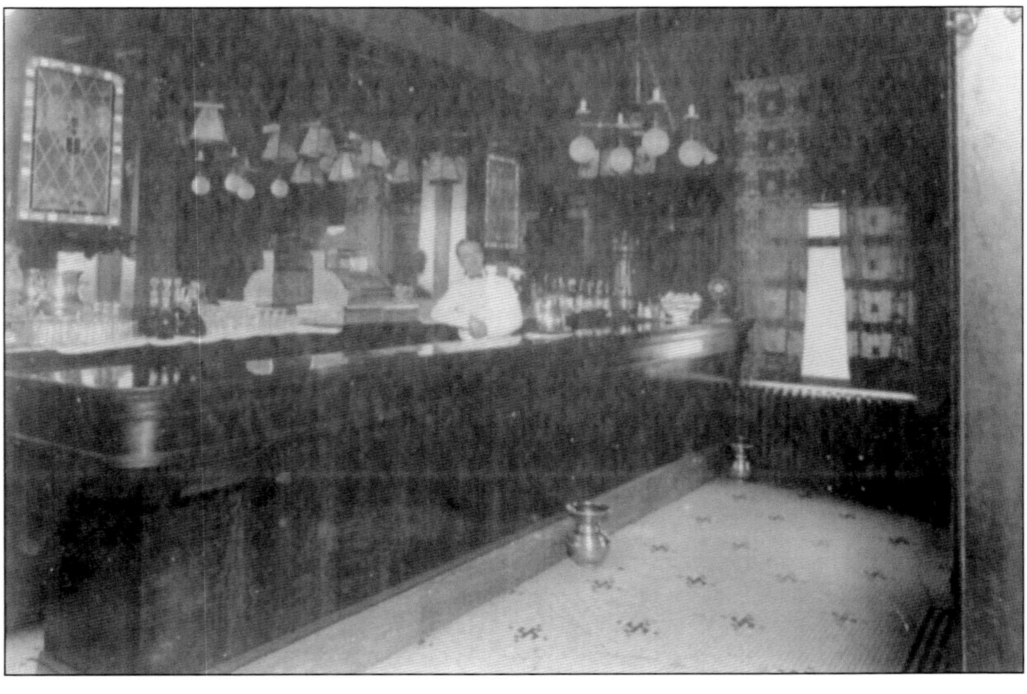

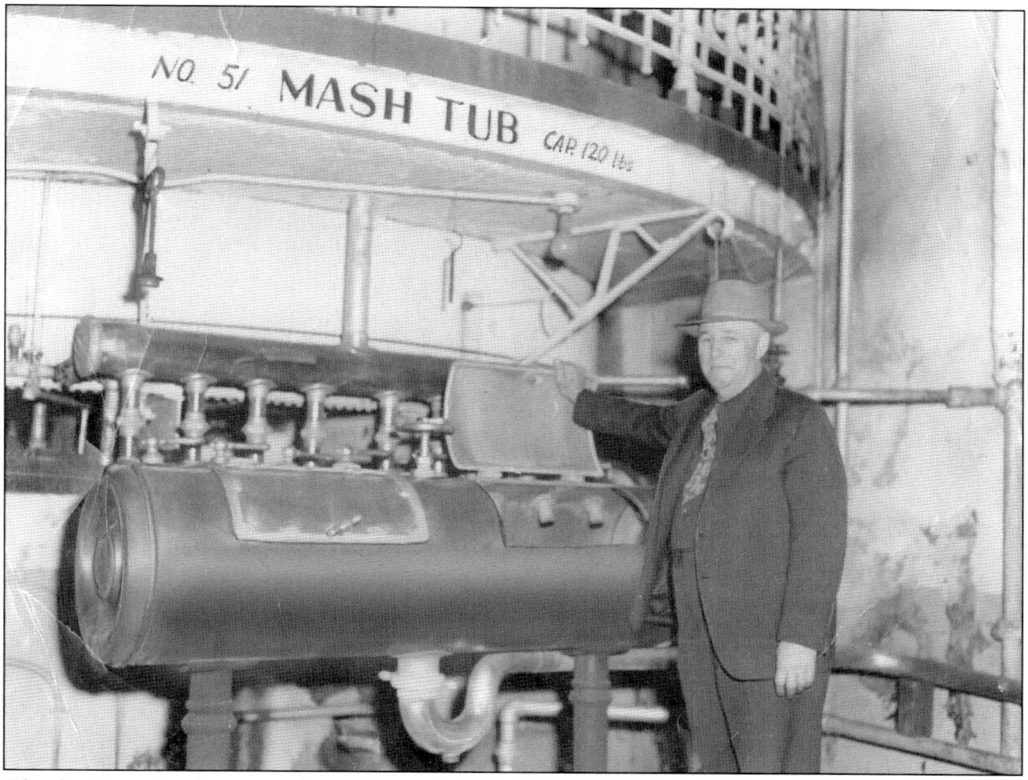

Charley Lingelbach, master brewer for the Walter Bros. Brewing Company, stands beside the mash tub in this 1951 photograph. Charley learned his trade from his father and grandfather, who brought the art with them from Germany. In the brewing of beer, mashing is an early process of combining the grain and water.

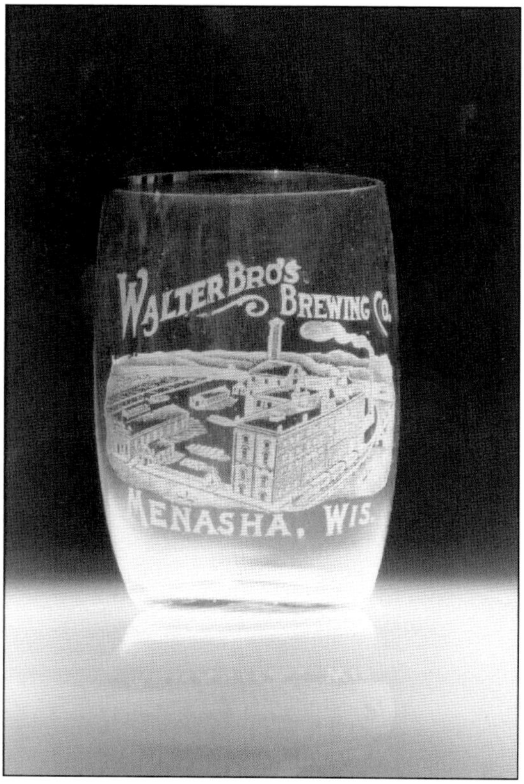

The detail of this beer glass, with its complex, etched design, makes it a collector's item for today that is considered a work of art. During its time, it was a distinctive way to show off the Walter Bros. Brewing Company facility; as an advertising medium, it did its job well.

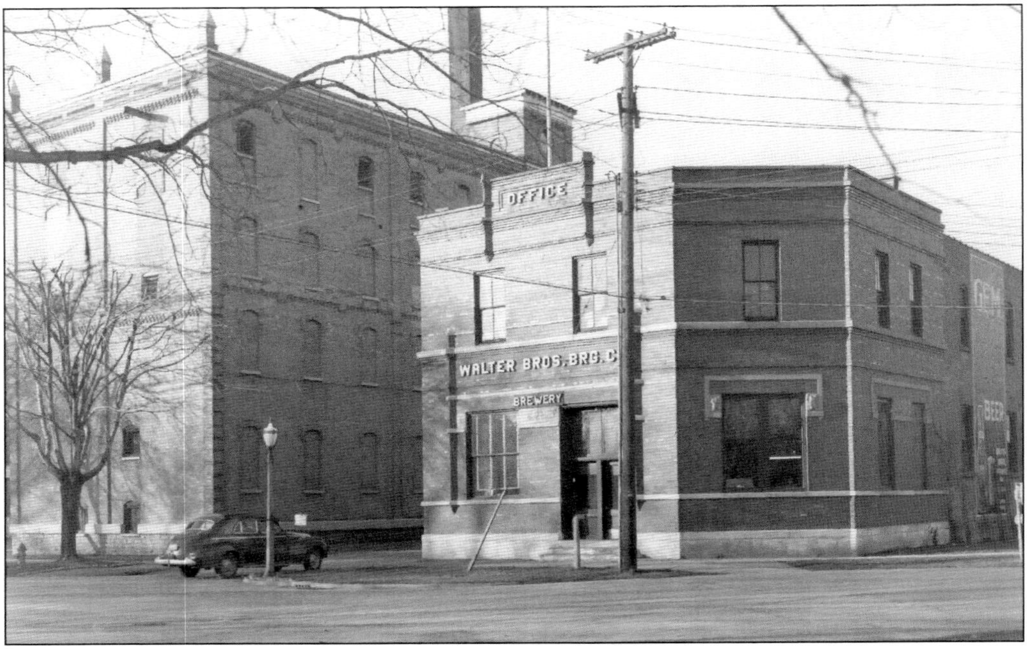

Purchased in 1888 by Christ Walter and his brothers Martin and Matthaus, the Walter Bros. Brewing Company brewed Gem and Gold Label beers. For many years, the other Walter brothers maintained breweries in many other Wisconsin cities such as Appleton, West Bend, and Eau Claire, as well as Pueblo, Colorado. Located next door to St. Patrick's Catholic Church on Doty Island, Walter Bros. was, by 1898, one of the largest brewers in the state. Christ Walter eventually became the Third Ward representative in the city council and president of the Board of Aldermen. The brewery stayed in business until 1956, and the facilities were razed in 1960.

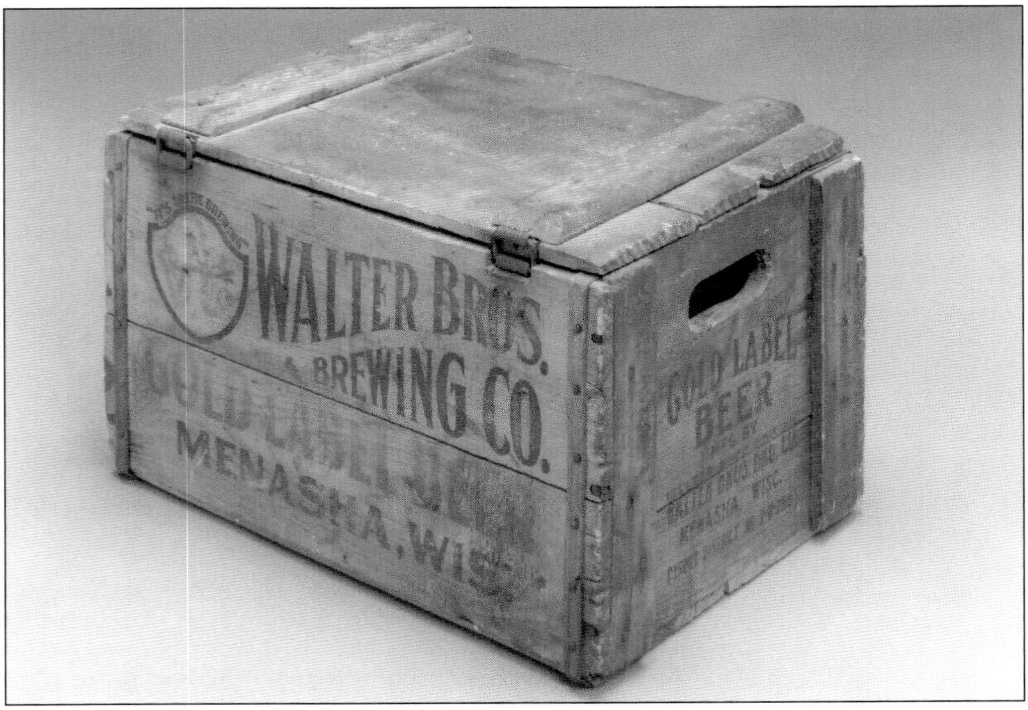

The Winz brewery was originally built on Manitowoc Street in 1860 by two men by the last names of Hall and Loescher. It changed hands many times before Werner Winz purchased all interests in the brewery in 1881. It burned down in 1895. The brewery pictured was built on the same site and remained in operation until Prohibition caused it to close in 1920. At its peak, Winz Brewing, also known as the Menasha Brewing Company, brewed 5,000 barrels of beer yearly and shipped them all over Wisconsin.

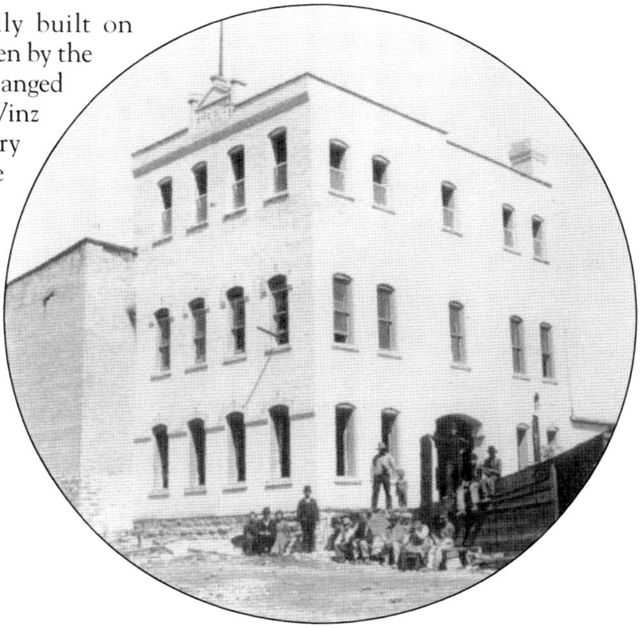

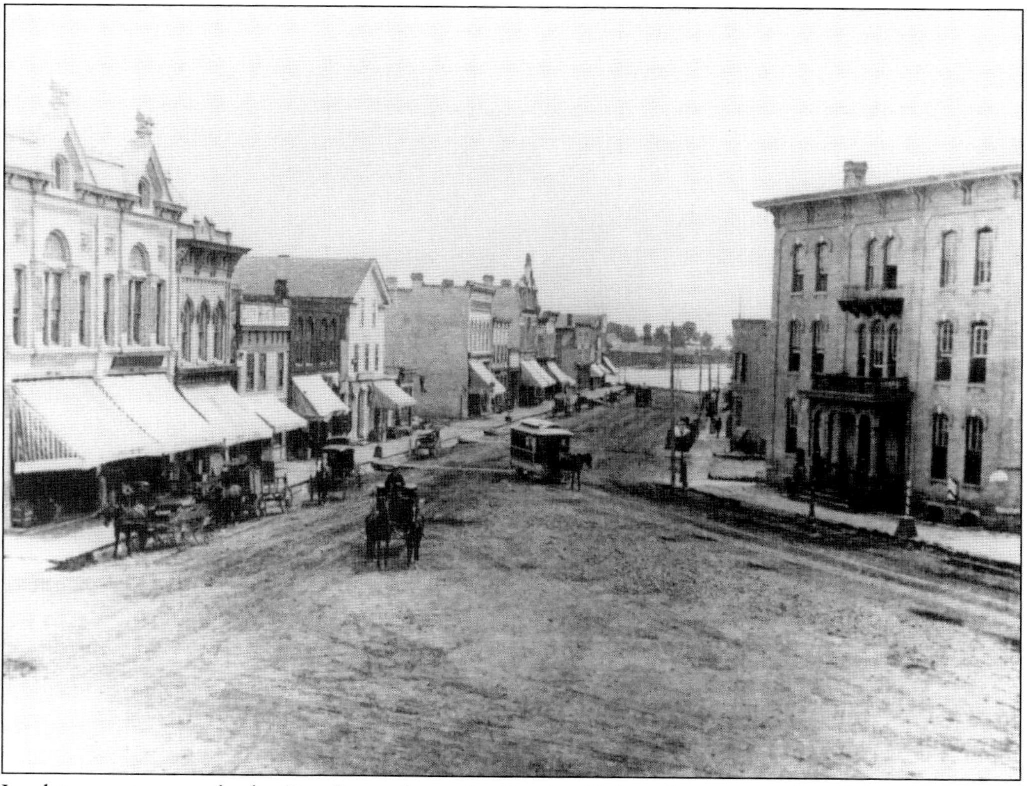

Looking east towards the Fox River from the Bank of Menasha corner, this 1888 photograph shows the R.M. Scott building (with awnings) fronting Main Street with the National Hotel across the street. Notice the absence of the flagpole circle, which eventually became a focal point on Main Street. It would be another 10 years before the streetcars became electrified. (Courtesy of Menasha Public Library.)

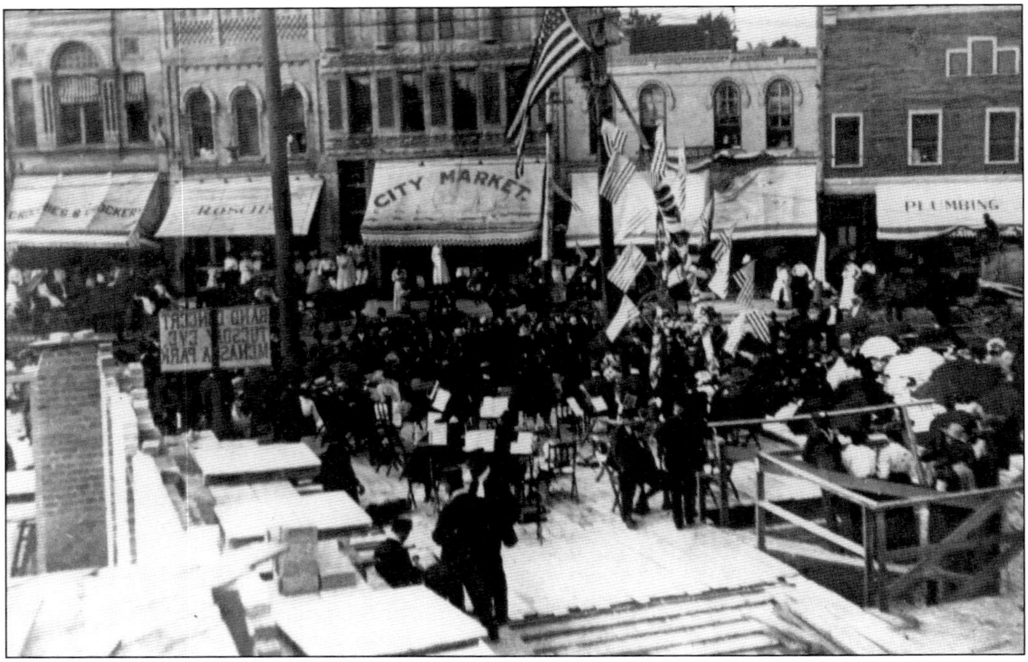

After the National Hotel burned down in 1901, R.M. Scott's widow announced that she would not rebuild it. Eventually, plans for a new hotel were developed by city fathers, and local manufacturers Christ Walter, Charles Smith, and Charles Howard resourced the project. Much of the citizenry turned out for the laying of the cornerstone of the new Hotel Menasha in 1905. Notice the sign facing Main Street, announcing the concert on Tuesday evening. The new hotel cost $35,000 and became such a hit, it required additions in 1911 and 1916. This example of Colonial Revival is the oldest instance of this type of architecture in Menasha.

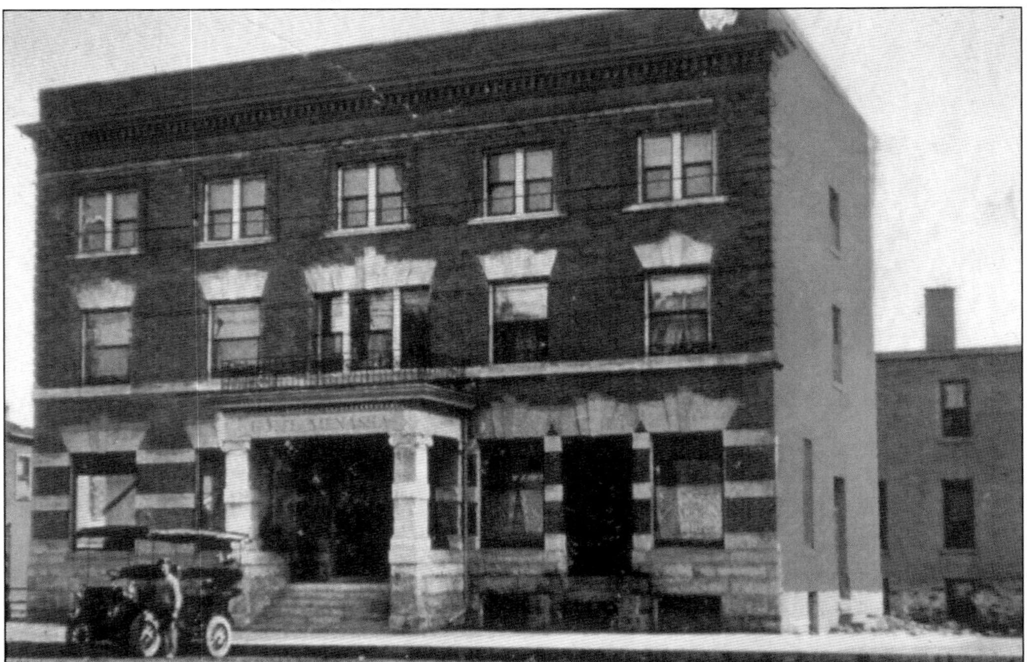

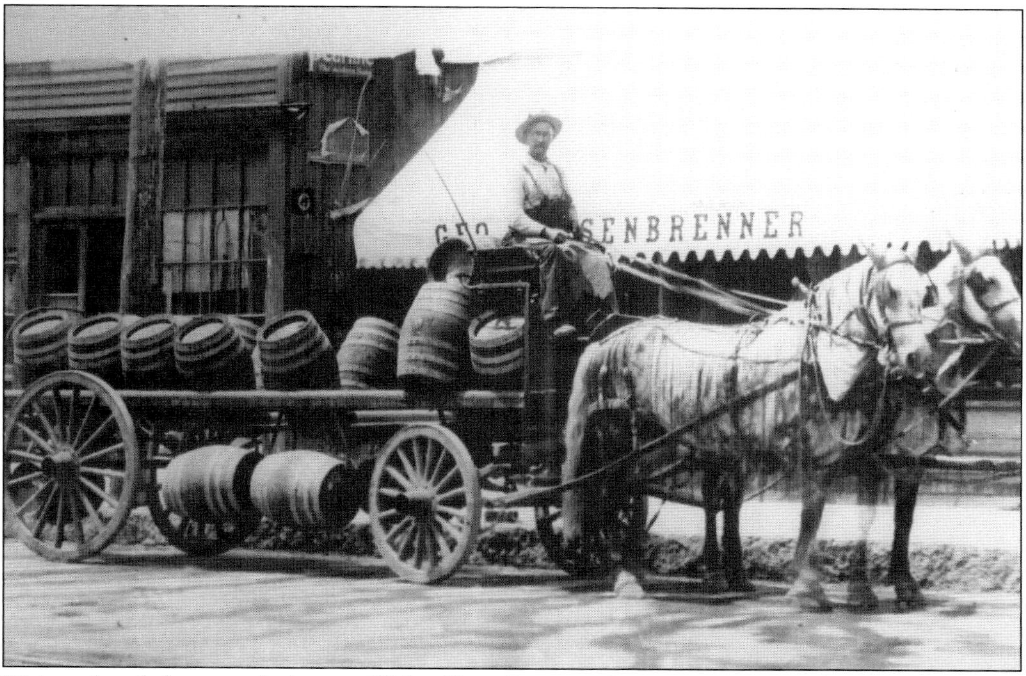

This undated photograph shows a Walter Bros. Brewing Company wagon in front of the George Sensenbrenner Sample Room, which was located at 292 Tayco Street in Menasha. Long before bottling became the norm, brewers dealt in barrels and kegs. A barrel holds 31.5 gallons while a keg is one-half barrel. A half keg or, 7.75 gallons, is referred to as a pony keg. (Courtesy of Neenah Public Library.)

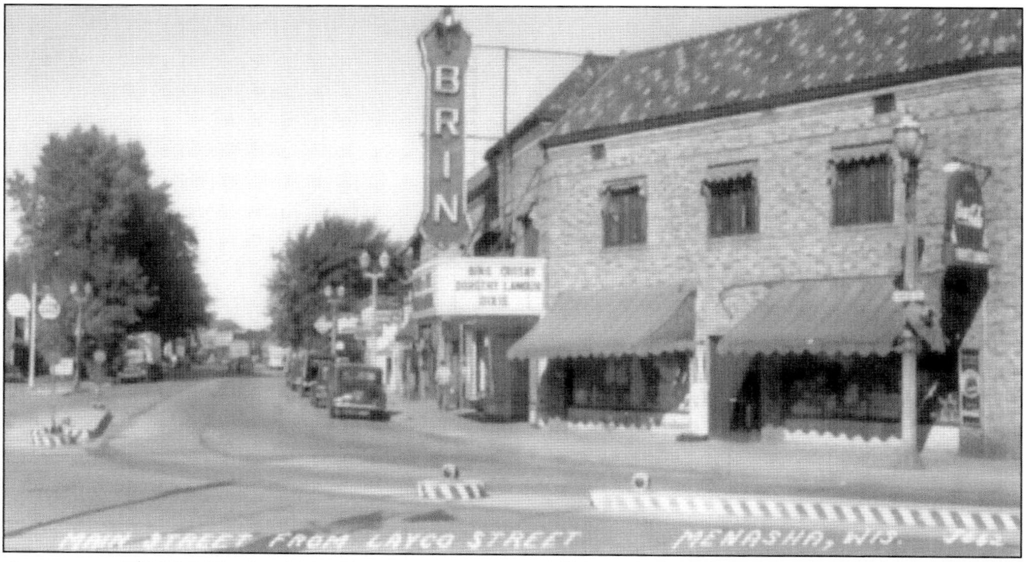

At a cost of $140,000, the Brin Theater opened in 1929, and though it was renovated in 1965, it closed in 1969; it was last operated by the Marcus Theater chain. Lack of plentiful parking was cited as a reason for its demise, and a news item from 1969 reported that the building would be razed. However, the building is still present today, housing several businesses. For its time, the Brin building was the largest commercial building in Menasha, housing a bowling alley, seven apartments, seven stores, and a 932-seat theater.

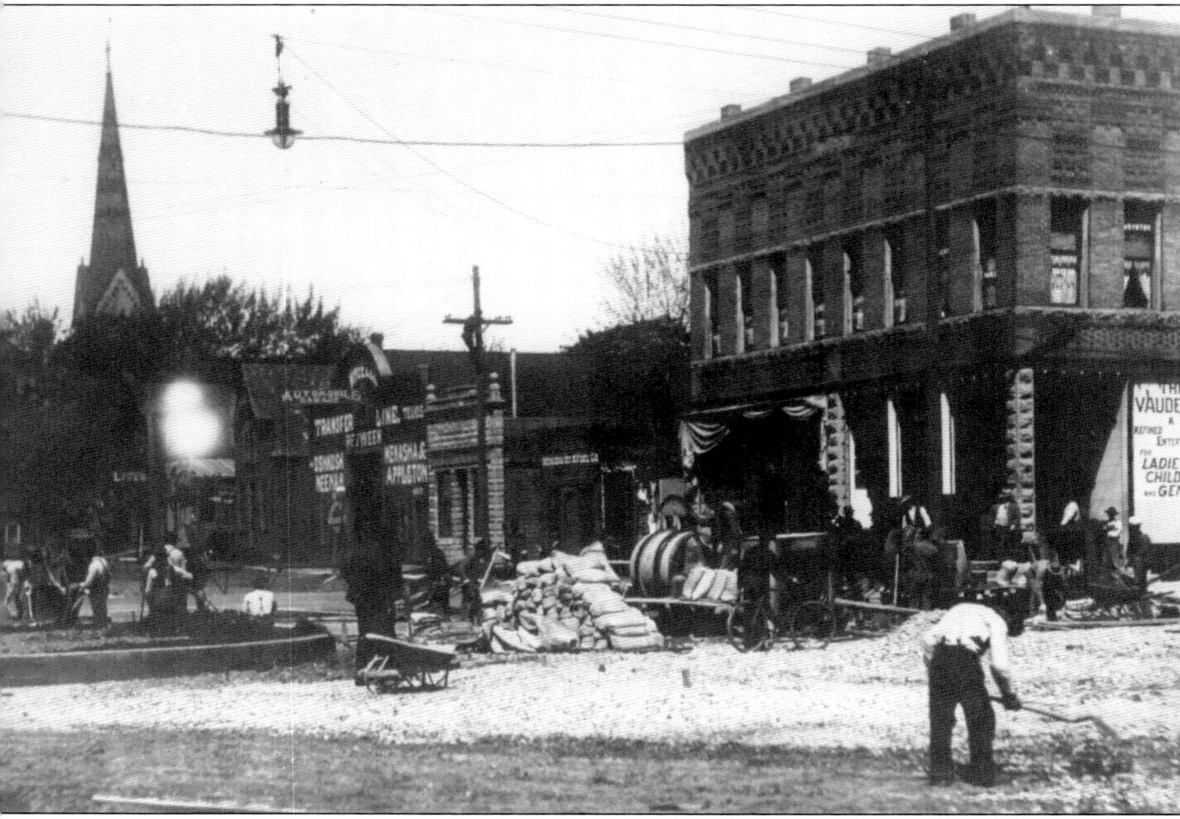

This photograph yields a wealth of historical information. Captured around June 1910, it shows the paving of the city square that was done in anticipation of the Benevolent and Protective Order of Elks convention about to be held in Menasha. The prominent building on the right, located at the corner of Chute and Milwaukee Streets, is the Vaudette Theater, formerly the Tuchscherer & Schlegel Department Store. Farther down Chute Street is the Menasha Ice and Fuel Company, and next to that is the Wheeler Transfer Line, a hub of transportation assets for the city of Menasha. Wheeler housed and provided transfer vehicles for all the train depots. His company ferried passengers to the local hotels and also provided livery and drayage services. Drayage is the transportation of goods for short distances and livery is the stabling of horses.

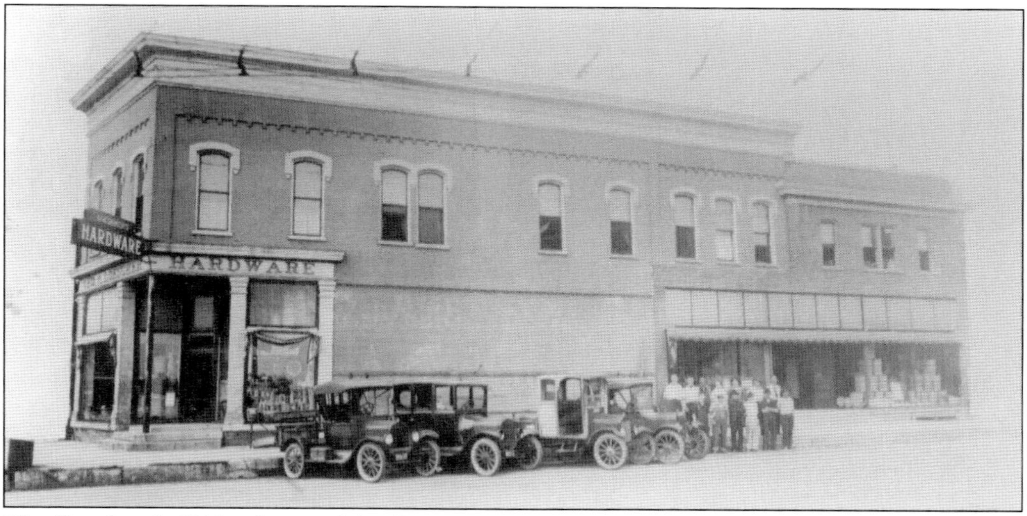

The October 1, 1910, edition of the *Domestic Engineering and Journal of Mechanical Contracting* reported, "The G.A. Loescher Hardware Company of Menasha, Wisconsin has recently completed the installation of a new heating plant in the city hall in that city." Loescher Hardware was one of the premier hardware companies within the city limits.

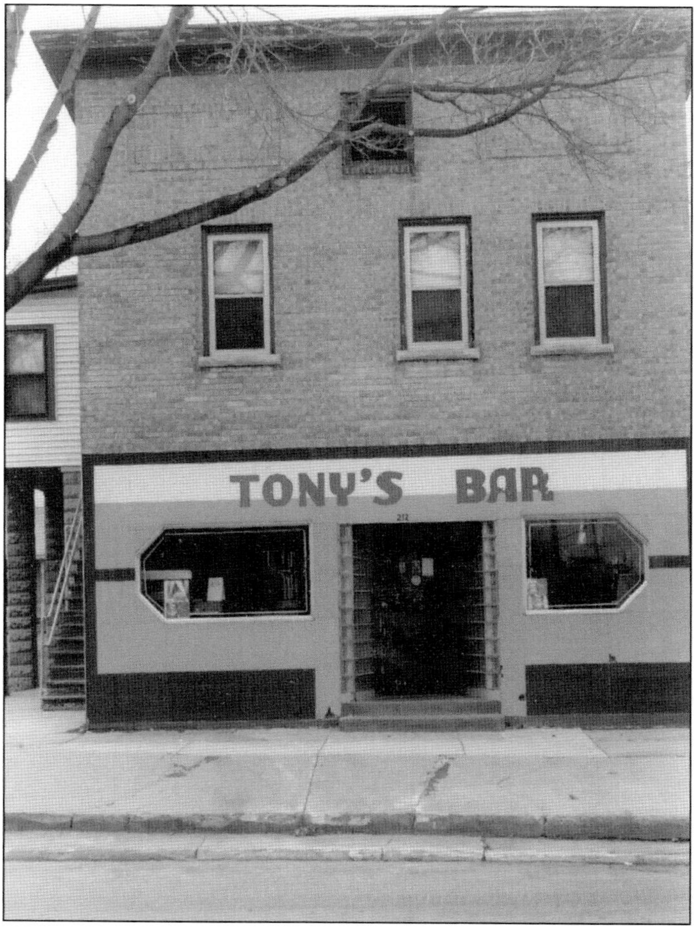

This building at Third and Manitowoc Streets was once slated to be a hotel for farmers. Businessman Henry J. McCabe planned this facility, believing accommodations catering to farmers using the adjacent plank road to Kaukauna and Appleton would lead to an increase in farm trade for the city. The structure was built in 1905, but it never became a hotel.

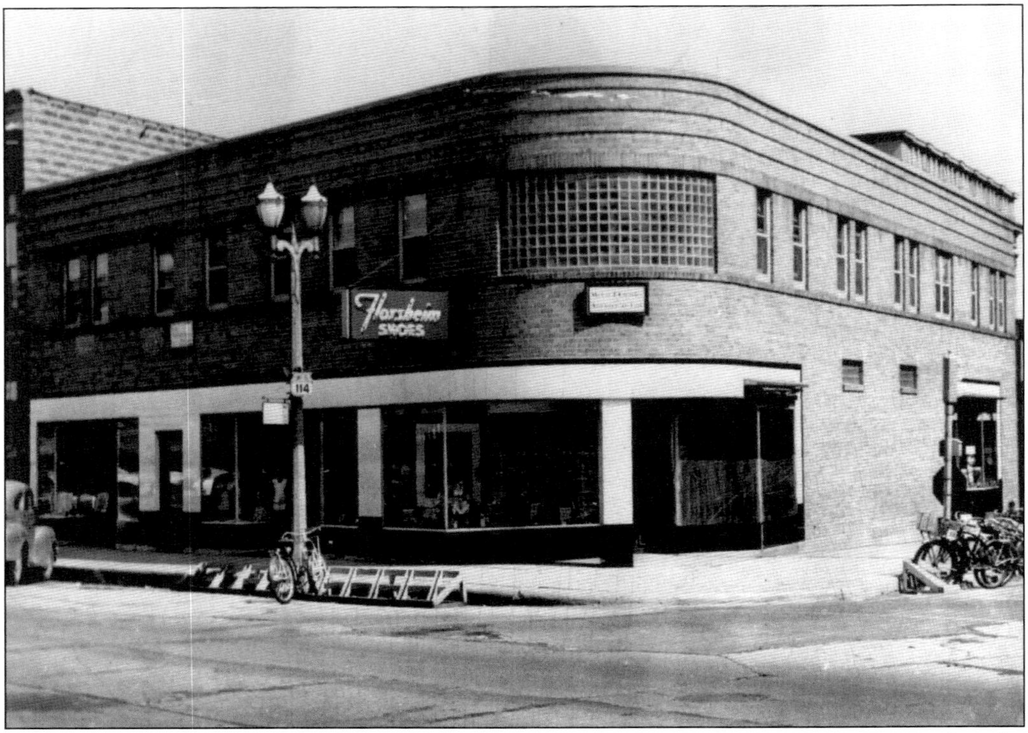

This version of the Tuchscherer Shoe Store at Main and Mill Streets, constructed after the devastating 1940 fire, is an example of the Art Moderne style of architecture that was in vogue from about 1930 to 1950. It is characterized by rounded corners, flat roofs, horizontal bands of windows, and the absence of historical references.

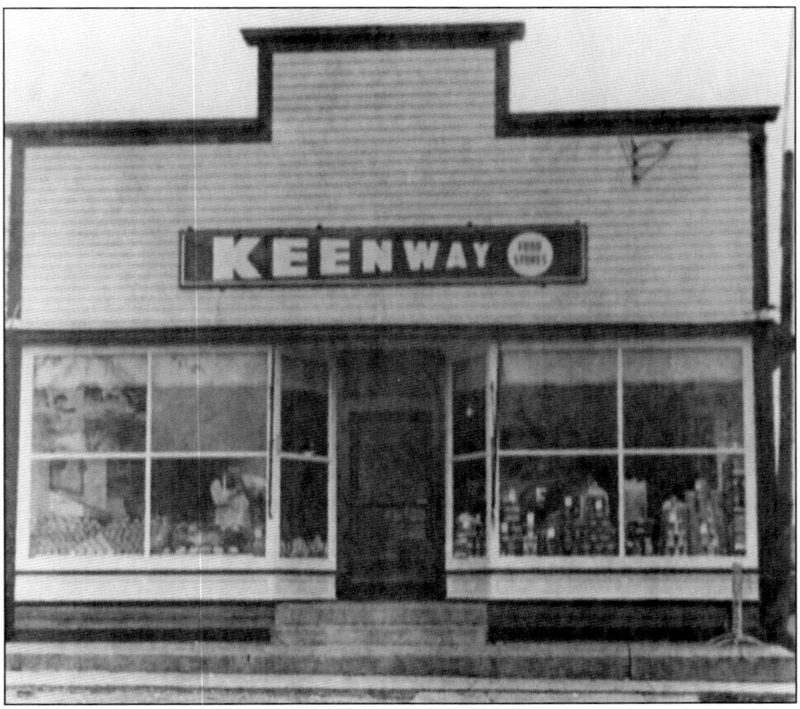

The Keenway Food Store was located on Manitowoc Street and owned by A.J. Seithamer, who ran the store from 1905 to the mid-1940s. It operated as a grocery for another 20 years. Keenway was a consortium of small groceries, like today's IGA, designed to help lower prices and consolidate advertising. Other stores were located in Oshkosh and Little Chute.

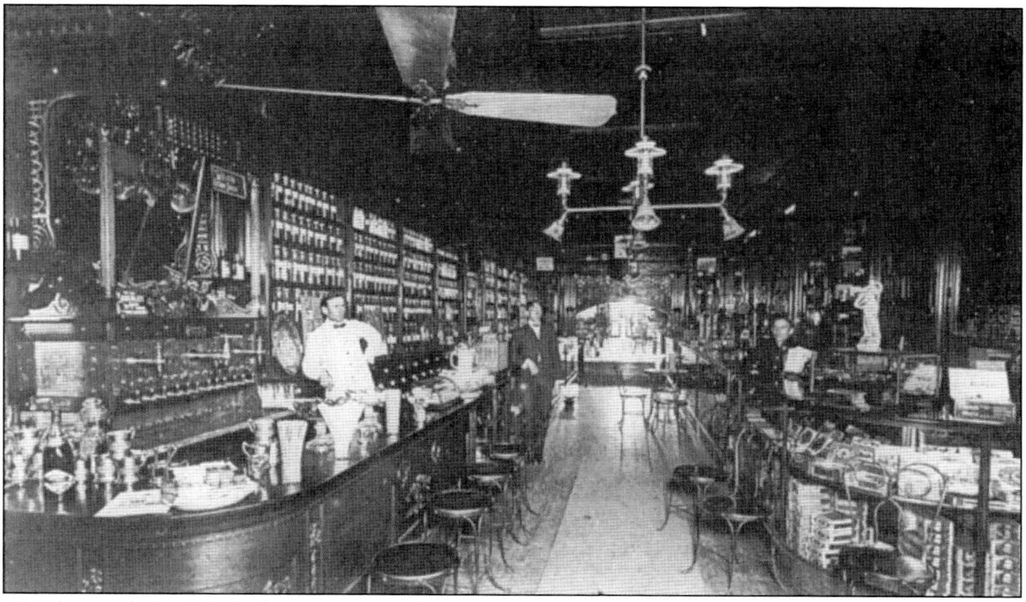

Charles and Emil Schultz opened a pharmacy in about 1910 next to Beck's Meat Market on Main Street, complete with a soda fountain. Soda fountains became popular in America due to the belief that carbonated water was good for the health. Many soft drinks were originally concocted by pharmacists; Dr. Pepper and Coca Cola were initially sold as patent medicines for 5¢ a glass. The Schultz brothers also maintained a store in Neenah. Emil Schultz stands at the right in this photograph.

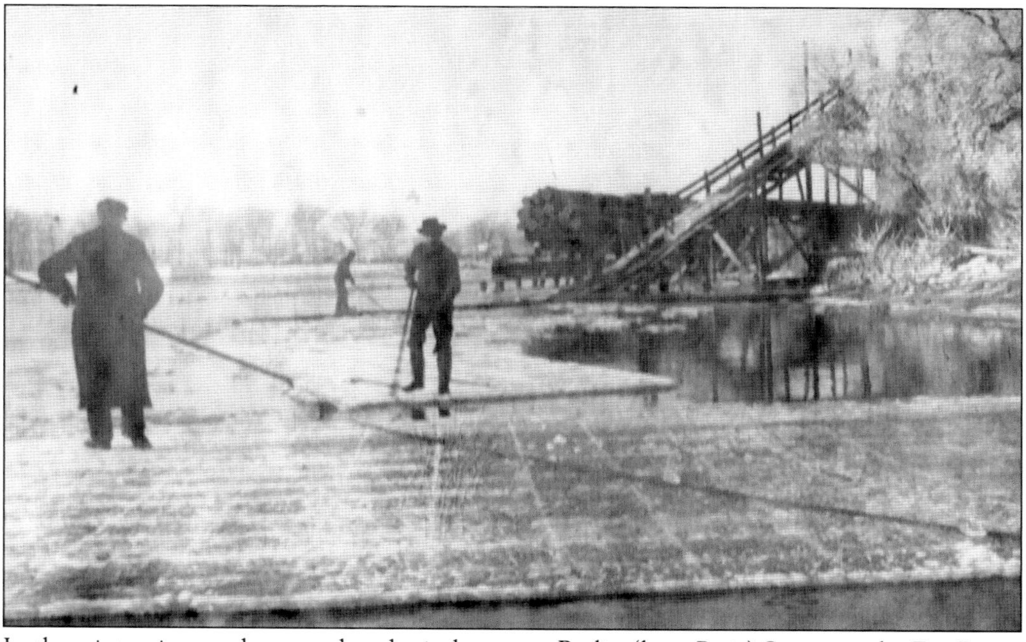

In the winter, ice was harvested at the icehouse on Berlin (later Paris) Street on the Fox River. Ice and snow would be taken into the icehouse and packed with insulation, often consisting of straw or sawdust. The ice would remain frozen for many months, often until the following winter, and could be used as a source of ice during the summer. This 1910 view also shows logs in the background that were floated downriver to Menasha Wooden Ware.

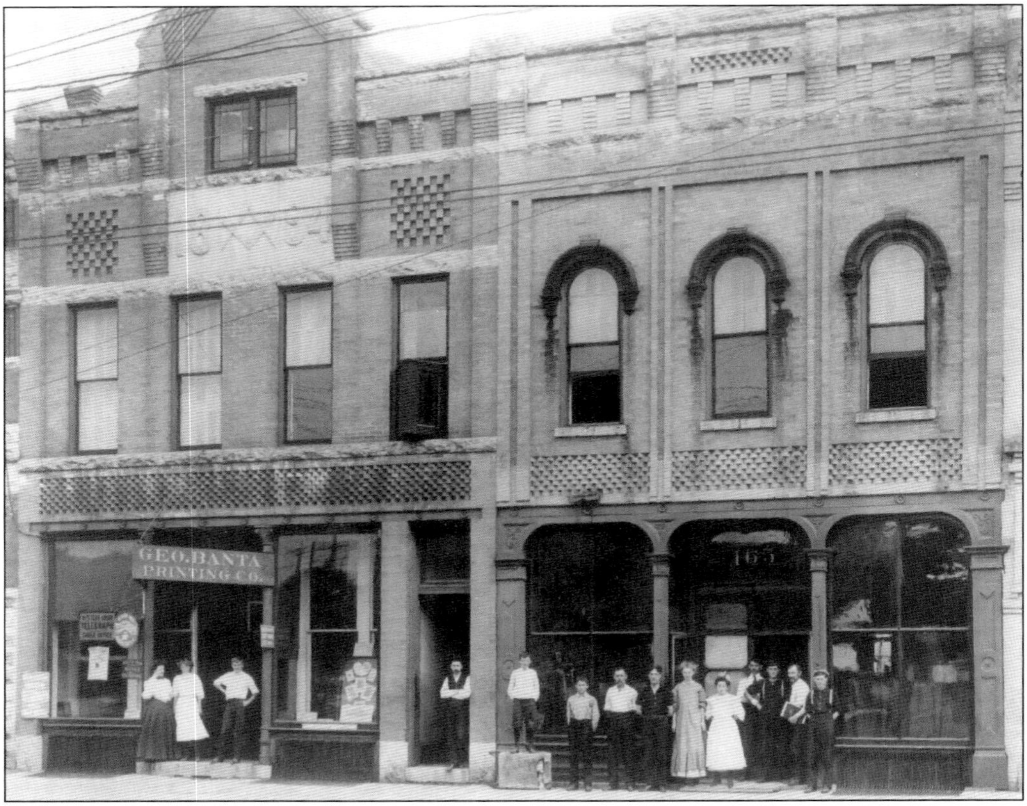

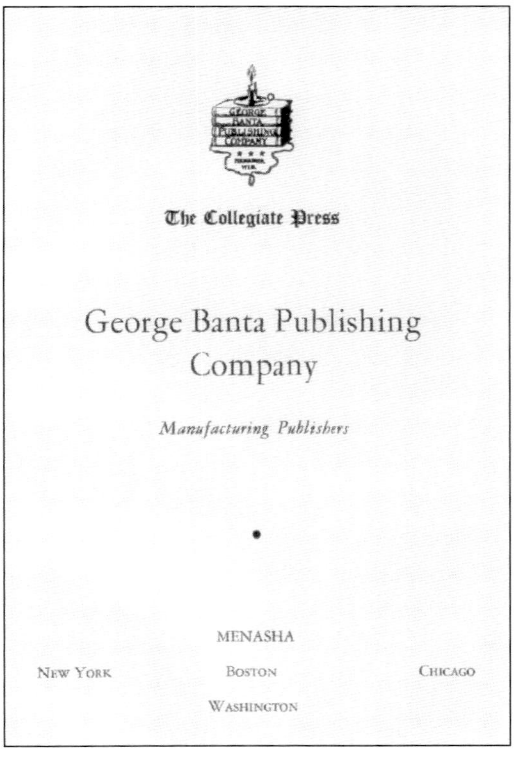

The 1905 photograph above shows the George Banta Printing Company in the Masonic Building. Located at 165–167 Main Street, the company moved to Ahnaip Street in 1911. George Banta Jr. stands in the left doorway, third from the left; the man standing alone in the center doorway is Archie McIntyre, a Western Union telegrapher. What had started as a hobby had now become an integral part of Banta's insurance business; items such as calendars, notepads, desk blotters, and the like were produced as promotional and advertising premiums for Banta's insurance customers. The George Banta Company was incorporated in September 1901. By 1930, it was printing some 130 periodicals. The ad at left from the 1917 Menasha High School annual, the *Nicolet,* reflects Banta's national focus towards business with mention of the commerce centers of New York, Chicago, Washington, and Boston.

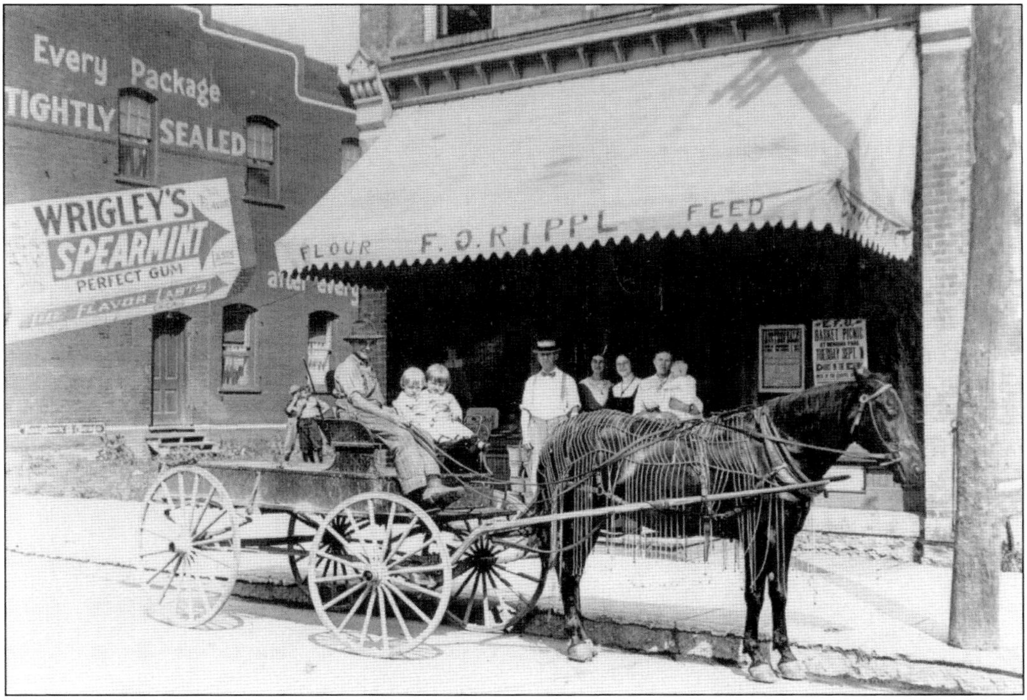

In about 1910, F.G. Rippl opened this grocery and feed store at 7 Tayco Street after operating a similar business on Kaukauna Street. His shop dealt in fancy and staple groceries, flour, and feed. For unknown reasons, the letter "G" appears backwards on the awning. Notice that the horse is wearing an ingenious device to shoo away flies. Shown in the c. 1916 photograph below are, from left to right, Grace Grassl, Theresa Rippl, delivery boy William Schnitzer, and proprietor Frank Rippl. Due to the size of the stores and the business philosophy of the times, self service was a totally unheard-of concept for most retail establishments.

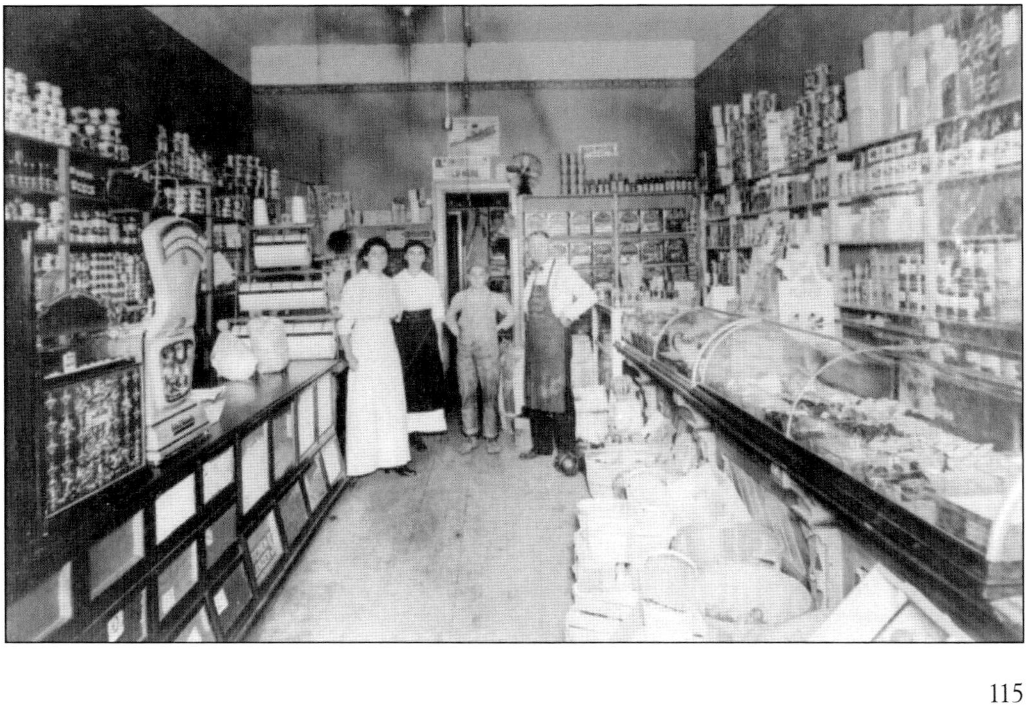

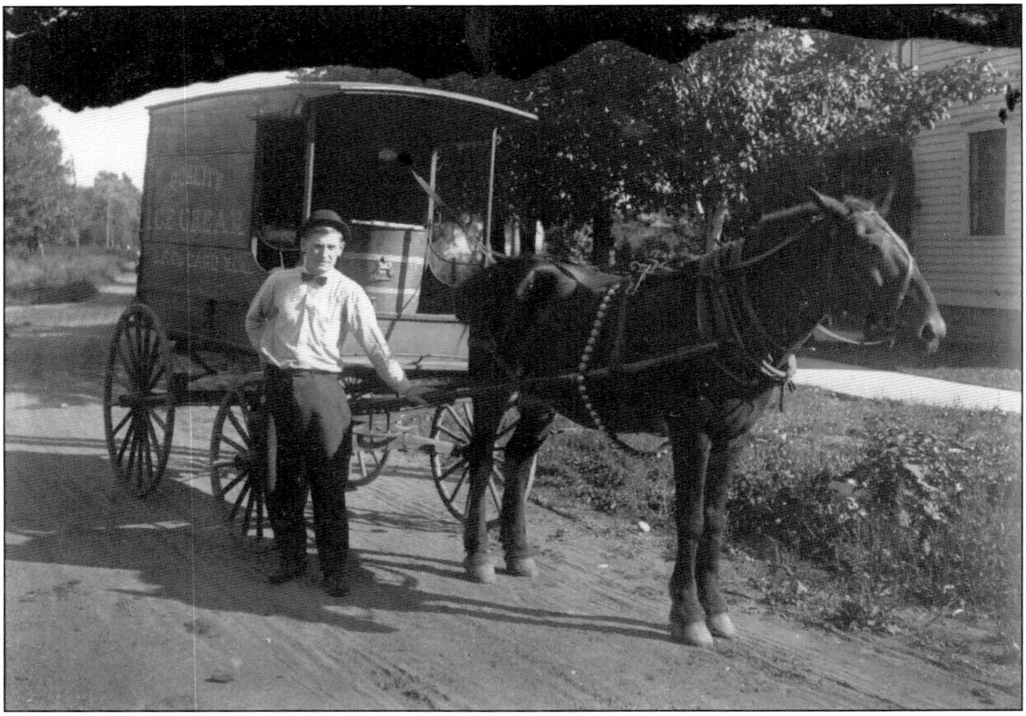

As a 19th-century forerunner to today's neighborhood ice cream truck with its nonstop music, John DeCaro sold penny ice cream cones from the back of his ice cream wagon. One presumes the jingle bells worn by his horse were enough to beckon his customers from their homes on a hot summer day.

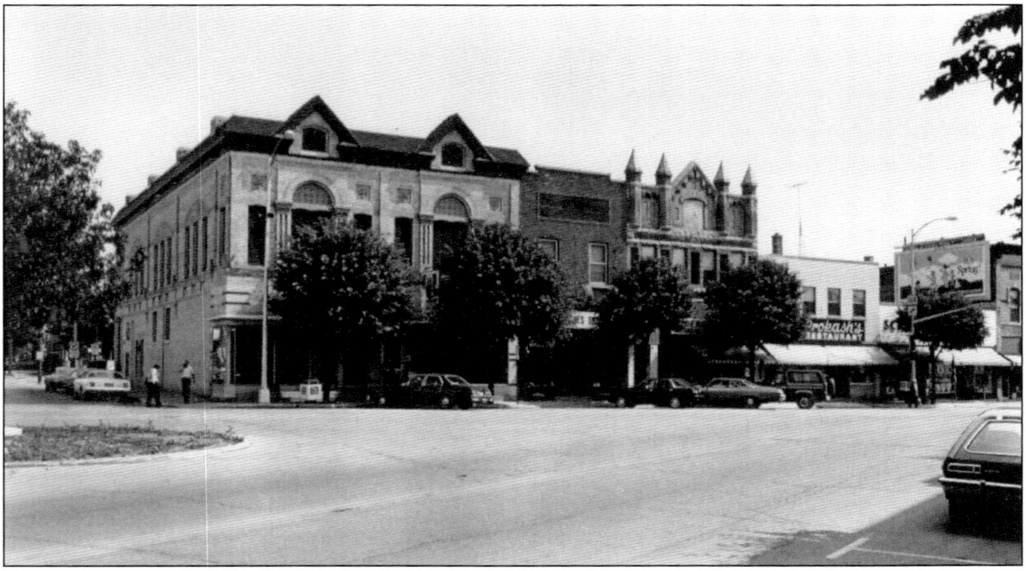

The R.M. Scott building at the southeast corner of Main and Milwaukee Streets has housed many businesses over the years. Shown here in the late 1970s is the city utilities offices. McMahon Engineering was on the second floor; next door was the Clothes Shop and above it was the local branch of the Independent Order of Odd Fellows, as evidenced by the engraved chain extant on the building.

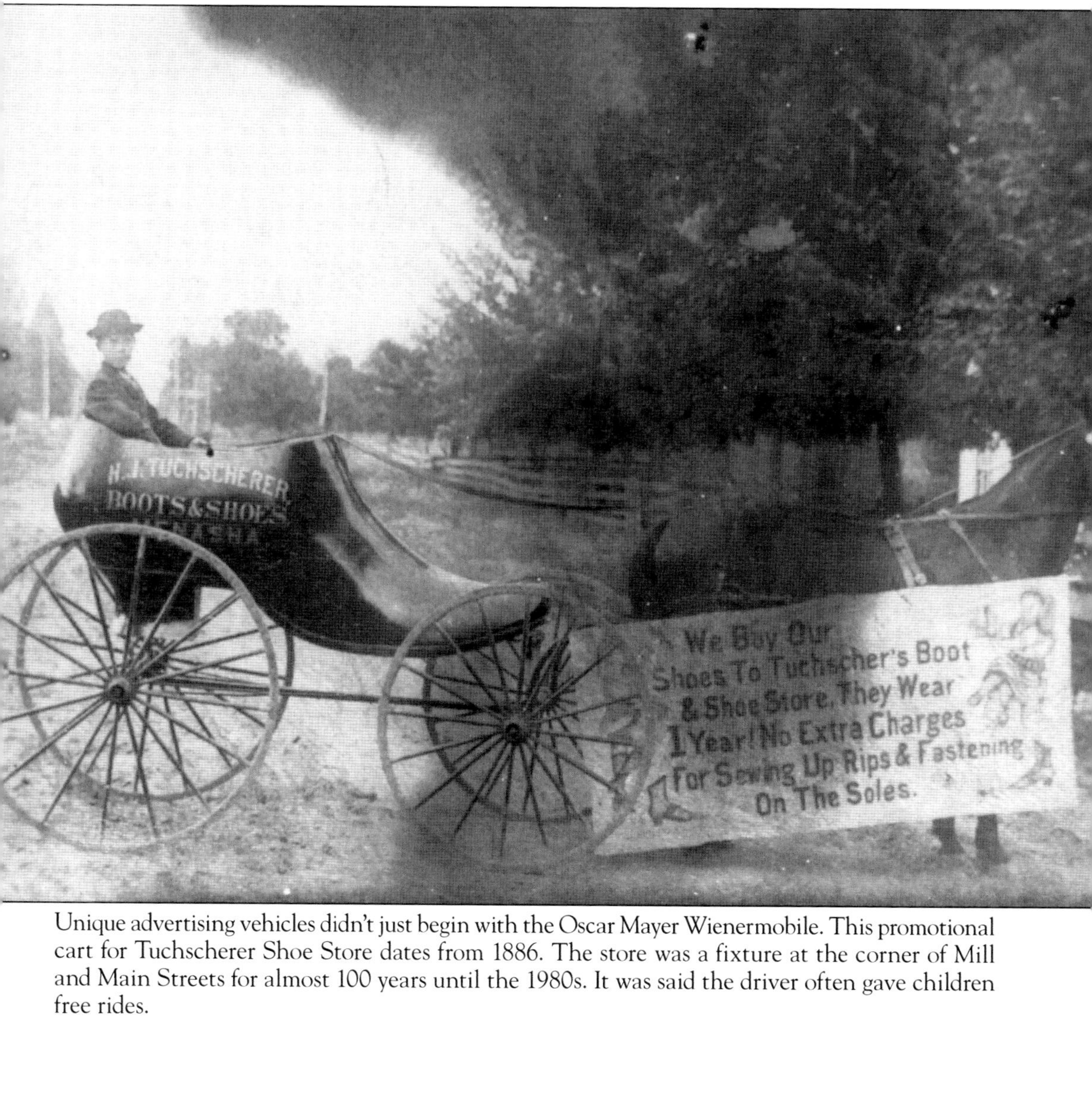

Unique advertising vehicles didn't just begin with the Oscar Mayer Wienermobile. This promotional cart for Tuchscherer Shoe Store dates from 1886. The store was a fixture at the corner of Mill and Main Streets for almost 100 years until the 1980s. It was said the driver often gave children free rides.

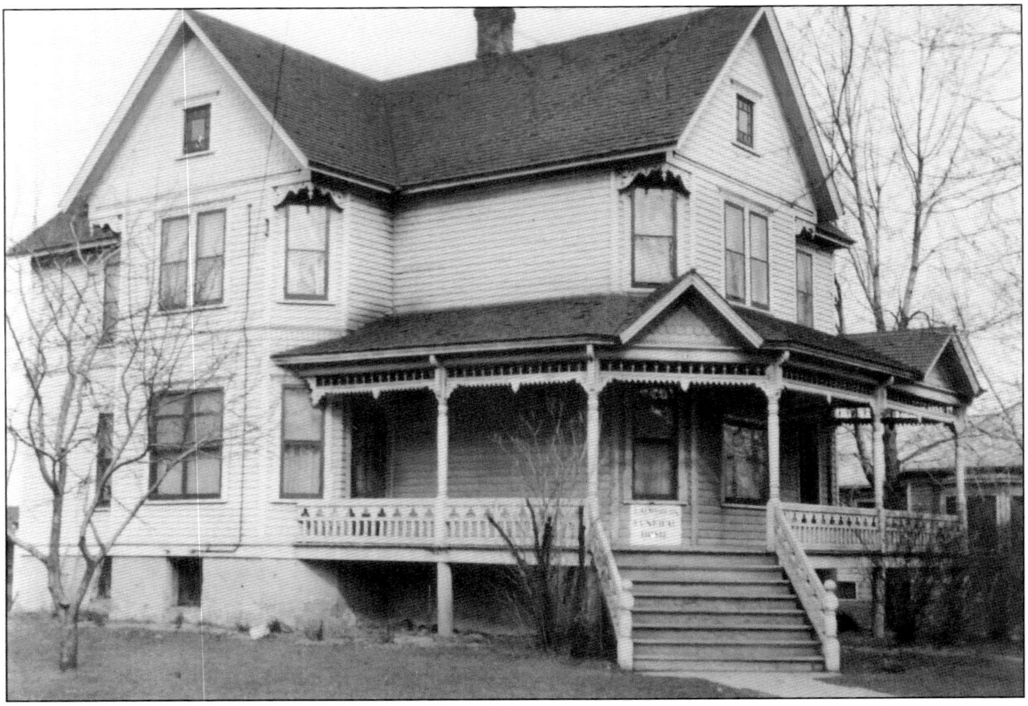

Over time, this house became the Laemmrich Funeral Home at 312 Milwaukee Street, the de facto Catholic funeral home in Menasha for parishioners at St. Mary's, St. John's, and St. Patrick's Churches. As evidenced in the photograph below, the home changed substantially to accommodate the business, including several structural additions and a new brick facade. During the holidays, for many years, its Christmas display, as seen below, was a Menasha tradition.

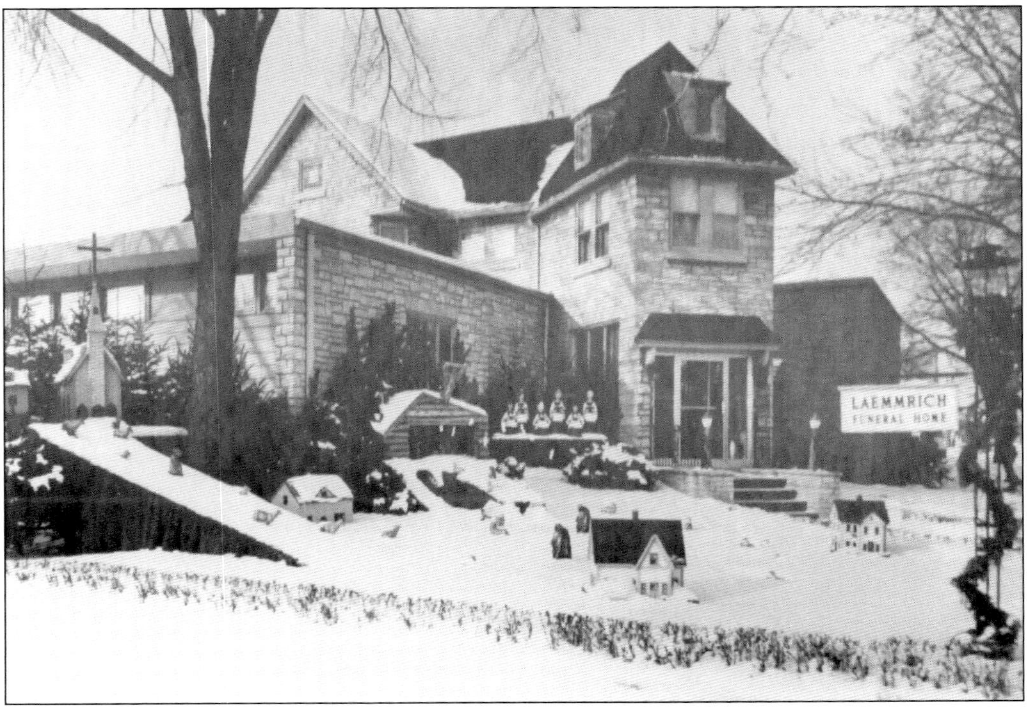

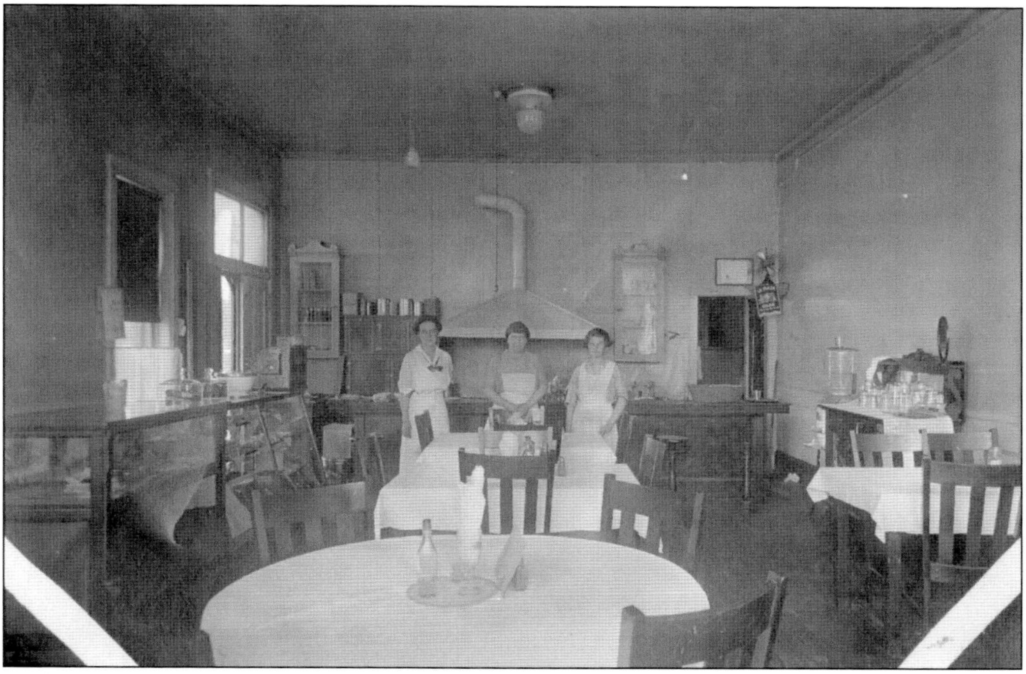

Otelia Mielke Maurer's restaurant on Main Street was a fixture for many years, offering wholesome food at affordable prices. Maurer (center) was a member of the Michael Mielke family, the innkeepers for the Fox River House at 232 Main Street. The other two women's names are unknown.

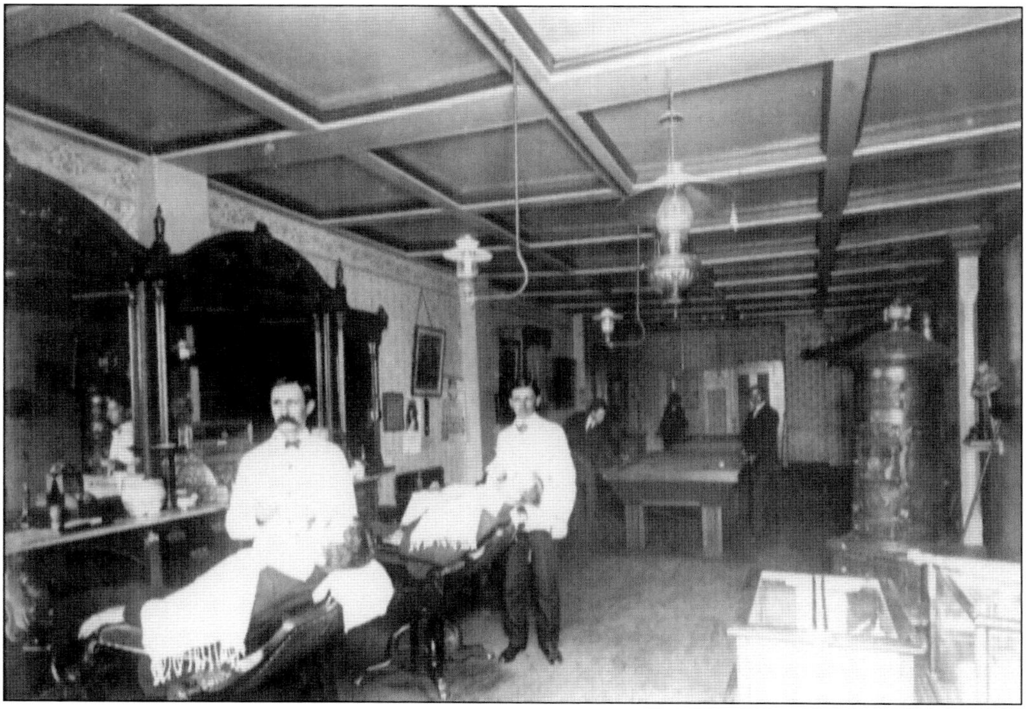

Walker's Barber Shop was located next to Tuchscherer's Shoe Store on the south side of Main Street. Joseph Walker (with mustache) was said to have had a reputation as being artistic with his clippers. With the pool tables in the back, it was a veritable social club for the men of Menasha.

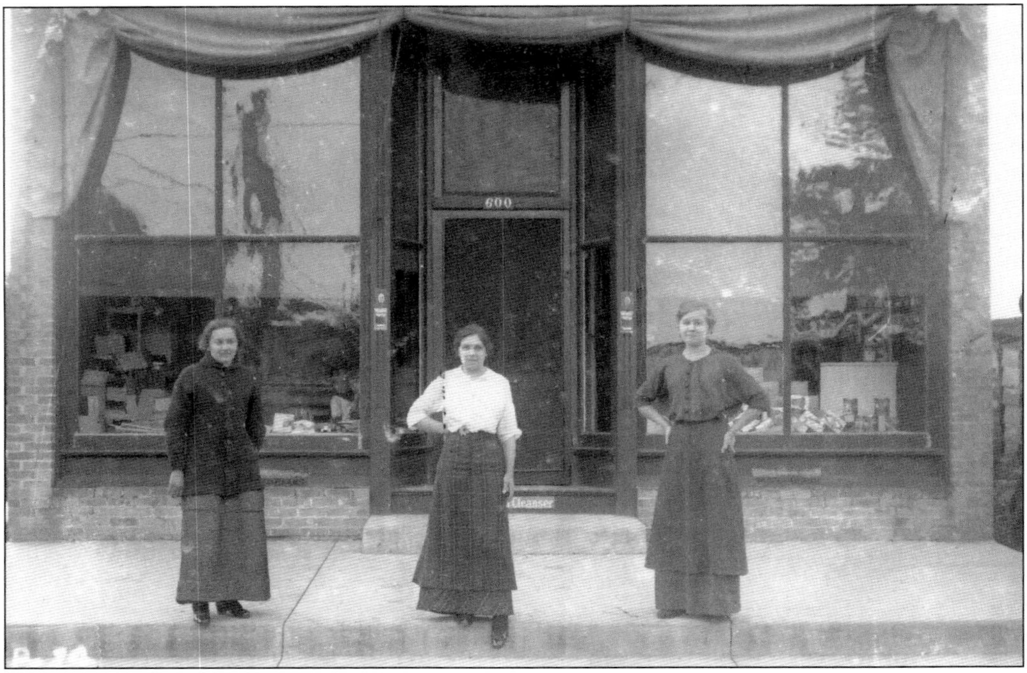

The Landig sisters stand in front of their family grocery in this 1913 photograph. Located at 600 Racine Street, it was directly across the street from the Wisconsin House, or Hotel Lenz. If one wished to place an order or schedule a delivery, their telephone number was 652.

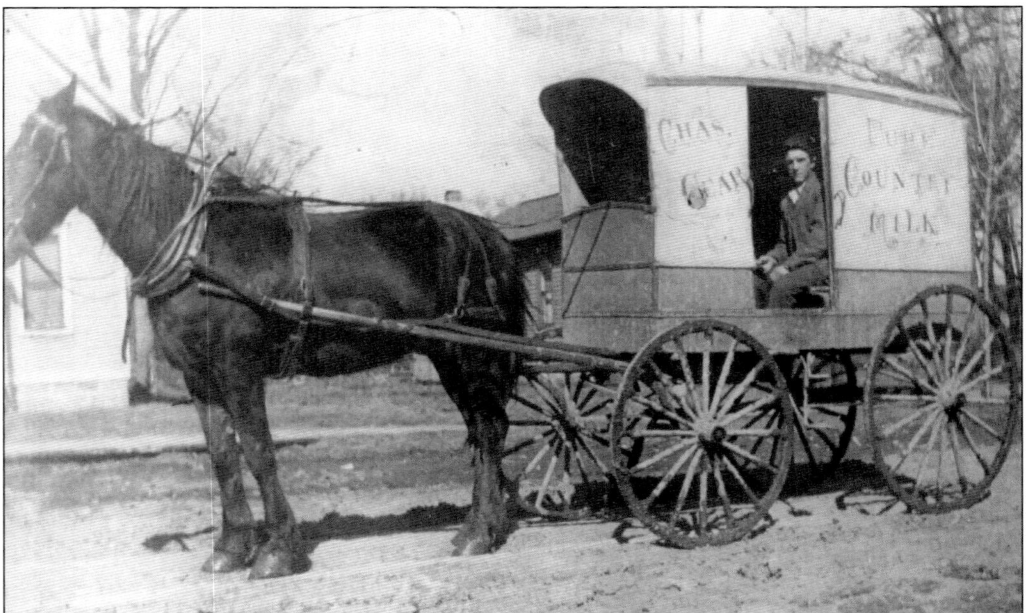

Charles Gear founded a dairy east of Menasha in 1883. In 1905, he moved his business to First Street where he modernized his operation, introducing pasteurization and homogenization. In the early days, Gear would drive down the street, ringing a bell, and fill the buckets and bowls his customers brought to his wagon, charging 3¢ to 5¢ per scoop of milk. (Courtesy of Menasha Public Library.)

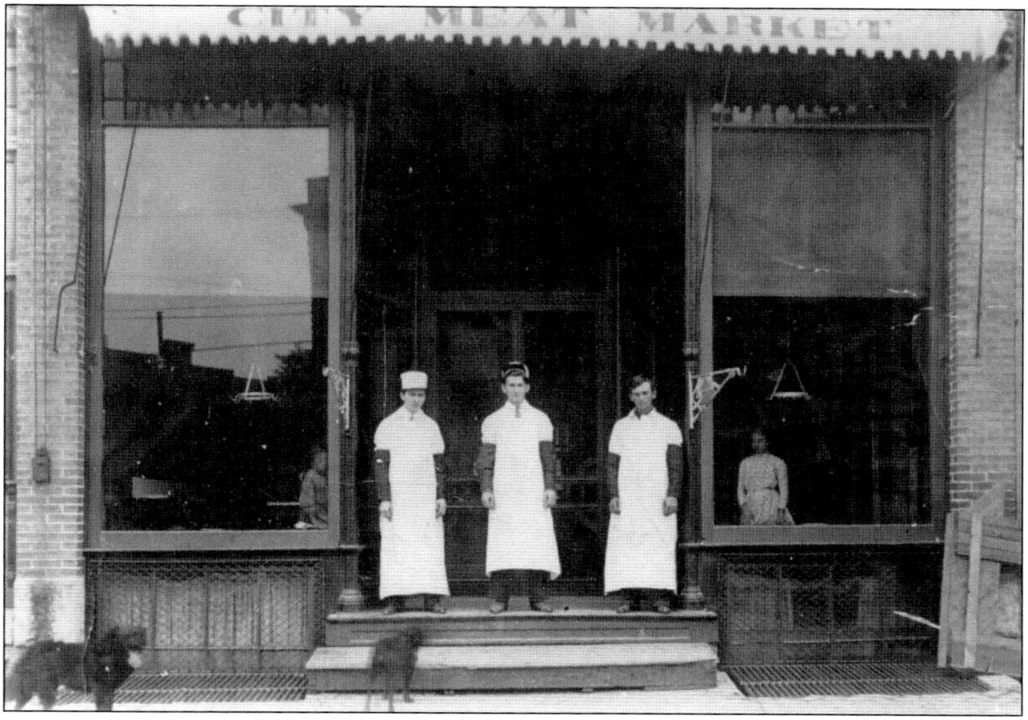

The Beck brothers pose in front of the City Meat Market, also known as Beck's Meat Market, at 186 Main Street. From left to right are Frank, Al, and William. Whether or not the canine visitors in this photograph received any free handouts is a matter of conjecture. The photograph below shows the interior view, where Nick Beck and his wife, Louisa, stand behind the counter. The sign high up the wall announces that this is a cash-only establishment. The walls display a fine array of sausages and sides of beef ready for a custom cut.

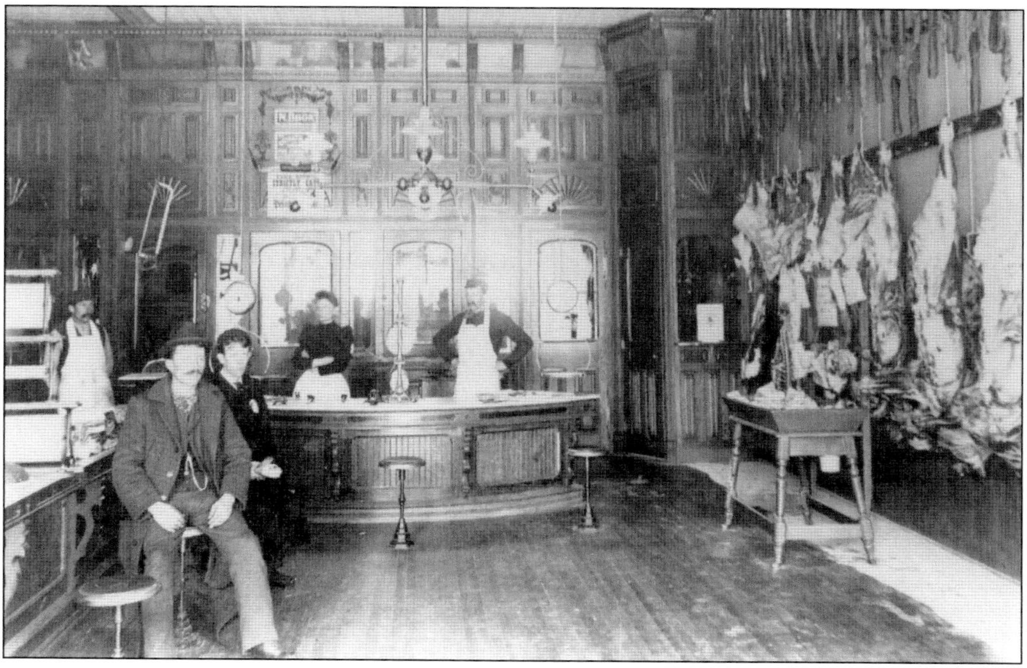

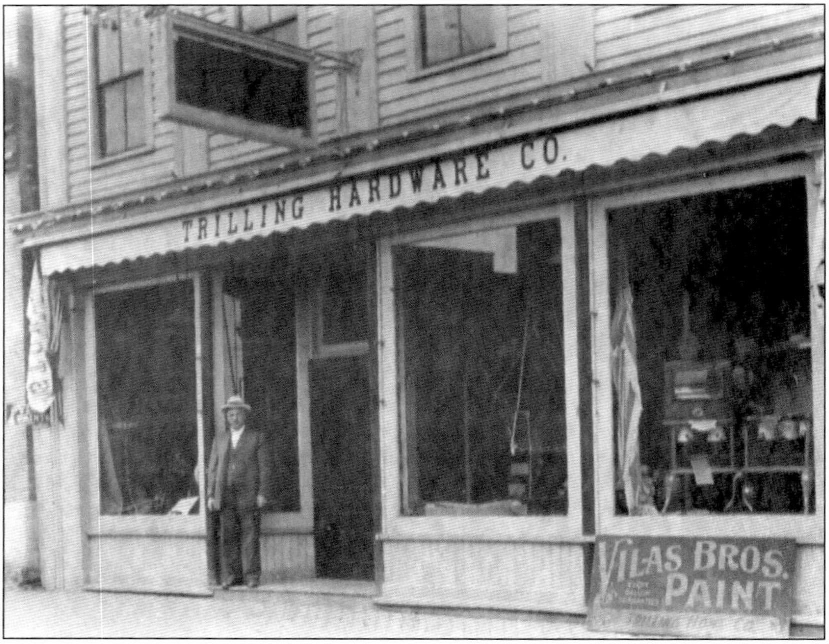

The Planner Building was built in 1885 by John Planner at 208 Main Street. Later, it became Trilling Hardware around 1912. This 1913 photograph shows owner Henry Trilling in front of his store. Among the tools and hardware, he sold stoves, guns, and ammunition. The Grand Army of the Republic (GAR) Hall was on the second floor. The GAR was a fraternal organization composed of veterans of the Union Army, US Navy, US Marines, and US Revenue Cutter Service who served in the Civil War. Notice the many cast-iron stoves for sale on the right side of the store. Henry Trilling's father had established this hardware store in 1856, so at the time these photographs were taken, this store was the oldest of its kind in the twin cities. The rear of the store featured an extensive repair department.

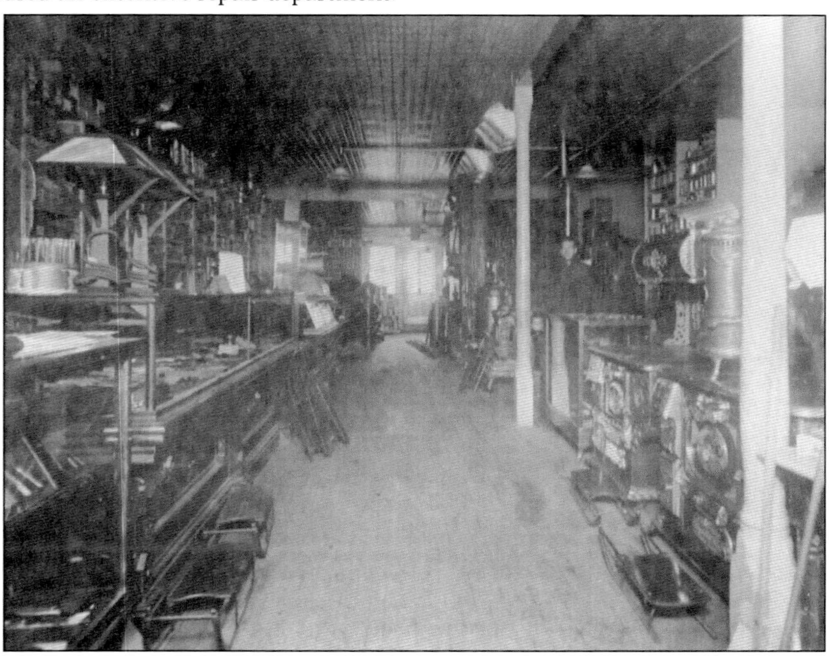

The National Express Company/American Express Company was located in the Tuchscherer building on Main Street. Standing in the doorway is Louis J. Ellinger Jr., who later became the Menasha postmaster. This photograph dates from 1898; notice the 46-star US flag in the window with the Puerto Rican flag. One can surmise that this commemorated the ceding of Puerto Rico, by Spain, to the United States following the Spanish-American War.

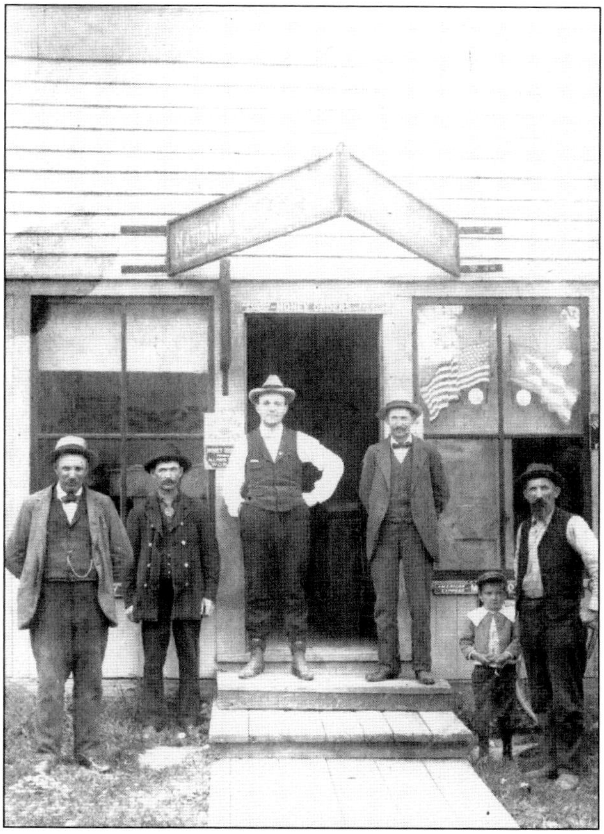

Morris A. Exley left Wausau in 1890 for Menasha and opened a meat market on Appleton Street. One year later, he settled in at Broad and Racine Streets, eventually moving to 234 Main Street. Pictured here from left to right are Raymond Landgraf, Joseph Henk, and M.A. Exley. As evidenced also at Beck's Meat Market, the butchers didn't seem to mind their customers getting a close view of their work.

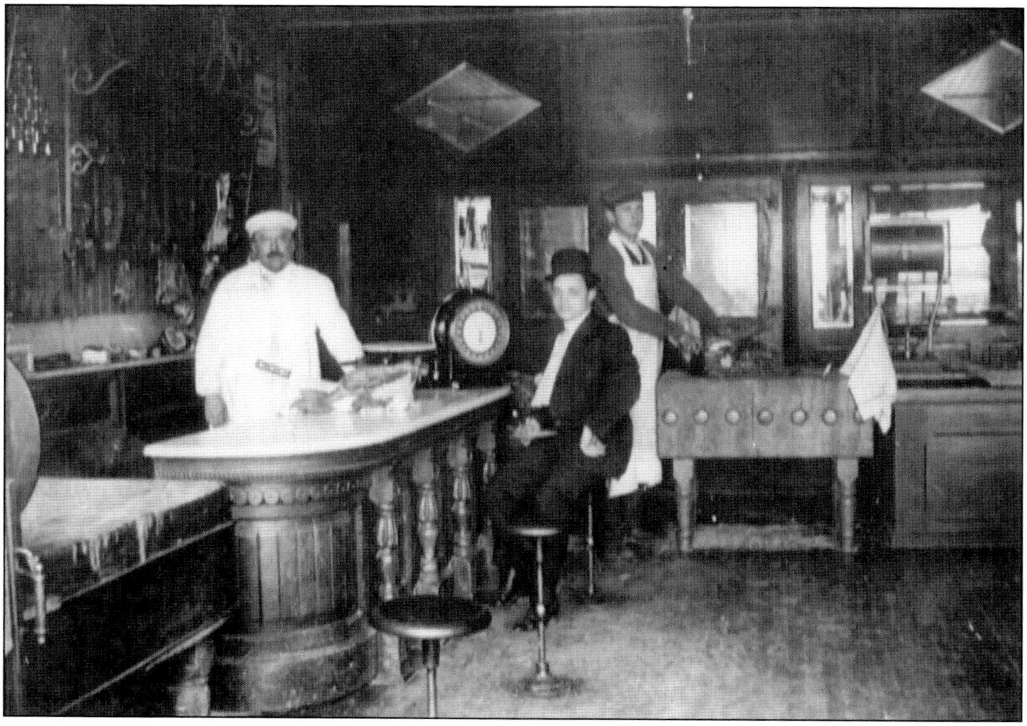

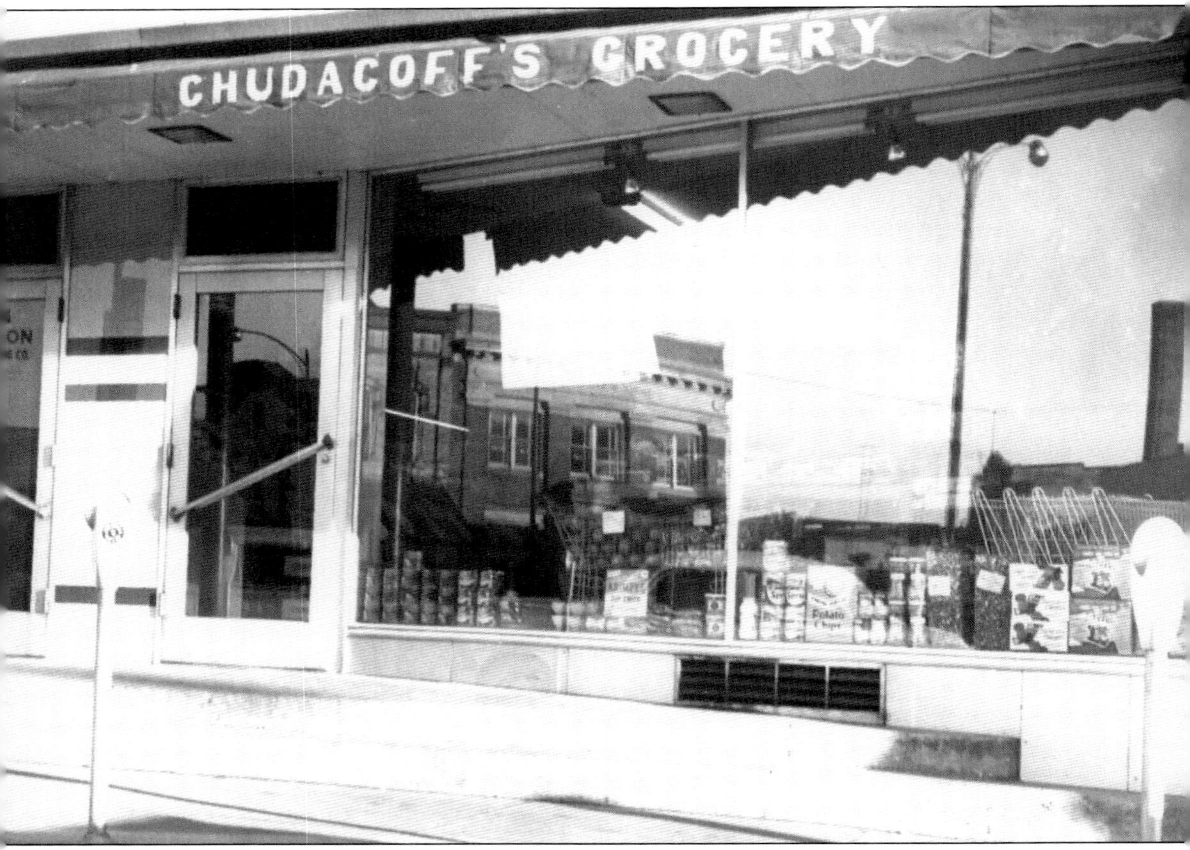

One of the many businesses in residence at the R.M. Scott building over the years was Chudacoff's grocery at 200 Main Street. Originally located at 182 Main Street, the original home of Schlegal's grocery, Chudacoff's moved farther west on Main in the 1960s. One can see the buildings of the Hotel Menasha block reflected in the glass window. Small neighborhood grocers such as this were the norm for much of the 19th and 20th centuries until the rise of the grocery chains. Many neighborhood groceries had specialized food lines or meats that drew their clientele, especially in more ethnic neighborhoods where the local language was spoken at the groceries and foods indigenous to the old country were still offered; residents felt comfortable shopping there. Another sign of the times is that most families had one car, if at all, and they walked to the store to get their groceries.

Bibliography

Adams, Peter J. and Peter A. Geniesse. *The Emerging Cities: Menasha, Neenah: Stories of the 19th Century*. Neenah, WI: Citizen Printing & Publishing Co., 1998.

Adams, Peter James and Associates. *Menasha Intensive Survey: Final Report, Menasha, Wisconsin*. Neenah, WI: Peter James Adams and Associates, 1986.

Auer, James M. *Centennial Memories: A Brief History of Menasha, Wisconsin*. 1953.

Augustin, C.J. *Semi-Centennial Souvenir Edition of the Menasha Press*. Menasha, WI: Menasha Press, 1898.

Glaab, Charles N. *Factories in the Valley: Neenah-Menasha, 1870–1915*. Madison, WI: State Historical Society of Wisconsin, 1969.

Goc, Michael J. *Land Rich Enough: An Illustrated History of Oshkosh and Winnebago County*. Northridge, CA: Windsor Publications, June 1988.

Harney, Richard J. *History of Winnebago County, Wisconsin, and Early History of the Northwest*. British Library, Historical Print Editions, 1880, reprinted March 2011.

Herziger, Caryl Chandler and Winifred Anderson Pawlowski. *Memories of Doty Island: A Link Between Two Cities*. Self-Published, 1999.

Lawson, Publius Virgilius. *History, Winnebago County, Wisconsin: Its Cities, Towns, Resources, People*. Nobu Press, 1908, reprinted March 2010.

Metz, James. *Prairies, Pines, and People: Winnebago County in a New Perspective*. Oshkosh, WI: Oshkosh Northwestern Company, 1976.

Neenah-Menasha, Wisconsin, Community Directory. Neenah, WI: E.G. Zabel, 1928, 1934, 1937, 1939 editions.

O'Regan, Suzanne Hart. *Ghosts in Sunlight: A Remembrance of Things Past*. Neenah, WI: Neenah Historical Society, 1985.

Saint Mary Parish, Menasha, Wisconsin: Centennial Celebration, 1867–1967. Self-published, 1967.

Smith, Alice. *Millstone and Saw: The Origins of Neenah-Menasha*. Madison, WI: Wisconsin Historical Society, 1967.

Smith Jr., Mowry and Giles Clark. *One Third Crew, One Third Boat, One Third Luck: The Menasha Corporation Story, 1849–1974*. Menasha, WI: George Banta Company, 1974.

Index

About the Menasha Historical Society

The Menasha Historical Society was organized May 3, 1956. With field trips, lectures, and seminars on topics ranging from genealogy to historical buildings, the Menasha Historical Society has, for the past 55 years, fulfilled its mission of preserving, advancing, and disseminating knowledge of the history of Menasha.

The Menasha Historical Society's Resource Center and Museum is located in the Memorial Building across from Smith Park at 640 Keyes Street in Menasha, Wisconsin. Meetings are held the second Thursday of the month, September through June (excluding February and March).

Mailing Address
The Menasha Historical Society
PO Box 255, Menasha, WI 54952

Website
www.menashahistorical.webs.com